Fr

EDITED BY JONATHAN ALEXANDRATOS
AND FROM MCFARLAND

*Articulating the Action Figure:
Essays on the Toys and Their Messages* (2017)

Free with Every Kids' Meal

The Cultural Impact of Fast Food Toys

Jonathan Alexandratos

McFarland & Company, Inc., Publishers
Jefferson, North Carolina

This book has undergone peer review.

All photographs were taken by the author
of items in his personal collection.

ISBN (print) 978-1-4766-8876-3
ISBN (ebook) 978-1-4766-5552-9

LIBRARY OF CONGRESS CATALOGING DATA ARE AVAILABLE

Library of Congress Control Number 2025016728

Front cover: (foreground) Wendy's Biggie Fries toy
from 1991 Wacky Wind-Ups Kids' Meal (author collection);
background cover photograph by Vinicius Tupinamba (Shutterstock)

Printed in the United States of America

*McFarland & Company, Inc., Publishers
Box 611, Jefferson, North Carolina 28640
www.mcfarlandpub.com*

Table of Contents

"I am hoping here only to tell a little, only so well as I may, about an ordinary house, in which I lived a little while..."
—James Agee, *Let Us Now Praise Famous Men*

Acknowledgments

The creation of this book would have been impossible without the support of so many. First, my community of "toy people" encourage me to keep pursuing my impassioned deep dives into our shared love, often appearing in SCUBA gear right next to me, seeking to unearth the next great mystery from far beneath the surface. These fellow divers include Dan Yezbick, Matt Kaplowitz, Christopher Bell, Shawn Crosby, J. Richard Stevens, Cathy Thomas, Emily Rosewood, Gina Femia (and their too-generous mother JoAnn Femia, who shipped me a big box of kids' meal toys gratis), Gigi Barreca, Andrew Tolch, Johnpaul Ragusa, Dan Treiber, Reina Mia Brill, Rajiv Mohabir, Hoyt Jacobs, John Rice, and so many more. There are also those explorers with whom I have had deeply educational chats coupled with even more frequent sessions with their online and in-print content. Those include Dan Larson, Pixel Dan Eardley, Brian Volk-Weiss, Andrew Jenks, Scott Zillner, and Stefanie Eskander.

My writing has been molded, so to speak, by teachers with whom I have been lucky enough to become friends. These experts in their crafts—Tina Howe, Vern Thiessen, Susie Moloney, and Nate Eppler—have meant everything in my commitment to bettering mine.

There are also those who have, over the course of years, held open the floodgates so that more plastic inspiration could reach my shores. My parents and grandmother were instrumental in developing my early love of toys, and my mother still leaves Happy Meal toys on my doorstep to this day. Dr. Tracy Bealer taught me new ways of seeing, studying, thinking, and being, clearing paths and making connections that I could not have imagined without her guidance. And finally, Jim, my toy collector cat, sat beside me with a look on

Acknowledgments

her face that I have anthropomorphized to mean "deep thought" on many nights where I explained to her the subtleties of an Australian McNugget Buddy, a Burger Chef Fun Meal tray, and a Dog N' Suds kid's toy.

Introduction:
Unpacking the Kids' Meal

CALVIN: If we don't all watch the same TV, what will keep our culture homogenous? We can't rely on monolithic networks to provide uniform national blandness anymore!
DAD: There's still McDonald's and Walmart.
—Calvin & Hobbes, in *The Days Are Just Packed*

We are what comes with what we eat. Or, at least, we can find ourselves in there, if we dig deep enough. In order to understand this, we will need to read the rhetoric of food and the various trinkets it can come with. Such practice is not without precedent. Dr. Amy Shuman, a folklore specialist, writes in "The Rhetoric of Portions," "Whether food is served in a family setting or between host or hostess and a guest, it can embody roles, expectations, and identities; and the behavior which accompanies the service may be interpreted as the expression of the feelings, attitudes, and sensitivities of the participants" (Shuman 72). Here, Shuman suggests that food contains and transmits messages from those involved in its delivery or consumption. For Shuman, even how much food is offered can be read for information about those serving it. I would expand this to say that when food contains non-edible items, such "expectations and identities" and "attitudes and sensitivities" of the food providers and consumers become amplified. Suddenly, there is excitement around who among the group will obtain the special item, what it will mean for their life, and how they will receive its meaning.

It could be argued, especially in a book analyzing the cultural impact of kids' meal toys, that a folklorist has no place. I disagree.

1

Introduction

While the elation of receiving a surprise Minion in a Happy Meal, or the disappointment of getting a toy already owned, is a modern phenomenon, the roots of those feelings extend into antiquity. The kids' meal toy is less a singularity, and more a rhetorical sum of the numerous food-attached items that came before it. To flesh this out, let's consider four hypotheticals, all constructed from facts of their eras:

1. *The Hypothetical Story of Maximinus.* If the name "Maximinus" recalls chapters of Latin language workbooks loosely translated the night before their due dates somewhere around sophomore year of undergrad, congratulations. You are in the right historical era. (You also may need a moment to collect yourself, if your experience learning Latin was anything like mine.) Maximinus lived, for our purposes, in 4th century CE Caesarea. Though a Middle Eastern city, the Roman influence there ran deep. Maximinus and his family did not have much money. As one year turned to the next, however, Maximinus hoped for the best. He had one thing going for him: his bishop was the man who would become Saint Basil the Great. At this time, Basil, busy earning that greatness, wanted to distribute money to his congregants experiencing poverty.

His plan was to commission the baking of a special bread. Each loaf of the bread would contain a coin. The families receiving the bread, therefore, would cut into it and find themselves slightly richer than they were before they ate. A tradition began that the person who found the coin in their slice would also receive good luck for the year. You can imagine Maximinus' elation when his piece of bread contained a much-needed slice of wealth.

While Maximinus is a fiction, the *vasilopita*, or "Saint Basil's Bread," is quite real. Some say that it actually has its origins in a siege of Caesarea, in which Basil asked the city for valuables in order to pay off the city's attackers (Saint Basil Academy). Charmed by the communal offering, the would-be enemy called off the siege and left without taking so much as an earring. Basil, left with the valuables, baked them all into loaves of bread and distributed them to the families of Caesarea. As if by miracle, each family, in this version of the story, received back the exact items that they gave. Aside from ignoring the reality of siege warfare in the 4th century, and the lack of evidence for an attempted siege of Caesarea at this time, *and* the impracticality of baking jewelry into bread, this story obscures the very reason Basil achieved sainthood in the first place: his acts of charitable giving. Here, Basil haphazardly returned what already belonged to the people of Caesarea. In the story that involves made-up Maximinus, which appears more prominently in retellings among religious institutions, Basil's generosity is made clear by his explicit interest in helping better the lives of the poor.

However, as I show through the next three hypotheticals, the establishment of one "correct" origin story is not nearly as effective as the existence of several potent ones. The fact that at least two, here, vie for prominence through fairly epic actions of social justice or political strategy (depending on which you hear) helps solidify the grandiosity of the *vasilopita*. The tradition travels through time, accumulating importance from many angles until all modern children know is the fact that it is capital–I Important in the most impervious sense. I know. I was one of those modern Greek American children.

In my case, the *vasilopita* was an essential New Year's practice. My eight-year-old-self had no doubt that the year's luck depended on whether or not I got that coin. (In a good year, it was a quarter. Occasionally, it was a dime or a nickel. In reality, it was whatever was in my grandmother's change purse when she baked it.) I not only cheated my way to victory, I also engaged in multi-faceted cheating. I cheated from all angles. I looked for silvery glimmers between slices. I lifted up the bread, which was about a foot in diameter, to see if anything circular sunk to the bottom. I looked for lumps. I let my unlucky slice crumble in my hands, and then demanded another without ever eating the pile of uselessness that lay before me. One year, I stole my father's quarter, thinking that the luck would come with it. Sometimes, my mother would rig the system so I got the coin piece immediately—a cunning display of mess-reduction tactics on her part.

But even if I found the coin fair and square, I had no clue if a "lucky" year was any better than an "unlucky" one. Ultimately, it didn't matter. The *vasilopita* never had to deliver on anything definitive—not its origin story, not the "luck" contained within it, not even the tastiness of the bread (I never enjoyed the flavor or the consistency as a kid).

It was the act of receiving a legend with my food that mattered. While I can imagine a family like Maximinus', or even a family today, being acutely thankful, in the practical sense, for the coin in their bread, for me, my gratitude was for the surprise of winning something meaningful. I didn't even know any of the origin stories of the *vasilopita* as a child. I didn't have to. All I knew was that there was money somewhere in that bread. Money, even in denominations as small as a quarter, meant power, especially at that young age. It meant I thwarted the boring but likely scenario in which I only received a slice of dry bread that I didn't even like. I was special. While everyone else just got food, I got something ... *else*. Something that makes my food, and therefore my self, stand out, even compared to the adults in the room, who were those with the most frequent and reliable access to money and power. Perhaps it's now no secret why I would grow up to hoard kids' meal toys from virtually every restaurant that offered them and then turn that obsession into a cultural study of the little pieces of special, powerful plastic that came with countless hamburgers, sandwiches, and nuggets. But we're not there yet.

2. *The Hypothetical Story of Juliette.* Here, our fictional Juliette was born in 12th-century France. Paris, let's say, because if you're going to go, go big. Twelve days after Christmas, for the Feast of the Epiphany, Juliette chose a slice of what we commonly call King Cake. It's circular, representing the path the Wise Men (or the Three Kings) took to baby Jesus Christ in order to shake the tail Herod put on them, according to Christian belief. Juliette was delighted to find her slice contained the *fève*, or bean,

representing the Christ child. This made Juliette king for the day, and, like the *vasilopita*, ushered in good luck for the year ("The Tradition of").

By 1870, long after Juliette took her last bite, the King Cake made its way to New Orleans, Louisiana, where the tradition changed into what most Americans know. This version of the cake is adorned in three colors: purple representing justice, green for faith, and gold for power. The bean or pea that would have been used as the Christ child stand-in during the 1100s would also eventually be replaced by a plastic baby, a less subtle nod to the desired imagery ("King Cake History"). In the 1950s, McKenzie's, a New Orleans bakery, added the new component, porcelain prior to its translation into plastic, to the cake for the first time, and the practice caught on ("Who Put the Baby In"). The outcome for finding the baby, though, remains somewhat the same (good fortune is still bestowed upon the discoverer), but now it comes with a price: hosting next year's King Cake party. The custom is directly connected to Mardi Gras in the United States, and is timed accordingly.

While the *vasilopita* has at least two origin stories, the King Cake is more of an evolving narrative. Its link to the Christian faith is inseparable, but the look of the cake itself has been added to over the centuries to take on even more meaning as it traveled across an ocean. The colors, by symbolizing virtues, serve as constant reminders of the ideals the King Cake expects its consumers to embrace. The circular shape, initially representative of the Three Kings' trail, is also accepted to mean a crown, which transforms the food into a figurative version of edible power ("Who Put the Baby In"). Transitioning the *fève* from a bean or pea to a plastic figurine implies the tradition is linked to modern advances in materials, though of course the more traditional options are still used in some cases. In the 1980s, the King Cake started to contain various fillings. Even the dough of the King Cake changes depending on region (in France or the United States), thereby creating a fluid, local experience by convention. This fluidity provides a contrast to the rigidity of Orthodox Christianity, and the more limited *vasilopita* recipes that exist. It allows for a wide appeal, as a King Cake can be made to match a variety of palates, and, in another example of keeping up with the times, can be shipped anywhere relatively quickly, a service many New Orleans bakeries offer.

That is how the King Cake first arrived in my New York City kitchen. When I heard there was a toy in it, I couldn't wait to dive in. Whether by luck or spiritual hand, I got a silver-colored, plastic Christ Child in my first slice. The excitement of this surpassed my childhood *vasilopita* memories. This looked like a toy. It could become an accessory to my action figures, some of which were the result of other (fast) foods devoured. Here, the baby, because of its toy-like nature, was easily stripped of its religious meaning (or, had I wanted, held to its intended esteem), and incorporated into a pre-existing collection. The coin of the *vasilopita* also adds to a collection, a collection of money, that can then be exchanged for a collection of, say, toys. However, to get a toy out of an edible "blind box" cuts out the middleman, the toy store, and allows a world to be built right away. Instantly, my Power Lords action figure had a baby. Reflecting on it now, I tend to see this fluid transition of the plastic form from Christ Child to toy baby as in-line with my reading of the King Cake as a whole. The story of the cake has as much ability to take on meaning as the figurine nestled within it. And when my toy, like the cake, is introduced into a new environment, the world of my preexisting toys, it integrates. This is another part of the appeal of toys that come with kids' meals: the ability to expand a child's imaginary universe right away by sparking the creativity that makes the recipient incorporate a plastic baby, a plastic chicken nugget, or a die-cast car into the story of their toybox. But unlike this example of instant gratification, we still have a few more years to go before this timeline hits the Happy Meal.

3. *The Hypothetical Story of Aki*. In 1878, roughly around the time Juliette's 12th-century King Cake was making its way to the United States, our next hypothetical friend, Aki, stood in a Kyoto bakery. She made something surprising to today's

dessert lovers. She took sesame and miso and pressed them into a mold, which was cooked over a flame. When done, Aki grabbed a fortune, folded it up, and put it into the hollow space inside the sweet cookie created by the mold. The result was called *tsujiura senbei,* or "fortune crackers." Aki looked upon her creation and, perhaps, considered it as another instrument in the symphony of food/object hybrids in which Maximinus' *vasilopita* and Juliette's King Cake are also players. However, Aki's *tsujiura senbei* were also distinct. Unlike the vague "good luck" of the *vasilopita* coin or the King Cake *fève,* the fortune was specific, automatic, and easily disregarded beyond its novelty. At this point, too, one would be right to have flashes of the Pac Man–shaped fortune cookies offered at the end of meals at Chinese restaurants. One would also be correct to wonder why this hypothetical is set in Japan. This is because, according to research done by Japanese folklorist Yasuko Nakamachi, the modern fortune cookie began, as described, in a temple bakery just outside of Kyoto in the 19th century (Lee).

By the 1950s, the fortune cookie was the final act of countless Chinese American restaurants, and has remained so ever since. It has become such a common ending there that many would assume the fortune cookie began in China. In fact, Nakamachi speculates that the cookie's leap from Japanese to Chinese restaurants happened in the United States during the 1920s and '30s, when Japanese immigrants in San Francisco owned restaurants that made American Chinese cuisine. From there, American servicemembers based in San Francisco would have received the fortune cookies, and then, upon their return from the war, requested them at their hometown Chinese restaurants, thus making the fortune cookie a phenomenon. While Nakamachi points out the Japanese roots of the cookie, Derrick Wong, an executive in the fortune cookie manufacturing industry, states that the cookie has spread through Chinese immigrants to the United States, as it is not popular in either Japan or China, currently (Lee).

For Dr. LuMing Mao, Professor of Writing and Rhetoric Studies at the University of Utah, fortune cookies perpetually exist in this "borderland" between nations. In his *Reading Chinese Fortune Cookie*, he writes, "like the Chinese fortune cookie, Chinese American rhetoric is a hybrid, too: it is born of two competing at the rhetorical borderlands" (Mao 145). LuMing's "hybrid rhetoric" posits that the essence of Chinese American communication is less a fixed point or definitive, logical set of references, but more of a spontaneous recognition that happens in conversations between specific Chinese Americans that usually reveal deeper truths about the experiences of all involved. Similarly, by analyzing the story of the fortune cookie as existing on the borders of at least three countries—Japan, China, and the United States—one can also appreciate the dessert as a hybrid, occupying an in-between space that can't extend past the limits of its own inanimacy. LuMing acknowledges this as the key difference between the hybrid rhetoric of Chinese Americans and that of fortune cookies: the *people* that live in the cultural "border zone" of China and America can emote, intuit, and otherwise "click" in conversation, whereas a fortune cookie cannot. In fact, the fortune cookie's fortune is almost disposable, often, as LuMing points out, not acted upon "beyond the confines of the restaurant" (Mao 147).

Modern kids' meal toys also occupy a hybrid border space. Perhaps that is often the consequence of an object being married to another completely unrelated item in the name of, in this case, Capitalism: one searches for the connection, and then, lacking one, settles into the middle space between the two. For kids' meals, the items offered aren't quite the "official" toys of a property, and they also aren't totally of the meal that's being eaten. There is nothing about a hamburger that necessitates a Beanie Baby or a Snoopy toy, *and* there is also the inescapable knowledge that the *Encanto* toy in my Happy Meal isn't as intricate as the ones on the toy store shelf. Therefore, while the kids' meal toy can just as easily be the baby in the King Cake, integrated into play however the consumer wants, it can also evoke an (intended) desire to either ask for the larger, more expensive toy at a Target or Walmart, or, due to some allegiance to perceived rules of maturity, pick the food-only "adult" items in an effort to leave behind the "kids" part of the meal.

On a recent visit to McDonald's, I witnessed exactly that. A child told his mother he wanted a Happy Meal so as to get the *Pokémon* promotional cards enclosed within. His mother loudly announced that, no, the Happy Meal was now off-limits, as the child's 12th birthday had apparently come and gone, and it was time to just stick to the McNuggets alone. I was about as disappointed as that 12-year-old. (I also felt a little called out, as I was there to order two Happy Meals *just* so I could get the *Pokémon* cards in them, with the food donated to a nearby unhoused gentleman.) I don't want to compare this to LuMing Mao's experience of rhetoric among Chinese Americans. As a white writer, I cannot pretend to understand that important bond enough to liken anything I do to it. However, just expanding on his work with hybrid spaces in general, there is something comforting about recognizing another person occupies that space with you. The in-between lands of existence can get lonely. It is nice to know others are there, even after so many have either chosen or been forced to choose a side. Perhaps part of me was sad to see that boy go.

4. *The Hypothetical Story of Jessie.* In June of 1992, our hypothetical eight-year-old Jessie was excited to sit down with her parents for dinner at McDonald's following her swimming lesson. She wanted a Happy Meal, as she often did, for lots of reasons. Though she didn't yet have the knowledge to make the connection to the King Cake, it was a way for her to find the *fève*, but with far better odds. In fact, it was a sure thing. However, that didn't change the excitement of getting a toy when a trip to the toy store wasn't on the agenda. This was as close to beating the system as Jessie could get. When it came to the power to go toy shopping, her parents held all the cards. But if she could manage to, somehow, miraculously, score some bright molded plastic under the guise of "dinner," Jessie felt like the tables had turned, and she had successfully thwarted her parents' intentions of keeping her small life barren of fun. Plus, the toys were always whimsical little contributions to her toy world, and she was thrilled to write them

Introduction

into her play narrative the way a writer on a soap opera might squeeze in a spontaneous evil twin.

This trip was different, though. When Jessie unboxed her meal, her parents were anything but happy. As their daughter took out a small, plastic, yellow car, with a spinning umbrella, and, seated in the cockpit, a bean-sized Batman villain called the Penguin sat ready for mayhem, Jessie's parents recalled the film where that very character bites off the tip of another person's nose and spews black bile, cheering on his own crimes as it dribbles down his chin. Jessie's parents were mortified. They were shocked that the company they trusted to protect the sanctity of their eating space had violated it so brazenly with the content of a PG-13 movie that, in their eyes, was far too adult for their child, or anyone else's. Jessie ate her meal, and was blissfully ignorant of her parents' disbelief, but, as their daughter played, Jessie's parents planned their next move.

They might have been one of the voices that shouted protest at McDonald's as a result of this promotion. One actual parent complained, "But why is McDonald's promoting this exploitative movie through the sale of its so-called 'Happy Meals'? Has McDonald's no conscience?" (Chapman). This person, summoning an oppositional tone reminiscent of Joseph Welch during the McCarthy hearings, uses the adjective "so-called" to indicate that perhaps the Happy Meal is ironically named if their parent company allows them to endorse distinctly un-happy, violent media through their toy promotions. Such complaints are not interested in what a kid might do with a Catwoman car or a spring-loaded Batmobile isolated from its source text. Instead, they have judged the film *Batman Returns* to be adult, and worry that the toys function as an insidious arm, pulling their children toward it. Even more egregious, this luring is meant to happen during a communal time that is, in many instances, a place for kinship and family: dinner.

This speaks to a deeper truth about the "stuff" that comes with our food. Whether it's the *vasilopita* coin, the King Cake baby, or the fortune cookie fortune, all are linked to some form of wholesomeness. The coin in the *vasilopita* is, by one origin story or the other, there to reinforce a distinctly Christian story, as is the King Cake's prize. The fortune cookie's Japanese roots tell us that this creation came from a bakery near a temple, linking it to spiritual practice. Beyond Kyoto, though, the fortunes themselves are nearly predictable in their positivity, however cliché it may be now. Even communal eating, on its own, has been read as a protected, safe space for those involved. Anthropologist Frances Garrett, et al., studied Tibetan communal meals as times when ritual is invoked to honor, construct, and maintain "appropriate and spatiotemporally situated community order" (Garrett 491). Their work demonstrates that meal sharing has, for centuries, been built in order for the people involved to exchange the intangibles of their relationships—love, kindness, respect—over the tangible goods needed to sustain life. Religious scholar Lawrence Schiffman points out that, in the case of the Dead Sea Scrolls, exclusion from the communal meal was a way to punish offenders (Schiffman 191). Schiffman believes that these ancient meals were "sacral," and therefore preventing one from joining them would have meant not just the denial of food, but the denial of the rites and prayers that may have accompanied it. Thus, it is not just that the sanctity of modern meals can be seen through family gatherings, Thanksgivings, dinners and lunches at religious places of worship, prayers before eating, and celebrations, but that this type of spiritual or pseudo-spiritual security has come with them for centuries. This is one cultural reason why violent and patently *gross* toys can be top sellers in toy stores, but can inspire outrage when paired with dinner.

The *Batman Returns* Happy Meal toys breached a contract some parents felt they had with one of their food providers. It seemed they felt as though they were promised an at least superficially safe environment for their meals in exchange for their money. As a result, Tim Burton has traced this outcry as the reason he was not hired to make *Batman 3* (Zakarin). In 1995, three years after the scandal, McDonald's took another pass at Batman, this time with the maximum amount of vetting around *Batman Forever*. McDonald's executives stipulated that they had to read the *Batman Forever* script before the film even began shooting, and they created a promotion that intentionally excluded Happy Meal toys (but included arguably some of the most fan-favorite glass mugs in their history). McDonald's led with the words they attempted to answer complaints with in 1992: that Batman is a promotion geared toward adults. The fact that, unlike with *Batman Returns*, McDonald's *Batman Forever* campaign did not feature toys provided evidence of their seriousness this time around.

This leaves kids' meal toys to occupy a unique cultural place. They are a node in a network of historical items that have supplemented food that demand an intertextual approach. Intertextuality, as Marsha Kinder notes, demands one study individual texts within the context of their "larger cultural discourse ... in relationship to other texts and their diverse textual strategies and ideological assumptions" (Kinder 2). Essentially, a text is linked to similar earlier and contemporary media that help assign it meaning. Kids' meal toys do not exist in a void. In addition to the above examples, the Cracker Jack prize, Depression Glass, cereal box toys, and many other object/edible pairings make for a sizable web that the kids' meal premium is nowhere near the beginnings of. Far more directly than my primordial historical examples, one can picture the delight of a child who opens their box of Cracker Jacks in the early 1900s to find a small toy inside. Likewise, Depression Glass, or the glass trinkets that frequently came with oatmeal or rice during the Great Depression as an incentive for buyers, speaks clearly to the excitement one felt as they received their *Batman Forever* Two Face glass from McDonald's in 1995. While the circumstances are undeniably different, the practice, and the feelings contained within it, bear more than a passing similarity to each other. Thus, kids' meal toys are modern incarnations of ancestral traditions. Their individual meanings in consumers' personal lives can obfuscate their presence as national, and indeed global, texts. They assist a general ritual—that of a meal among family or friends, under very specific conditions. They expand what borderlands can be, as objects sandwiched between toy store and restaurant. They are not the coins in our *vasilopitas*, the *fèves* of our King Cakes, or the fortunes of our fortune cookies, yet they are, in some ways, expected to adhere to their legacies of safety, surprise, and wholesomeness. They are paratexts that can cross over into textuality themselves.

In the coming chapters, I explore the kids' meal toy as this cultural phenomenon, at times interrupted by my own history with them. This book is not a catalog of kids' meal toys, meticulously organizing and depicting each one. That work has already been done expertly, at least per McDonald's Happy Meal toys, by Joyce and Terry Losonsky, whose myriad, picture-filled volumes showcase these items by decade and region, as well as many other collectors who have contributed similar volumes. Other notable resources for anyone seeking work in this area include Meredith Williams, Bobby Beauchesne (@ConsumerTC on Instagram), and Glen Mullaly, among many others. Additional material can be found online via sites like AllFastFoodToys.com, the r/kidsmeal subreddit, and many social media pages devoted to sharing and trading kids' meal toys and collections. While I have relied on some of those sources for this book, I also incorporate interviews with the creators of kids' meal toys and other experts in the field. Alongside this, I use pre-existing scholarly theory from literature, comics, and toy studies in order to not just understand kids' meal toys, but "read" them. The writings of theorists like Walter Benjamin and Jean Baudrillard have helped me to locate kids' meal toys as objects of both art and collection. Other writers such as, most notably, Jonathan Gray and Henry Jenkins, pop culturalists who unpack what it means for media to produce many spin-off products, allowed me to place the kids' meal toy in time. Through them, I have come to understand the kids' meal toy as an object that is at once temporal, political, and (para)textual. Though this introduction reaches far back in time in order to start from a place that recognizes the kids' meal toy as a timeline point in a long history of items that have altered the eating experience in one way or another, the remainder of the book zooms in closer. I follow the kids' meal toy through its origin(s) and creations, and then down the rabbit holes of theory. This includes explorations of race, gender, collecting, destruction, fads, theater, and, ultimately, ourselves. All of this is done to serve one purpose: to argue

Introduction

that kids' meal toys find meaning as texts that burst binaries. They are at once meaningless playthings and controversial message vessels, representations of race and in conflict with it, fan objects and corporate mascots, and temporary and permanent. Though individuals may see them as one of those two options, culturally, they are both—and more. In their permanence, which is located in collector nostalgia, source media, and the durability and availability of their materials, kids' meal toys preserve a pop culture legacy in a concrete way. However, even the most detailed studies of toys and modern media omit them from the conversation. By leaving kids' meal toys out of the study of pop culture, one neglects narratives—or, as some of the folklorists in this introduction might say, artifacts—that live in states of flux, and, as such, are easily molded by their consumers, frequently children, into meaningful, if often temporary, characters in playworlds that can abide by the source texts from which the objects were derived, alter said media, or ditch it altogether in favor of wholly imagined play. Through lifting the veil on what the kids' meal toy is, and then diving deep into its applications, this book firmly affixes these playthings beside the already-established texts of pop culture. To cover that ground, my chapters at times operate like kids' meal toys, bagged at first, and then, ideally, burst open to live alongside the others collected.

In order to do this, though, I need to set some parameters. Because the range of kids' meal toys is vast and diverse, one book can only cover so much. In addition to trading cataloging for analysis, and therefore admitting that the goal, here, is not to speak to every toy, but those that break the seals of their little fast food baggies and address the greater study of these objects, I limit my study to U.S. kids' meal toys, generally speaking. That kids' meal toys are a global phenomenon deserves more than I can possibly give it. The intimacy of one child receiving one, say, She-Ra figurine from a Sonic Kids' Meal overwhelms the truth that kids the world over are not only having the same experience but are also doing so with toys that will never be seen in North America. The aforementioned Losonskys created two volumes under the *McDonald's Happy Meal Toys Around the World* title in order to showcase the range of these international

14

products, and even those just barely scratch the surface. While I have fond memories of a family trip to Greece in which I noticed, in a McDonald's, that the Happy Meal toys offered there were of a type that baffled me, I am in no position to analyze how those items impacted Greek culture, nor, even more so, other cultures to which I do not belong. However, within the United States, I intentionally select toys from a range of fast food chains. Many times when talking with friends, I will conventionally interchange the terms "kids' meal toy" and "Happy Meal toy." This speaks to how ubiquitous McDonald's has become in branding these toys. This book resists that urge. It is inaccurate to suggest that any one fast food chain "owns" the kids' meal toy. Many restaurants have produced them, and, in so doing, have created a spectrum of objects that run from the scientifically cute (McDonald's McNuggets) to the utterly terrifying (Roy Rogers Critters). I have come to see these variations as genres, and to favor one over another risks a less complete analysis.

Finally, I would be lying if I said my motivation, here, wasn't at least partly personal. In this introduction, I have established, if only barely, a history of object/food pairings meant to shape eating experiences using hypothetical characters. Let me end this introduction with a fifth story, this one not fiction but autobiography, focused on a subject who also invades the chapters to come. When I was a kid, one of those young ages whose number can only come with a margin of error thanks to my then-developing brain, my uncle took me to a McDonald's in Pittsburgh, Pennsylvania. I was there on a family trip, but it was just us two who had broken away for some food. On the counter by the cash register, there was a domed display containing the Happy Meal toys one might receive during the then-current promotion. It was clearly pediocularity,* or Daniel Thomas Cook's term

---

*The ethics of pediocularity are debatable, with many arguing that appealing directly to children, who do not have the analytical development to reason purchasing decisions, is unethical. However, one sees it constantly in fast food restaurants of the 1970s–early 2000s where full-size and countertop displays contained kids' meal toys at a child's eye-level, hyping kids into excitement over their "favorite" of an assortment. Other less pediocular examples of such advertising include translites, which promote kids' meals on stores' menu boards, and opened samples some restaurants put on display behind their counters.

Introduction

for the placement of products to be in the sightlines of kids rather than adults, at full volume (Johnson 93). Within the display stood the Super Looney Tunes Happy Meal, produced in 1991 to coincide with the DC Super Powers action figures, but not released until 1992, the same year as that controversial *Batman Returns* line. But I didn't know any of that then. All I knew was that I loved them. They were the perfect combination of two properties seminal to my little life: superheroes and Bugs Bunny. At that time, liking superheroes didn't exactly make one's life easier. Even as children, we comic book fans knew to stick together. Comics and comic book characters were treated by those around me as wastes of time, members of a "junk" medium better off forgotten. The Looney Tunes had a bit more clout, but even they were seen as distractions from the "real" learning I was supposed to be engaging as an elementary school student. However, in that moment, it dawned on me, in some way, that something could be made *for me*. Even better, the thing made for me was offered to others, others who might also love the two things I loved. Looking back on it now, I must have felt some version of a confluence. I could imagine comparing the figure I got—a Bugs Bunny that became Superman (or Super Bugs) with the help of a snap-on plastic costume—with the ones my friends would get (the Daffy Duck/Batman [Bat Duck], the Petunia Pig/Wonder Woman, or Taz/Flash). Then, I could see my uncle, the Looney Tunes fan, and my father, the comic book collector, play along, too. And behind them, there would be waves of people who found some sort of cathartic release in these toys, just as I did. Again, I don't mean to suggest I was thinking in these terms then, only that I could sense a toy like this could provide me with something I desperately wanted as a geeky only child: instant community. These toys made such an impression on me that, when I grew older, I purchased two sets of them on the secondary market—one bagged, one to play with. Next I found and bought that very display next to the cashier that intrigued me so much then. Now I own the wax sculpts for that promotion, and have spoken with some of the makers of those prototypes for this book. Anything that creates this type of a response in someone cannot be void of meaning.

Just as, perhaps, Maximinus after discovering the *vasilopita*

16

coin, and Juliette after the *fève*, Aki after her fortune, and me after my Super Bugs, I hope this book will call together others who, excited by one person's discovery, come to see what all the fuss is about, only to learn that the real blessing, the real luck, the real playtime, is getting to build our shared world of little, surprise toys together.

CHAPTER 1

"A prize in every box"

Establishing a Kids' Meal Toy History
and Its Broader Socio-Political Intersections

"Some food, some fun, it's all inside this Happy Meal."
—Happy Meal slogan, 2007–present

This book has two primary aims: one practical, the other theoretical. This chapter is devoted to my work's practical goal of histori-
cizing the origins of kids' meal toys and the ways in which they are
produced. Further chapters will then theoretically deconstruct the
kids' meal toy so as to study its relevance to scholarly conversations
in which it is currently absent and explain its cultural staying power.
This is necessitated by the kids' meal toy's role as a paratext, or, as literary theorist Gérard Genette defined the term, a piece of scaffolding built to surround a primary narrative to support its transmission.
In the world of kids' meal toys, this is best seen in the way, to offer
one example, the 1989 *The Little Mermaid* Happy Meal toys from
McDonald's (paratext) aided in the telling of *The Little Mermaid*
story (text) by Disney. However, because, as theorist Jonathan Gray
points out, "paratexts often take tangible form," we have two different paths to analysis: (1) we can study how the "tangible form" interacts with its intangible story, and (2) we can dissect how the "tangible
form" came to be (Gray 6). It is wise to take interest in both, as each
has unique power to deconstruct the kids' meal toy's cultural impact,
whether that be as objects that leave a physical mark on the world
they were created into, or as literary dendrites extending from a central node of text.

Before we can break apart the kids' meal toy, though, we need a primer on how they were put together. In the interviews I conducted with kids' meal toy consumers and creators for this book, a common trend emerged. The vast majority of people I spoke to could recall with ease their favorite kids' meal toy and the reason(s) why they held that particular item in such high esteem. However, they also, understandably, admitted to massive gaps in their knowledge of kids' meal toys in general. Among casual consumers, there was a sense that kids' meal toys emerged out of the ether: plunked into a branded bag, and dissolved again until the next noteworthy promotion which may have come in a month, a year, or a decade. There was often shock when the discussion shifted to the kids' meal promotions that happened outside of their awareness, fast food giveaways from decades past, toys from smaller chains, or the prevalence of these items in today's market. This suggests that one's relationship to their kids' meal toys is deeply personal, which, in a way, is by design. When we are kids, these surprises typically appear as if by magic. It was not until I reached my tween years, at earliest, that I even noticed fast food employees putting the kids' meal toys into their boxes as orders were being filled, and I was in my late teens before I learned you could simply ask to buy these playthings independently, and have some degree of choice over which one(s) you purchased (thank you, Burger King *The Simpsons Treehouse of Horror* promotion). Before this, fast food chains had succeeded, in my case, in making the experience of getting a kids' meal toy mystically intimate, which of course only heightened the importance of these objects. They may have still been special had I seen them as pre-planned waves of toys given evenly to customers, but the fact that they felt like representations of a one-on-one relationship I had with my favorite fantasy worlds via the conduit of restaurants I craved most made them, in the best examples, urgent and deeply treasured.

But as I have also found in discussing kids' meal toys with collectors for this book, those "best examples" vary from person to person. I will insist that the McDonald's McDino Changeables Happy Meal represents a high watermark of kids' meal promos, but others have just as fervently maintained that Burger King's *Lord of the Rings* kids' meal takes the cake, and more still have stood up for myriad others.

Through this, one starts to develop a fairly accurate picture of kids' meal toys as rotating promotions that each try to cast as wide a fandom net as possible so as to make each wave the "favorite" of a given group. Once one starts to see beyond their own treasured toys, questions arise around how many "nets" have been cast, for how long, and for what reason. Luckily, we have answers.

The Burger Chef Revolution

To understand the rise of the kids' meal toy, one must first be grounded in the story of modern fast food. The current archetype of the fast food restaurant—a sometimes kitschy or maybe sterile uniformly branded building in which an array of standardized fare is prepared quickly, as if on an assembly line, and sold to customers who have the option of dining in, taking their food to-go, or driving "thru" all for a cost generally lower than a "sit-down" establishment at which waiters take orders for meals created more delicately—spread rapidly after World War II. As Alex Park writes in "The Wartime Roots of the Global Fast Food Boom," "The industrial economy that had ended the Great Depression and closed out the Second World War had turned inwards, building prefabricated homes and four-door sedans instead of tanks and planes" (Park) This evokes the post-war suburb, stocked with new families, war veterans pivoting into early careers, and the American commute, whose speed increased via mass produced cars and a freshly-launched interstate highway system. Industry also aimed its wartime efficiency at post-war initiatives like farming. Says Park, "When chemical manufacturers stopped making munitions and started making fertilizer, they supercharged corn production, setting off a livestock explosion which has never abated" (Park) This agricultural revolution created more food inventory that chains such as McDonald's, which was rapidly reproducing across the United States in the '50s, could easily access to fuel their business. Combined with the Baby Boom and the restructuring of American living spurred on by the return of countless soldiers, an efficient, dependable, consistent

21

eating option like the one offered by fast food chains fit right into the zeitgeist.

And emerging fast food chains knew it. Companies that existed pre-war like White Castle and Bob's Big Boy began to expand and innovate. As soon as 1956, Bob's Big Boy began marketing to kids with their *Adventures of Big Boy* comic book, as well as other in-store premiums. McDonald's, which emerged during the Second World War, transitioned from a small operation owned by two brothers to Ray Kroc's constantly evolving franchise. Further, many new chains crowded the field of fast food, all clamoring to make the most in-demand product rallied under post-war American values. Advertising, recruiting, and franchising all echoed this sentiment through their appeals to patriotism. Ads for McDonald's consistently featured a drawing of their restaurant, a building whose design traded practicality for artistic license, adorning the sides of the bright, glass-heavy burger stand with large golden arches whose purpose was solely to trigger easy recognition, even at a distance, of the company that erected this monument to, as those same advertisements often said, "America's burger." These restaurants were not solid brick fortresses that could stand a chance against bombs or could go dark in the event of an air raid. They represented a country past all of that, in which citizens could feel safe even outside, lit by the bright fluorescents of a white, yellow, and glass boldly visible roadside stand. As Alan Brody, et al., state in their thesis *Peculiar Capitalism: Fast-Food Franchising and Entrepreneurship in Postwar America*, "From drive-in to drive-up to drive-through, fast food outlets became a worldwide symbol of American enterprise, capitalism, and preeminent business model" (Brody 14). The idea, here, is that working for a new fast food chain meant class mobility, financial prosperity, the potential for upward mobility, and access to the promised, and jingoistic, "American Dream" visualized during this time as an anti–Communist manifestation of individualist wealth generated by anyone with enough of the enterprising spirit needed to grow it. While such framing fundamentally ignored all of the institutionally racist, sexist, and other discriminatory factors that prevented, and continue to prevent, equal, or even sizable, realizations of this dream, franchising attempted to define a specific path to it.

Though franchising, or the process by which an independent operator comes to own a location or locations whose trademark is controlled by a larger corporation, is an old idea, existing both in the United States and beyond it for centuries, certain developments unique to 1950s America created new franchisees at an exponential rate. According to the International Franchise Association,

> Franchising's emergence in the post-war 1950s took advantage of pent-up consumer demand, an abundance of available franchisees with the returning veterans, and capital provided by separation pay and the G.I. Bill. However, the most important post-war event to benefit franchising came in 1946 with the enactment of the federal Lanham (Trademark) Act. Under the act, property owners were able to safely enter into licenses with third parties—an essential requirement for franchising to expand [International Franchise Association].

In other words, because of the G.I. Bill's funding of veteran endeavors, corporations like fast food chains could appeal to returning soldiers by tying the expenditure of their government benefits to a new life that allowed them to "be their own boss" in the American economic boom they fought to provide. Furthermore, the Lanham Act would ensure their investment by making it illegal for an unlicensed party to use a registered trademark without paying the necessary cost to become a franchisee. Because of this, a company like, say, Burger King, who started franchising operations in 1954, could promise franchisees that their fees would guarantee exclusive access to their brand, and all else unique to that specific company. This map took potential post-war franchisees from the income received via their G.I. Bills to fees paid to protect their ownership of a reputable, national (or international) branded business under the Lanham Act, and resulted in a sea of new operators who emerged into the fast food franchise boom of the 1950s.

However, by the transition into the 1960s, many found this route to success an undelivered promise. As Brody writes, "by the 1960s, the numerous failed enterprises show an industry beset by risk while defending its declining reputation.... Many potential entrepreneurs fell victim to fraud, while others encountered a powerful industry propaganda machine" (Brody 12). This suggests that the fervor of the 1950s franchisee also excited the decade's franchisors, some of whom leapt into a crowded fast food market with inflated pledges of financial enrichment on which they could not deliver. Chains like McDonald's experienced well-known success, but other corporations collected franchise fees and, when they failed to develop the markets to house their new crop of operators, left the hopeful store owner holding the bag. Corporations did their best to maintain some semblance of respectability, but, by the mid-'60s, the lived experiences of those dejected by failed ventures built on hollow assurances of success created a need for the fast food status quo to shift.

One common case study for this type of fraud stems from the "Minnie Pearl's Fried Chicken" scandal. During the '60s, franchises were sold for the yet-to-be-built fast chicken restaurant that was intended to compete with Kentucky Fried Chicken. Franchisee buy-in was extreme, the stock price of the company soared, and all before a single restaurant was opened. As recorded by Bill Carey's *Fortunes, Fiddles, and Fried Chicken: A Nashville Business History*, once Minnie Pearl's Fried Chicken finally opened a limited number of restaurants out of the hundreds that were franchised, they largely failed to turn a profit, but that all happened after a small percentage of insiders sold off their stock in the company, making them a hefty sum. The debacle included Tennessee political candidates, state newspapers, and celebrities Minnie Pearl and gospel singer Mahalia Jackson, whose name was going to be lent to another chain created by the same corporation (Carey). This large-scale erosion of the American franchise model garnered national attention, with *The New York Times* devoting a front-page story to the matter. If post-war legislation and U.S. infrastructure redesign made a compelling, worry-free case for franchising, scandals like this throttled back a portion of that enthusiasm, giving pause to some who may have otherwise jumped head-first into helping the corporate growth of new fast food chains. However, this was only one of the problems faced by fast food companies in the 1960s.

Competing brands also faced a near-saturated market. Of the twenty-four largest currently-operating fast food chains, seventeen of them began in the 1950s and '60s, with a plethora more if one includes those that are no longer in business. This includes mainstays like McDonald's, Burger King, Wendy's, Taco Bell, and Sonic, among others (Sulem). Unlike Minnie Pearl's Fried Chicken, franchising helped each of these restaurants spread quickly across the nation, finding new markets, and new profit, every quarter. Given the massive number of companies, and the huge quantity of locations under each, there was a great deal of pressure on each to prove why they stood above the rest. While McDonald's tied their burgers to American identity through ads that proclaimed themselves "America's favorite," Burger King touted the "Whopper," a filling, flame-broiled, "meal-on-a-bun" that could not be found elsewhere. With Bob's Big Boy burger being the signature sandwich of their 550 1965 locations, and the Big Shef emerging that year to fill Burger Chef's approximately 400 menu boards, McDonald's put out its competing Big Mac in 1967, giving what was at the time the company's 700–800 stores* their first taste of their now-legacy sandwich. Restaurants like Taco Bell could stand out on its cuisine alone, and Sonic was the only large chain able to boast its "drive-in" feature that accommodated America's expanded car market, but the fight for customers' attention, and money, was still as aggressive as ever.

So, with the need to assure franchisees that they were buying into a profitable company capable of delivering on its promises, and corporate innovation fueling the uniqueness of chain identities, it makes sense that the fast food market of the 1960s started to become more full-throated in its appeal to an essentially untapped demographic: children.

McDonald's began this pivot in 1963 when they introduced Ronald McDonald, "the Hamburger-Happy Clown," on TV via three commercials seen in the Washington, D.C., market. In the 1950s, Ray Kroc started franchising McDonald's restaurants and famously did not limit franchisee creativity. As long as franchisees paid their fees, and ran their restaurants with a degree of uniformity and a work

---

*As of 2023, McDonald's had 40,275 worldwide locations.

ethic up to his standard, they had some latitude in terms of suppliers and individual store details. This attracted advertising executive Oscar Goldstein, who became a D.C.–area franchisee himself. Because of his work in the ad world, Goldstein knew Willard Scott, who had just portrayed the sensational Bozo the Clown on WRC-TV in Washington from 1959 to 1962. Understanding that Bozo was instantly recognizable to most U.S. children at the time, Goldstein asked Scott to use his clown personality to bring a younger audience to McDonald's. While McDonald's does not officially assign a creator to Ronald McDonald, Scott writes the clown was his idea in his memoir *The Joy of Living*, a claim supported by McDonald's Northeast Division President Henry Gonzalez in a 2000 *Today Show* segment (Scott). This early fusion of children's appeal and restaurant operations worked, as Ronald McDonald has been steadily representing McDonald's internationally for sixty years and counting as of this writing. However, although Ronald McDonald became a globally-known phenomenon, in 1963, his presence was only slowly growing. As a result, another mascot represented the company in a crucial way to complete the task of winning over a younger demographic.

In 1964, McDonald's introduced its earliest kids' toy. Not affiliated with any particular meal, the "Let's Go to McDonald's" dexterity puzzle required players to gently rotate a metal milkcap-sized cylinder so that two small pinballs settled into corresponding indentations in the bottom plate. When they did, they formed the pupils of Archie McDonald's eyes. Archie McDonald was a short-lived McDonald's mascot who filled a brief period between the end of Speedee's tenure and the full start of Ronald McDonald's. While Ronald McDonald is most often associated with the chain's kid-friendly appeal via the Happy Meal, Archie McDonald stood for an era when the company frequently did not require a purchase in order for a child to receive a prize. In addition to the dexterity game, Archie McDonald was also used to advertise giveaway trick-or-treat bags and pins, all free to children who asked for them. The slogan that appears on the dexterity game's surface, "Let's Go to McDonald's," further emerges on print advertising and other promotional items

featuring Archie McDon-
ald. If Speedee repre-
sented quick service for
adults with an appetite,
Archie encouraged kids
to exert their influence
over their parents in order
to manifest a McDon-
ald's visit. Indeed, children needed no money at
all to get something from
the experience, and the
company understood that
parents would likely agree
to impulse purchases
once at the restaurant. In

An early fast food kids' premium: the 1964
Archie McDonald dexterity game.

other words, Archie McDonald walked so Ronald McDonald could
run.

As unique as Archie was, and Ronald McDonald is, however,
one should note that many fast food chains of the time produced
ads aimed at kids. A brief look at 1960s Burger King advertisements
reveals many depicting a child consuming a Whopper, with some
even going so far as to use a clown. Wendy's, which emerged in 1969,
featured a child's image as their mascot, and an implied, name-only
association with a popular Harvey Comics "Good Little Witch." Taco
Bell used the image of a young, cartoon boy in their ads of the 1960s,
though this mascot, which utilized nearly every facet of the stereotypical Mexican caricature, does not offer much in the way of positive messaging. And of course, as mentioned previously, Bob's Big
Boy had been printing its own comics since 1956. All of this is to
say: fast food chains could not have significantly stood out during
this time with conventional advertising-based outreach to children.
More innovation was needed if one company was to overtake the
others in the race for the children's market.

Enter Burger Chef. Though a nearly forgotten relic today, Burger
Chef was a fast food chain that achieved prominence during its

decades-spanning run. The idea began in 1954, when Frank and Donald Thomas patented their "flame broiler" which produced a burger patty taste distinct from that of other chains. (Currently, Burger *King* still markets its burgers by mentioning this cooking method by name.) In 1957, the brothers, along with Robert Wildman, opened their first Burger Chef location. By 1966, the trio had 440 stores operating in the United States, and were "the fastest-growing hamburger chain in the country and the second largest behind industry leader McDonald's" (Sanders). Their restaurant building design was unique, with white and red beams housing large glass windows, a chef mascot adorning its large sign. Burger Chef eateries were bright and spacious, offering guests not primarily a place that served the practicality of food consumption, but the pleasurable enjoyment of a space built to be stayed in. When the restaurant shifted from its early drive-in format to a sit-down style layout, as McDonald's would also do, they further emphasized the joy of lingering in their vibrant buildings. As noted previously with other chains, Burger Chef, too, appealed to kids in the 1960s through cartoon children that brought their menus to playful life. In this way, Burger Chef joined the mainstream fast food trend of generating in-house mascots that could either reflect child faces back to them, or, like Ronald McDonald's clown, employ characters with which kids were already familiar. However, Burger Chef also went one step further.

These mascots, created by many fast food corporations, work as paratexts that give their products significance. As Jonathan Gray notes, "[Advertisers frame what they sell] not simply by telling us to buy such products or services, but by creating a life, character, and meaning for all manner of products and services. Hype, in short, creates meaning" (Gray 3). An oft-repeated, by Gray and others, caveat about media states that they cannot tell consumers what to think, but what to think about. An advertising line saying some version of "Buy our product" cannot sell on its own, as it cannot convince enough people that they have a need or desire to do so. However, to give, in the case of fast food, a hamburger "character" means that, now, there is a narrative surrounding the product, and it is often a story in which consumers play an essential role. Mascots serve as

Chapter 1. *"A prize in every box"*

paratexts that tell this story, and promotional embodiments of those characters become tangible paratexts of their own, allowing consumers to take that narrative home with them and participate in it further. This stokes the "hype" to which Gray refers. It is the yearning and excitement within consumers generated by paratexts that promote the *story* of a fast food corporation's hamburgers so that customers feel as though they are buying more than simple sustenance. With kids' meal toys, as with children's media, the ethics of this are debatable. Certainly, for critics like Stephen Kline (marketers limit the imaginations of youngsters through the products they sell them) and Thomas Englehardt (television producers and marketers cloak 30-minute commercials in shows presented as narrative independent of advertising), it is insidious to embed a product in a structured story and use paratexts to sell the narrative, and thereby the product, to kids. Others, like Dan Fleming, may see toys like these as reflections of what is popular, responses to a market that already has a demand for a specific product. Whatever the relationship between marketer and consumer, these corporate mascots told the story of the food they represented and its link to the people who would ideally eat it. However, the fact that a corporation understands a story must be told about their product does not mean they necessarily know the best way to tell it. This has given rise to many promotional attempts to sell fast food to varying degrees of success.

In the late 1960s, Burger Chef began giving away promotional items designed with young people in mind. For example, in 1967, Burger Chef commissioned the agency Bridges/Sharp/Van Tassel, Inc., to create a series of "book covers" that featured restaurant branding, games, pop culture parody, and personalization opportunities. These book covers were single sheets of paper large enough to wrap around the cover of a hardback textbook, thereby transforming an academic tome into a surface for play. One featured prompts like, "Draw groovy threads for 'Sticky,'" next to an illustration that very closely resembles English model Twiggy. Nods to social protest, 1960s sitcom characters, and popular comic book characters, always distant enough from the official licensed property so as to avoid infringement, interweave a busy landscape of Tic Tac Toe, empty

29

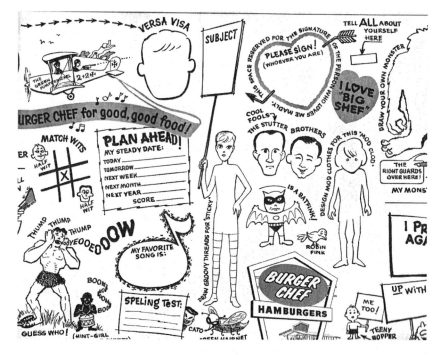

A 1967 Burger Chef promotional book cover.

faces to be filled in, and space for information commonly entered into a daily planner. All of this combines to form an item clearly targeted at a tween/teen crowd who would understand the more mature references contained on the book cover. It promotes Burger Chef, but also teeters on edginess, a way of appealing to young people in search of representations of the nonconformity to which they are drawn, especially amidst the social movements of the 1960s, and the pop culture that interacted with it. By all accounts, these book covers were not a major draw that pushed young people toward Burger Chef (though, the chain was also prospering, and it is difficult to weigh the impact of any one factor on that growth), they speak to the formation of the chain's identity as one that wants to capture the youth market—not just kids, but teenagers, too.

As Burger Chef entered the 1970s, this interest would only intensify. According to Burger Chef historian Scott R. Sanders, "Most of Burger Chef's promotions during the 1970s were targeted toward children" (Sanders). At the start of the decade, this is best represented by Burger Chef's revamp of their store signage which changed the chef mascot illustration from a slightly more realistic drawing to a rudimentary cartoon that resembles a conventional kid's doodle.

But, in 1973, Burger Chef changed the fast food game by being the first restaurant to introduce a kids' meal. Named the "Burger Chef Funmeal," the menu option was "designed for children and consisted of a hamburger, french fries, a small drink, a dessert item, and a toy set into a take-home tray decorated with Burger Chef characters" (Sanders). The Funmeal shrunk the portion size of an adult meal and paired the food with a toy that, unlike the 1967 book covers, played to the desires of young kids, rather than the teen set. Given its novelty, it is understandable that Burger Chef historian Sanders notes the Funmeal as "enormously popular" (Sanders). In 1973, the chain still enjoyed the #2 slot in the national rankings of top fast food restaurants, and Burger Chef's Funmeal innovation is surely relevant to their success. However, another aspect of Burger Chef's identity, and possibly their prosperity, can be found by reading the Funmeal toys themselves.

An early 1970s Funmeal promotion featured four rings, each of which represented a different Burger Chef monster mascot. These monster mascots would be featured across many Funmeal promotions throughout the 1970s. The cartoonish characters included Fang, a vampire; Angel, an ogre in a schoolboy uniform playing with a yo-yo; Seymore, a stereotypical robber cape-clad and obscured by a wide-brimmed fedora that evokes a scarier Hamburglar; and Jethro, a mace-wielding, decomposing Frankenstein's monster. These creatures are each combinations of the humorously shifty and genuinely scary. Angel, for example, bears no resemblance to a monster one might conventionally recognize, and, on top of that, he twists a child's school uniform into something sinister as it conflicts with his imposing body and blank stare. Angel, for lack of a better description, very clearly isn't one. Jethro's malevolence is even more blunt. Of the four monsters, he is the only one of them to literally carry a weapon. His arm that holds the mace looks as if it is mid-extension, and that, combined with his face that is nearly a

Early 1970s Burger Chef monster rings.

skull whose skin has shrunk around it, creates a character who one could actually see doing harm. These are not Ronald McDonald, "Hamburger-Happy" and ready to usher kids into a warm and safe environment; these are Burger Chef monsters, characters who might exist in the Count Chocula universe on a good day, and they are very ready to scare the Funburger out of you.

The early 1970s saw several iterations of these Burger Chef monsters. Appearing on the company's unique cardboard trays, a nod to Frankenstein's monster called Crankenburger, joined by other Universal Studios clones, comprised the narrative comics and masks that encased the Funmeal. These interactive trays created play environments for kids to use with their promotional toys, creating a fully-formed experience for child consumers. Much like cereal boxes, jokes, comic strips, and punch-out collectibles covered nearly every inch of the Funmeal trays. While these comics embraced monster characters, the cartoonishness of their illustration style exchanged Burger Chef's 1960s-era edginess, and even the grotesqueness of their Halloween rings, for a softer, more kid-friendly approach.

In fact, the rings and the trays neatly encapsulate Burger Chef's step-by-step progress toward patently uncontroversial material that would give few parents pause. The book covers were not conventionally frightening, but they did push the boundary of subversive social commentary more than items from other fast food chains. Their efforts were inescapably corporate, but they also effectively hid their mass market "squareness" by appealing to a generation seeking nonconformity to restrictive social norms. Burger Chef book covers represented a company that lived within conventional fast food

A 1974 Burger Chef Funmeal food tray.

expectations, but was unafraid to challenge them, too. The Funmeal monsters pushed these boundaries as well, but differently. Where the book covers were surprisingly encouraging of rebellious social satire, the monster collectibles were unexpectedly willing to tap into kids' love of horror, an area not many fast food chains were willing to go at the time. It is no surprise this strategy worked. Plenty of children enjoy horror. As pop culture writer Joshua Pantano writes for *The Ithacan*, "Regardless of how tough these situations might seem, children learn that they can get through them by being brave, and horror lets them engage with these conflicts in a safe and controlled environment" (Pantano). While, for Pantano, these "environments" are books, movies, and TV shows, Burger Chef, through their monsters, effectively said that fast food meals count, too. After all, a child has the same ability to put down a scary toy as they do a frightening book. If they do not quickly disengage, though, the child will find, with the Funmeal monster collectibles and other texts, that the joy of moving through the horror to realizations of safety can be its own reward. A child is unlikely to shrink from Jethro in the same way they might run from *The Shining*, but that does not negate the fact that the fight-or-flight possibility is there for both. The book might get shut, or read privately, but the Jethro ring may initially cause repulsion, but then be worn as a triumph over the initial fear, or a talisman that serves a fantasy narrative of the wearer. Either way, the rings, like the book covers, encourage some sort of growth on behalf of the young person consuming them, and, in that way, they understandably unite as Burger Chef products.

Throughout the 1970s, Burger Chef continued to pioneer kids' meal toys successfully. This payoff was so great that competing chains, intentionally or not, echoed Burger Chef's innovation. When Burger Chef built products around its scary universe of monsters, other chains crafted promotions bearing the faces of their own sometimes frightening characters. As Burger Chef moved into licensing intellectual property for Funmeals, starting with their 1977 *Star Wars* offering, the competition also began exploring the benefits of material not created in-house. Had Burger Chef maintained its market share past the 1980s, it may be more widely seen as first out of the gate on many of these practices. However, with Burger Chef's 1982 sale to Imasco, many of their locations either closed, or converted to Hardee's restaurants, a brand also owned by their new parent corporation. This opened the door for the number one fast food chain in the world to dominate the kids' meal toy market by an even wider margin.

The Emergence of the Happy Meal

As Burger Chef entered its redesign phase in the early 1970s, so did McDonald's. If the 1960s were a test decade for both restaurants to issue sporadic toy giveaways and kid-centered advertisements, the 1970s were the years when these restaurants fully integrated kids' meal marketing into their menus. Starting in 1971, McDonald's created commercials that told the story of the hero and villains of the new McDonaldland. The hero, initially, was Ronald McDonald, but he was soon joined by other do-gooders like Officer Big Mac and Mayor McCheese, McDonaldland professionals with hamburgers as heads. The villains included the sandwich-swiping Hamburglar, the shake-stealing Evil Grimace, and the Filet-O-Fish pirate Captain Crook. These heavies were not perhaps as scary as Burger Chef's eventual cast of misfits, but they were just as menacing. However, at the time of their debut, some argued that the real criminals lived not in McDonaldland, but in the real McDonald's Corporation and its advertising agency, Needham, Harper, and Steers.

In 1968, Sid and Marty Krofft created *H.R. Pufnstuf*, a children's TV show that showcased the brothers' puppeteering talent. The show became popular, and, in 1970, Chicago-based ad company Needham, Harper, and Steers approached the Kroffts because they wanted to win a marketing deal with McDonald's. To do this, Needham wanted to make commercials for a new, live action McDonald's fantasy universe called "McDonaldland" based on the Kroffts' *H.R. Pufnstuf*. In court-documented letters between the Kroffts and Needham, the ad agency recognized that they needed to pay the puppeteers fees for their work. In a later phone call, Needham told the Kroffts that the campaign had, in fact, been canceled. But, according to the case, this was far from the truth. The McDonaldland contract had already been awarded to Needham, and the project was a go. Without paying the Kroffts, Needham poached the puppeteers' designers and voice actors to create their McDonaldland characters. McDonald's wanted this effort to extend beyond TV spots, so the McDonaldland bunch would adorn toys, hand puppets, pins, and print material alongside their small screen launch. In every iteration, the McDonaldland cast bore a striking resemblance to the Kroffts' *H.R. Pufnstuf*, which resulted in the lawsuit *Sid & Marty Krofft Tele. v. McDonald's Corp.* which went to trial in 1973, and was ultimately decided in 1977. The Court found McDonald's liable, and a $50,000 award (about $250,000 in 2023) was given to the Kroffts (*Sid & Marty Krofft Tele. v. McDonald's Corp.*, 1977). Throughout litigation, McDonald's ramped up their production of commercials and tie-in toys that used the McDonaldland characters. While the judgment cost the fast food juggernaut the use of some characters, it by no means eliminated McDonaldland, and the campaign earned McDonald's far more than it lost in payment to the Kroffts. As its biggest competitor, Burger Chef, began its descent in the late 1970s, McDonald's proved itself nearly untouchable, weathering a Court loss as if it was a slap on the wrist.

As the case moved through the justice system, McDonald's capitalized on Burger Chef's Funmeal idea by crafting its own "Happy Meal." Having several years of Funmeal examples behind them meant McDonald's could enter the kids' meal game having learned from another company's successes and failures. The Happy Meal concept went through two earlier stages before evolving into the kids' meal that is still a feature of modern McDonald's restaurants. In 1975, McDonald's began fusing McDonaldland characters with kid-directed food via projects like the Sea Bag. In a way, this product combined two earlier Burger Chef ideas: the Funmeal and The Mariner. As discussed earlier, the Funmeal included small-sized food and a toy, but The Mariner was a fish-and-chips-style plate aimed at adults. McDonald's did not offer strips of fried fish, but they did sell their branded Filet-O-Fish, which comprised the "Sea" portion of the Sea Bag. Also included were a regular size order of french fries and cookies shaped like McDonaldland characters. Using the cookies with the cartoon image of Captain Crook on the paper bag, the Sea Bag was available to all, but unmistakably designed with kids in mind.

Outside the United States, though, one franchisee may have even beat the Sea Bag to the punch, building an even more kid-friendly option for smaller stomachs. Yolanda Fernández de Cofiño and her husband Jose founded the first Guatemalan McDonald's in 1974. In a video Fernández de Cofiño made for McDonald's, she explained that she noticed children could not finish the larger portions that were standard for McDonald's regular meals. As a result, she created

Chapter 1. "A prize in every box"

a "children's menu with a smaller burger, smaller fries, a small soda, and a small sundae," also including a small toy from her local market with the "Cajita Feliz" for her new "Ronald Menu" ("Un homenaje a la"). Though we know Fernández de Cofiño purchased her franchise in 1974, it is uncertain when, exactly, she realized the portion sizes were too large, and that invoking the name of Ronald McDonald, per the "Ronald Menu," would help kids find food meant for them. As such, it is hard to say whether Fernández de Cofiño's idea predated 1975's Sea Bag, if it happened concurrently, or if it was slightly later. Through Fernández de Cofiño's participation in the 1977 World Franchisee Convention, it is known that, by this year, McDonald's executives were aware of her creation, and encouraged her to present it to others at this event. Even if Fernández de Cofiño's concept came after the Sea Bag, the way she geared her meal specifically and explicitly toward children, and included a toy with the food, locates her idea much closer to the eventual Happy Meal than Captain Crook's implicitly kid-friendly Sea Bag.

After the '77 World Franchisee Convention, McDonald's Regional Advertising Manager Dick Brams contacted Bob Bernstein at Bernstein-Rein, a communications firm that had been retained by McDonald's since 1967, with a request to make the official version of Fernández de Cofiño's idea. This began the next phase of the idea, where the bits and pieces of primordial Happy Meals would combine to make the colorfully-boxed, toy-accompanied signature kids' meal. The first design to emerge from this was 1977's Fun-to-Go Meal, whose cardboard box featured either a buildable McDonald's restaurant complete with cut-out food and trays, or a comic strip that wrapped around the container which was similar in style to the 1978–1979 *Ronald McDonald* cartoon printed in the Chicago Tribune. The "Fun-to-Go" name was used initially because McDonald's was also trying to promote their new "drive-thru" service, and the "to-Go" piece of the branding highlighted the quick, take-home nature of this option. The Fun-to-Go Meal was regional, limited to the Kansas City market, and typically came with a paper promotion like a Ronald McDonald "heat transfer" T-shirt iron-on or a "Fortune Burger" scratch-off fortune, mimicking the central reward of a fortune cookie. Much like Burger Chef's early promotions, each of these were branded with in-house mascots as opposed to licensed properties. The Fun-to-Go Meal tested well enough to evolve the idea into the "Happy Meal," changing the name on the box and increasing the activities it offered. On these early Happy Meal boxes, kids could play matching games, solve riddles, and finish drawings of Officer Big Mac. These boxes resembled the activity-laden Burger Chef book covers, but for a younger set.

Though Bob Bernstein gets much of the credit for being in charge of the Happy Meal's box design, he was not the artist behind the cardboard container's whimsical cartoons and games. That man was illustrator and storyteller Simms Taback, who would go on to win a Caldecott Medal in 2000 for *Joseph Had a Little Overcoat*, a book he began in 1977, around the same time he was illustrating the Happy Meal box. The art for both is similar: large-bodied characters with small-pupiled faces and realistic shading to make the figures pop off the page. Where the comic strips offered basic renditions of the McDonaldland gang, Taback brought these characters to life through vivid yet still very playful images. This playfulness was central to Taback's art, as he often found depth in characters with a quirky relationship to the world. In this way, it is fitting *Joseph Had a Little Overcoat* was a product of Taback's Happy Meal period. In the book, Jewish farmer Joseph starts the story with an overcoat. As Joseph ages, so does the coat, shrinking first to a jacket, and then, eventually, when there is only so much fabric left, a button. Joseph finally loses the button, but still has the story of the overcoat, which is what he is narrating in the book. He ends by stating the lesson of the tale: "You can always make something out of nothing" (Taback 18).

I think of the kids' meal toy in much the same way as Joseph does the overcoat. When the toy is first received, bagged and brand new, it has an outsized role in the receiver's play, perhaps even being the only toy at the table, if one is dining in. As the owner ages, the toy shrinks, maybe not physically (though, if pieces are lost—that, too), but in terms of relevance. Maybe it is relegated to a toy box. Maybe it is only hauled out occasionally, a pinch hitter called in

Chapter 1. *"A prize in every box"*

when the MVP dolls and action figures are out of service. Down the line, maybe it even finds its way onto a desk, chipped paint marking its years. Often, kids' meal toys are lost by their owners, much like Joseph loses his small button. However, like the overcoat, one still has the story of their toy, how they first encountered it, what it meant to them, and its larger importance. *Joseph Had a Little Overcoat* was Taback's way of showing that even the littlest, lost objects can have big impacts through their stories. This book is my way of saying the same.

Once Taback completed work on the Happy Meal box, it was put into midwestern test markets in 1977 where, as expected, it succeeded well enough to go national. Many of the July 1979 *Ronald McDonald* comic strips in the Chicago Tribune thus end with a final panel that announces the new Happy Meal. This panel features a revised box that, stylistically, does not appear to be from Taback. This art is far more similar to that of the comic strip, and uses a circus theme to present the jokes and riddles reminiscent of the '77 version. If Bob Bernstein got his Happy Meal box inspiration from watching his son interact with the games on the backs of cereal boxes, as he claimed, then both Taback's box and the update captured this well ("Who Really Invented"). In place of the paper premiums more typical of the Fun-to-Go meal and the early Happy Meals, the 1979 release contained small items like rings and pencil toppers that bore the images and sculpts of McDonaldland characters. These prizes were closer to what Burger Chef offered, with McDonald's character rings being formally similar to their competitors, though obviously featuring different mascots.

By the end of that year, McDonald's moved the Happy Meal into

An example of the types of rings McDonald's offered in the 1970s.

another territory Burger Chef had been two years earlier: licensing. In 1977, Burger Chef licensed the Star Wars intellectual property for use on their Funmeal boxes and in promotional items. This resulted in C-3PO Funmeal trays, in addition to variants featuring other characters, that could be punched out along perforated lines to create a paper Droid or other piece of the Star Wars universe. The base of these containers, where the small drink, burger, and fries plugged in tray-style, also looked like the surface of Tatooine. Burger Chef also offered collectible Star Wars posters that could be purchased in-store with a large Coke. While this promotion did not yield any plastic Star Wars toys, it did, according to a 1977 flyer, pair the Star Wars Funmeal with a free "Speed Strip Racer," which was essentially a small race car—not quite an X-Wing, but a fast vehicle, nonetheless. Likewise, the December 30, 1979, *Ronald McDonald* comic strip ends with an ad for "McDonald's Star Trek Meal," which boasted, "There's an official Star Trek prize in every Star Trek box" ("McDonaldland"). Indeed, with Star Wars already taken, McDonald's licensed the *other* "Star" property, Star Trek, for its first Happy Meal based on a concept not created in-house. While the Happy Meal box was not as intricate as the Funmeal's—it was just a continuation of the July 1979 construction with Star Trek branding instead of the McDonaldland circus—McDonald's did create five plastic toys to promote *Star Trek: The Motion Picture*. Interestingly, the promotional material removed the word "Happy" from the equation, referring to the product as the "Star Trek Meal," despite having all the other features of what we now think of as a conventional Happy Meal.

These toys fused the McDonald's Happy Meal toy style with Star Trek's broadest motifs to create a promotion that expanded the worlds of both. The five prizes included were a Star Trek wristband, a comic viewer, a "secret compartment ring," a mini board game, and a press-on graphic featuring characters and symbols from the sci-fi film. None of these toys were meant to replicate any of the props used in the Star Trek film or TV shows. Instead, they took generic objects and rebranded them, through stickers or molded images, as Star Trek tie-ins. The wristband, for example, would have had no connection to Star Trek unless one put on the stickers that came with the item which would then freckle it with the faces of Kirk, Spock, Uhura and others. In this way, McDonald's used a strategy similar to the one employed by the makers of rack toys, or toys that were sold cheaply in drug stores, and would often be the same item with a rotation of different stickers branding it as a different pop culture property each month. The secret compartment ring, however, is a bit more of an elaboration on previous McDonald's premiums. Prior to the Star Trek Happy Meal, McDonald's offered rings engraved with the likenesses of McDonaldland characters, as noted previously. These rings also bore engraved images, but of Star Trek characters, ships, and insignia as opposed to in-house mascots. The Star Trek markings were also featured on the "secret compartment" section of the ring, a tiny box attached to the ring piece capable of holding approximately four Tic Tacs. This prize shows McDonald's interest in building on what they had created prior with new innovations that could make consumers feel as though they are receiving a novel product.

Saturday is a FUN DAY

Buy a Star Wars Funmeal

and

get a speed strip racer FREE

A 1977 Burger Chef *Star Wars* Funmeal ad mentioning the "speed strip racer."

The box art, too, represented similar progress. Drawn by artist Ron Villani, the illustrations could not be more of a departure from Simms Taback's playfulness. These drawings of characters like

Free with Every Kids' Meal

Mr. Spock were dark, realistic, and complex. Today, one might see them and think of the photoreal oil work of artists like Alex Ross. If the previous two Happy Meal boxes suggested a light and whimsical tone, this one was serious, asking its observers to accept its graphics with the same big screen gravity they might take in the grandiose effects famously used in *Star Trek: The Motion Picture*. However, the box did still conform to Happy Meal standards in other ways. Each box, amidst this weighty art, featured jokes and even a belching U.S.S. *Enterprise*. Therefore, one could read this entire promotion as McDonald's attempt to both honor its (then-brief) Happy Meal history and add the distinctiveness of new properties to its oeuvre.

This set the tone for Happy Meal progress post–1979. It would be a combination of in-house McDonaldland character toys and licensed prizes from popular properties. As Burger Chef lost restaurants, McDonald's maintained its place as industry leader, and rose, through the Happy Meal, to become the world's largest toy distributor (Darren). As competing restaurants like Burger King, Hardee's, Sonic, Arby's, Subway, Long John Silver's, Taco Bell, Pizza Hut, and so many others entered the kids' meal game in the 1980s and '90s, many of them followed the Burger Chef/McDonald's formula: use restaurant-specific mascots in some promotions, and licensed properties in the majority.* While the success of this depends on the restaurant and the promotion, McDonald's sold about 50 million Star Trek Meals across 4,500 restaurants. So, when Paramount's Director of Merchandising and Licensing Dawn Steele said in 1979, "Coca-Cola and McDonald's were willing to pay millions for the tie-in on top of spending tens of millions to pay for network advertising to promote our film," one can imagine the fast food giant saw a healthy return on their investment ("20 Things You").

While some industry professionals like Steele embrace licensing, others are not so sure. According to critic Ellen Seiter, "Marketing

---

*Some may recall that, while Burger Chef was doing its Star Wars Funmeals, Burger King began selling supplemental Star Wars glasses. This started in 1977, with the debut of the movie, but was not integrated into a kids' meal, as Burger Chef's Star Wars offerings were.

professionals warn of numerous pitfalls in toy licensing. Licensed products can fail because of overexposure, parental objections to graphics or other associations with the character, a short 'shelf life' for popular characters ... a bad product mix ... and, finally, because of the fickleness of children as a market and rapid changes in their tastes" (Seiter 199). Essentially, licensing is a gamble. When a source property is clearly in the spotlight, buying a costly license for its toys comes with fairly good odds of a healthy return. Still, how-

While this store display item was created in 1996, it asks a question that transcends time.

ever, said successful property could fail its licensees if it grows to become so abundant that there is little demand and more consumer fatigue. Other factors could also interfere with success, such as poor toy construction, content that appears too adult once parents evaluate it, and the rapid shifts in kids' tastes. Considering all of this, licensing can still be a winner, but it is by no means a sure thing.

But more than just this profit, through their kids' meals, fast food chains proved that they could deliver on the wealth promise of the 1940s and '50s. Stymied by franchisee scandals, the kids' meal came at just the right time to provide data that might convince would-be operators to make the leap. Kids' meals proved to this demographic that kids and families would eat at their restaurants, as these locations now had items truly exclusive to them. One could get a hamburger anywhere, but only McDonald's had *Star Trek: The*

Motion Picture toys. In that same way, kids' meal toys also allowed fast food chains to stand out in a crowded field. As future chapters will discuss, tie-ins with fad properties provided enough of a reason for plenty of customers to choose one specific chain over another, even going out of their way to do so. If Star Trek could move 50 million Happy Meals, future promotions linked to, say, Beanie Babies at the height of their craze could easily replicate that. With the concept of the kids' meal toy being, generally speaking, a win, chains had only to refine the processes of making and selling kids' meal toys, steps that proved a bit more complicated than one might initially assume.

How to Make a Kids' Meal Toy

By 1979, the engine that would drive both licensed pop culture and in-house properties to the kids' meal toy market had started. The 1980s would move these toys from novel yet often low-quality items to a constant staple of fast food experiences whose intricacy and fan appeal would expand over time. This would give rise to essentially all of the kids' meal premiums regularly remembered, from McDonald's McNugget Buddies to Burger King's *The Lord of the Rings* interconnected figurines, to the massive Pizza Hut/KFC/Taco Bell promotion for *Star Wars: Episode I: The Phantom Menace*. As stated previously, there are many print and online resources designed to provide those interested with comprehensive lists of released kids' meal toys over the decades. This book, however, is better served by dives into specific toys, as it aims to provide depth over the easily accessible breadth that has been the focus of kids' meal toy writing previously. As such, this section will use the 1994 McDonald's *Animaniacs* Happy Meal toy promotion as a way to study the process by which a kids' meal toy is made.

To be sure, these steps may look different for various toys from different restaurants, but, thanks to interviews with one particular designer who worked on the *Animaniacs* Happy Meal, details of this line's development can be presented, with industry generalities to be extrapolated from there. I interviewed toy designer Shawn Crosby in October and November of 2021. Crosby noted that, growing up, he did not have many of the most current toys, so he started tinkering with the ones he had. From this, he gained a knack for building out play features that would keep him, and any kid, entertained by the otherwise-forgettable toy. He also recalled playing with toys like Irwin's Girder and Panel sets, which allowed users to build large skyscrapers that resembled those that might become stomping fodder in a Godzilla movie. The skills Crosby learned while customizing his own childhood toys played directly into his work as a toy designer. Thus, Crosby had an established career prior to his work on the *Animaniacs* line, working on a number of projects for toy giant Mattel, including prototype action figures for movies like *Demolition Man* and *The Last Action Hero.* Once he fell into kids' meal toy work, he played a role in the creation of 30–40 such premiums in addition to all of his other work in the industry.

This is true of most toy designers I have spoken with. None that I know of exclusively work on kids' meal toys. They have extremely diverse portfolios filled with myriad projects, no two of which are truly alike. Frequently, they work for big toy companies (Mattel, Hasbro, Playmates) or toy design studios like Varner Studios or Anaglyph Sculpture. From casual conversations I have had with these designers, I get the sense that the industry is small, in that people network and form connections regardless of primary employment company, and those friendships lead to work across production houses. It is common, then, for a toy designer to work for Mattel, but take on freelance projects elsewhere should they decide. Some of these freelance projects may bring them to design studios like Varner or companies that specialize specifically in kids' meal toy creation such as Alcone or Spin Magnet. These companies are less known than, say, Mattel or Hasbro, but they are where fast food corporations typically turn when they need kids' meal toys.

This cross-pollination will be important when Crosby discusses how he came to *Animaniacs*, but, before that could happen, McDonald's needed to get there first. As is the case for most kids' meal toys, the final products start with the union of a media company and a fast food chain. How money changes hands has a lot to do with the property in question. If, for example, McDonald's wants to run a Marvel Happy Meal, they will surely pay Disney a high fee for the license, as the properties contained under that superhero-filled banner are sure-fire moneymakers. For a less popular license, though, the fees paid by the food corporation may be negligible to non-existent, as the restaurant chain's promotion would help the media production company more than the other way around. There is not one way a toy property arrives in a kids' meal; instead, it can arrive via a range of routes. Crosby supported this when he said, "I don't have input on the toy line. Sometimes that comes from a parent company like Disney, sometimes that comes from a food company, and then sometimes it comes from the middle ground toy design company" (Crosby). Thus, the contract that begins a kids' meal toy promotion depends on what is being promoted, how strong the relationship is between the two companies, and the size of the companies involved. This captures both the benefit and drawback of licensing outside properties. Fast food chains may get access to pre-established, popular characters which will drive people to their restaurants, but, for the likenesses at the top of that food chain, they will need to pay a handsome sum. Of course, generating in-house toys around restaurant-based mascots has its own plusses and minuses: the chain does not have to engage in a contract with a big film production studio like Disney, but they do have to spend quite a bit of money to generate original characters and make the public aware of them prior to their promotions in kids' meals, much like Burger Chef and McDonald's did in the 1960s and early '70s.

Since *Animaniacs* is an Amblin Entertainment/Warner Brothers Animation property, and both are large companies in the early '90s, one imagines the contract between them and McDonald's was complex. Though *Animaniacs* became a phenomenon, it was not yet released when McDonald's initially agreed to be its Happy Meal distributor. (While the toys were distributed in 1994, they all bear "1993" stamps, indicating a possible earlier production date. *Animaniacs* premiered on September 13, 1993, on Fox Kids.) Therefore, while one imagines there would be a fee of some kind paid by McDonald's, it may not have been as large as it would have been for a well-known property that was more of a sure thing. When McDonald's once again distributed *Animaniacs* Happy Meal toys in 1995, the fee, then, might have increased, given the show had become a success, unless of course the second promotion was also covered by the initial contract.

Amblin/Warner Brothers Animation were also fairly secretive about their new property, and had developed much of the Happy Meal toy design prior to it even reaching the production stage. This hints that the studios believed in *Animaniacs*, their 30-minute animated kids variety show which often featured segments starring the Animaniacs, three zany half-dog-half-cat hybrids who cause comedic mayhem, and other series regulars like Pinky and the Brain, lab rats with visions of world conquest, the Goodfeathers, gangster pigeons, the eternally grumpy Slappy Squirrel, and others.

Once an agreement is reached between a license holder and a fast food chain, a third company will typically be contracted to make the toys. These companies can sometimes be given lots of creative freedom to come up with toys on their own. Other times, the license-holding media company or the fast food chain will deliver materials to the toy design company with instructions to produce work that actualizes their concepts. In those cases, the job of the toy designer becomes not to create their own idea, but to replicate what they were given exactly.

Crosby got this project the same way many toy designers get their work: it was assigned to him. As toy designer David Vonner mentioned in *Sun Hero Magazine*, "There's usually a product manager that has everything divided out, then you have designers under your product managers" (Shobe 25). Here, Vonner is referring specifically to his work on toys in general, but, given that product managers are responsible for distributing the workload on all of a company's toy projects, one can reasonably assume this process works, in some cases, for fast food premiums, too. Other toy designers have told me that kids' meal toy work is, artistically, seen as less desirable than that for toys sold in toy stores due to its disposability and limited range of options (a toy in a Happy Meal will typically not have the articulation and accessories of a 6-inch action figure one buys at Target, for instance). In these cases, designers may take kids' meal toy work if it is assigned to them, or if the project adds to income generated elsewhere. However, Steve Varner, head of toymaking giant Varner Studios, was nothing but enthusiastic about kids' meal toy design. In an email to me, Varner referred to kids' meal toys as "McToys" and happily reflected on his decades of sculpting them, which included the iconic McDonald's McNugget Buddies (Varner). For Varner, this toy genre is an underappreciated one, filled with popular playthings that tend to disappear next to the legacy giants like Transformers and G.I. Joe. Thus, there is no singular industry take on sculpting kids' meal toys; it simply depends on the designer.

Before, I mentioned that Crosby came to kids' meal toys by way of cross-pollination from his work at Mattel. As he explained, a colleague of his came to him and asked if he wanted to partake in "government work." When Crosby inquired what was meant by "government work," he learned that this was shorthand for work outside his primary company. He accepted, and this "government work" turned out to be the *Animaniacs* Happy Meal promotion. For Crosby, this work had the allure of an additional paycheck, and played to his strengths as a designer. He took the job by choice, and was interested to learn more. That, however, proved difficult. According to Crosby, "We didn't have a demo reel for it, to see anything about the characters. All we had were these sketches. So [the toy design company] brings me these sketches, and I don't know what they are. They're like rabbits? Dogs? They turned out to be Animaniacs. They're like, 'Can you make these toys?' And I'm like, '...yes. Can you tell me what these are?' And they're like, 'No...'" (Crosby). Those sketches turned out to be front, side, and top drawings of Dot's Ice Cream Wagon, a soon-to-be Happy Meal toy.

The 1994 McDonald's *Animaniacs* Happy Meal promotion eventually had eight toys in the United States. They were: the Bicycle Built for Trio (a bike that had the three Animaniacs—Yakko, Wakko, and Dot—teetering atop it), the Goodskate Goodfellas (a skateboard with the gangster pigeons on board), the Upside Down Wakko (the Animaniac riding a bike inverted), Slappy & Skippy's Chopper (a motorcycle for two squirrels), the aforementioned Dot's Ice Cream Wagon (a wheeled pushcart helmed by the Warner sister), Mindy & Button's Wild Ride (a roller coaster car with a dog and a toddler at its mercy), Yakko Ridin' Ralph (an Animanica riding a security guard who clings to wheels), and the Pinky & the Brain Mobile (the lab rat duo in a modified penny-farthing). Given what Crosby said, one assumes the toy

Chapter 1. "A prize in every box"

sculpting began for all of these with outline sketches turned over by the parent studio. That was certainly the case for Dot's Ice Cream Wagon. For this toy, designers like Crosby had to figure out not just how to mold the vehicle as drawn, but how to make the action feature, a pop-up ice cream cone that emerged from the cart's storage hold, work. Luckily, questions like these do not usually fall to just one person.

At toy production houses, designers typically specialize, though one person may have several specialties. As David Vonner says of his time as a sculptor, "Some guys aren't just designers, you know, they're also painters or model makers and sculptors, so they can contribute even more widely" (Shobe 25). Shawn Crosby's specialty was the "hardware," or pieces of a toy that need to be molded in styrene, a material harder than the wax that is usually used to sculpt parts of toys. In the case of Dot's Ice Cream Wagon, the cart itself would be made by Crosby in styrene resin, and the likeness of Dot affixed to it would be sculpted out of wax by someone who specialized in that material, as Steve Varner of Varner Studios does. It is important to note, here, that Steve Varner mentioned his shop switched over to digital sculpting in 1999, so that means this process is more computerized today than it would have been in 1993/1994, but, because the *Animaniacs* promotion is of this older era, it is more accurate to describe the prototype building process as a manual one. As the prototype of the toy is formed, its action features are tested, and a "choke gauge" is used to assess whether the item has parts small enough to be a choking hazard. This requires one to see whether parts will fit through a small loop on a choke gauge, meant to represent the opening to a child's throat. This is especially important for kids' meal toys, as they are distributed widely, to very young children, and, if any toy should prove too hazardous for a 0–3-year-old, an "Under 3" toy must be given to prevent the risk of harm. The ultimate idea, here, is to get to a "master," or essentially a functioning prototype of the toy. At a big toy design studio like Varner, designers have all the resources they need in-house to get to this stage and beyond.

But just because, in the case of the *Animaniacs* Happy Meal, the look of the toy was laid out from the get-go, this did not mean artists like Shawn Crosby never thought about the object independently of its plans. In fact, Crosby has thought philosophically about the kids' meal toys he made frequently. Crosby said, "For me, as a toy designer, it's fine if it's connected to a license, that's inevitable, but you have to think about the merit of the toy on its own" (Crosby). The "merit of the toy on its own," to Crosby, means that the end result should hold up as an object of fun regardless of one's familiarity with the property it represents. Crosby thought fondly of the pop-up surprise ice cream cone in Dot's Ice Cream Wagon as a source of this merit. He also considered other toys that simply represented a character, with no other action feature built into the item, as reliant solely on one's interest in the likeness they represent, and this, for Crosby, robs the object of a play value that he views as essential to its cultural purpose. This is, I would argue, a useful philosophy for a designer of kids' meal toys, as these items, more than other playthings, must appeal to the broadest swath of consumers, and cannot be restricted to only the demographic familiar with their source material. This complicates the notion that kids' meal toys are entirely paratextual, or created solely to surround or promote a source text. If these toys are engineered to appeal beyond such parent narratives, they are imbued with a level of textuality on their own, allowing them to fit into consumer play stories as characters and objects native to those individual tales instead of the mass market story with which such an owner would be unfamiliar. In other words, the viability of a kids' meal toy on its own allows consumers to craft equally independent stories with it. At this point, the toy ceases to be the product of a large media company and becomes an original character contributing to a play narrative just as novel, and, arguably, just as valid. Though Warner Brothers can put millions of dollars behind making sure consumers know *Animaniacs* canon, none of that negates the play invented by a child that side-steps the "official" story. When Crosby mentioned this stand-alone play value of toys, I instantly thought of the playthings I have purchased simply because they "looked fun," and for which I am still ignorant of the property from which they stemmed.

Once the design team has a master, they will use this to produce further examples of the toy. Masters are painted, so that the color scheme, or "paint apps," of the toy can be evaluated. The master will also be used to produce molds, which will create hard copies of the eventual toy. These hard copies will be studied to see how well the master replicates out of a mold. The molding process usually shrinks the toy slightly, and reduces some of its detail. If anywhere along this process designers need to edit a part of the sculpt to better suit packaging or safety needs, they have the opportunity to do so before the toy moves into mass production. Once the toy's final look is approved, what Crosby calls the "perfect ones and some rough copies" are sent off to their mass production factory, which, for kids' meal toys, is usually in China. There, the masters are subject to "tooling," or the breaking down of the toy into its individual parts so that it can be molded and assembled in mass production.

At this point, the onus of production shifts overseas, and U.S.–based design shops monitor progress as those factories move ahead. This is an area where more scholarship is needed. Images of Chinese factories as described by writers like Leslie T. Chang in her book *Factory Girls: From Village to City in a Changing China* and the short documentary *Santa's Workshop* by Lotta Ekelund and Kristina Bjurling compose a grim collage of work there. While a single factory can produce numerous items, however, none of those in these sources are specifically depicted as making kids' meal toys. That said, one 2000 article in Hong Kong's *South China Morning Post* reported that a factory contracted by McDonald's to produce Happy Meal toys allegedly employed 400 child workers who worked 16-hour days for 1.5 yuan (roughly 25 cents USD) per hour. In 2006, China Labor Watch reported that "thousands of workers" at the Henry Plastic Toy Factory, a contract manufacturer for McDonald's (and others) in Dongguan, protested poor working conditions and extremely low wages, resulting in 10 protester arrests (China Labor Watch). While these reports are troubling, they are also incomplete. Many of the labor conditions in China and Southeast Asia are typically shrouded in secrecy, with only hints of broader violations reaching the U.S. public. Some may understandably assume surreptitiousness, but the toy industry is one that requires confidentiality. It is important that toy designs are not circulated prior to planned release, as to do otherwise would leave the line vulnerable to the ambitions of other companies who may want to seize a market share soon directed toward a competitor. Still, though, the same could be said for many industries, and a number of them have been subject to far greater transparency than is currently available in this case. The best writing that is not directly investigative of overseas human rights abuses can do is remind readers that this area needs more clarity that current public disclosures cannot provide. Such probing is often resisted in kids' meal toy fan communities, too, as the product is so closely associated with words like "happy" and "fun," and these facts are anything but. This is, of course, an obstacle it is up to us to overcome in order to demand consumption be as close to ethical as possible. For now, in the midst of this, factory workers assemble, paint, and bag kids' meal toys marked for distribution in the United States and/or other markets.

Once orders for kids' meal toys are filled, boxes of thousands of these objects are shipped and distributed to individual restaurants. From there, the restaurants issue the prescribed toys on an often weekly basis, where they fall into the hands of consumers of all ages. This is where the producer of the original media, the fast food corporation, and the toy design studio can discover the impact of their creation. Shawn Crosby explored this moment from a range of angles. He noted that, while kids' meal toys are "an afterthought" that is designed only to keep kids occupied for the duration of their meal, care should still be taken in how that time is filled. Crosby said, "the company has to be careful what they give kids because crayons will end up on the tables, stickers will end up in the restaurants, and that's one reason why I think toys are really preferable" (Crosby). This comment adds a layer to the kids' meal toy world that does not apply to toy store purchases. It indicates how the kids' meal toy is, in many ways, a product that exists in a specific environment, and that elicits certain unique behaviors. For a toy found at a toy store, the item tends to remain in-box until the hopeful owner takes it home. At a fast food chain, this is possible, too, through take-out orders, but for dine-in customers, these toys are opened at the restaurant tables.

This is cemented in the commercials for the *Animaniacs* Happy Meal, in which kids wheel the toy vehicles across McDonald's tables within inches of their hamburgers and chicken nuggets. Not only that, the animated Animaniacs are there, too, giving the commercial a magical interaction between fantasy and reality. Through advertising materials like this, restaurants encourage kids to use these toys as a way of relating to the space. This transforms the kids' meal toy from a conventional toy to an object that, like a magic wand, turns a table into a race track, a seat into a ramp, and a french fry into a speed bump. Therefore, kids' meal toys become one of the few, if not the only, toys in the vast world of playthings to unite place and visitor so whimsically.

By understanding how kids' meal toys are made, one earns a deeper understanding of what they do, and how they function. Through the process of production, designers move the toy from a concept attached to a specific property to a three-dimensional object that functions beyond its source text. Once the toy transcends its text, it breaks out of its paratextual bubble, no longer serving to solely promote, but also to entertain, as Crosby said, "on its own merit." Once it can do that, it gains the power to disconnect other places and items, like fast food restaurant tables, from their root meaning so as to imbue them with a world just as magical as the one the kids' meal toy inhabits. Perhaps this is the reason kids' meal toys endure, despite disposability being in their DNA. They attach themselves to an experience, the experience of a fast food restaurant, by transforming that moment into something beyond the bounds of the known world, something that can only exist within the realm of transformative play.

The Impact of a Kids' Meal Toy

Kids' meal toys are a reward, not just to the child who earns one, but, ideally, to the companies who promote them. Historically, media and toy corporations who insert their paper, plastic, or plush paratexts into kids' meals have hoped to provide consumers with a gateway into their mainline products, or sustain an already-enthusiastic market for their wares. Many fast food toy premiums can provide business case studies for understanding what successful and flawed pursuits of these outcomes look like. Such analysis can also capture larger moments of controversy for toy and fast food companies that formed perhaps imperfect unions to craft meals made unhappy by unexpected litigation. Here, I have enumerated a series of lesser-known kids' meal toy promotions in order to discuss the ways in which they speak to the broader impact of such premiums.

1. 2002 McDonald's LEGO Galidor Happy Meal

At the turn of the 21st century, LEGO experienced a sales slump. By 2004, this decline meant a 40 percent drop in sales, and debts around one billion dollars ("Lego-lution"). Galidor, a line of LEGO-made action figures, was expected to revitalize the brand. In 2002, the company turned to McDonald's for help. The LEGO Galidor Happy Meal was born. LEGO historians David C. Robertson and Bill Breen see the move as wise in their book *Brick by Brick: How LEGO Rewrote the Rules of Innovation and Conquered the Global Toy Industry*. Galidor, at the time, was essentially unknown to U.S. consumers, "and from a delivery perspective, the company's plan to package Galidor characters in McDonald's Happy Meals was a clever way to connect with American kids (especially those who had previously ignored LEGO), as well as open up another source or revenue," say Robertson and Breen (Robertson 59). This shows that LEGO wanted the Galidor Happy Meal to be an introduction to the brand, betting that the brand recognition started in a McDonald's restaurant would create a desire for the product that would hop over to the shelves of toy stores. The Happy Meal, it was thought, could grow an audience. Ultimately, it could not. Galidor is almost universally seen as a massive failure for LEGO, and it would seem generating an enthusiastic audience is beyond the power of kids' meal toys alone. This prioritizes toy design and source media storytelling above kids' meal marketing and its ritual of collection and consumption, suggesting that, if interest in the primary product is not present, the fast food promotion will struggle to change the public's perception.

2. 2001 McDonald's LEGO Bionicle/Diva Starz Happy Meal

If Galidor represented a low point in LEGO history, Bionicle, a different line of buildable figures from the company, was so successful it helped dig the brand out of its financial crisis. In 2001 alone, LEGO Bionicle earned $160 Million, representing booming sales. Thus, its presence in a Happy Meal, coupled with the girl-marketed option of Diva Starz dolls, was the opposite of Galidor's. Where Galidor's Happy Meal acted as an introduction, Bionicle's was part of a larger saturation sustaining excitement for a popular fad toy. Robertson and Breen note that, by the time the Happy Meal landed, Bionicle merchandise existed as lunchboxes, Nike sneakers, cereal premiums, T-shirts, and, of course, the toys themselves (Robertson). Coupled with Diva Starz, a huge hit at the time for its parent company Mattel, this Happy Meal contained toys marketed to boys and girls that had both already garnered significant attention. Here, the kids' meal's role was clear: keep the trend going, and offer consumers another piece in their likely already robust collections. In this case, the Happy Meal had a much easier time sustaining interest than generating it, as it would try to do for Galidor.

3. 2002–2008 McDonald's Madame Alexander Happy Meal

Madame Alexander has been paired with Happy Meals seven times between the years 2002 and 2008. Each time, the dolls were offered in conjunction with a promotion marketed to boys, with *Teenage Mutant Ninja Turtles* and *LEGO Batman: The Video Game* among them. This is noteworthy within a discussion of licensing, as Madame Alexander could be viewed as what Ellen Seiter calls a "high end" license, in that the dolls have a 100-year history in which they have been known for selling some incredibly expensive pieces. But Seiter also identifies other licenses as "mass market," and these would cover most licensed kids' meal toys, including the boy-marketed ones mentioned previously: they are drawn from pop culture cartoons and mainline toys that are, themselves, generally fairly cheap (Seiter 198). The Happy Meal itself is mass market, too, in that it prides itself on its affordability and availability. So that raises a question around the power of the kids' meal: do these promotions have the power to move licenses from "high end" to "mass market," and what would be the benefit of doing so? Certainly, for Madame Alexander, the upside would be in announcing to fans of the pricey dolls that wealth is not a prerequisite for brand engagement. And to other potential collectors, high end licensors can say that wealth is not a requirement for participation in the brand narrative. Indeed, Madame Alexander has many lower-cost items today, and I read their presence in kids' meals as a statement that the company would embrace a mass market presence to attain greater market share. If, as Seiter believes, mass market licensing, such as that for popular superhero franchises like Batman, is key to not only profit-making but also to decision-making around which properties will continue to occupy movie and television screens, a high end licensor might seek to convert to a mass market license, and I posit that kids' meals are one potential convertor in that process, as evidenced by the Madame Alexander premiums (199).

4. 2003 McDonald's Bratz/*He-Man and the Masters of the Universe* Happy Meal

Though the 2003 *He-Man* McDonald's promotion has become a fan favorite for its use of highly articulated action figures, it is the Bratz side of the promotion that offers the better case study. Cultural historian Orly Lobel writes of MGA head Isaac Larian that, at the time, "Larian [was] no stranger to litigation with the giants, not only Mattel, not only with his own brother, not only with most of his own attorneys, but also with McDonald's over the licensing of Bratz for Happy Meals" (Lobel 46). The conflict stemmed from ownership over the hugely successful Bratz dolls, with Larian arguing against Mattel that they rightly belonged to his toy company, MGA. However, the McDonald's lawsuit, according to Bloomberg, was not over ownership, as the fast food chain had no claim to that, but the sculpts of the toys in the promotion, to which Larian objected.

Chapter 1. *"A prize in every box"*

The lawsuit was settled, but it left an interesting footnote in kids' meal toy history (Bloomberg). The suit was built upon an argument over the artistry involved with making the premiums, forcing a question around how "loyal" such toys must be to their source material. To be sure, the 1979 *Star Trek* Meal contained toys that resembled nothing in its parent film. By the 2000s, however, expectations had changed such that licensors and consumers expected a more explicit connection between promotional item and licensed intellectual property. After all, one of the largest draws of the *He-Man* promotion were the striking similarities those figures had to the mainline versions in toy stores. This speaks to the growth of the kids' meal toy by demonstrating that, by the turn of the 21st century, the market for such items had grown so significantly and the money put into such licensing arrangements became so large that the practice of producing a kids' meal toy was expected to be more refined than it was in the 1970s, when a McDonald's eraser would do. One can then use this to contrast 2023's kids' meal toys, many of which are generic portraits of their source characters made with exaggerated, cartoonish heads of plastic or plush. These shifts can also indicate cultural preferences that changed with the advent of Funko Pop!, the popular vinyl figures that feature blank facial expressions on enlarged heads, a difference from the early aughts' interest in hyperrealism in toys represented by outfits like McFarlane and Art Asylum. In this way, the kids' meal toy becomes a brief encapsulation of mass market toy trends.

Kids' meal toys materially impact large groups of people before, during, and after their production. Prior to the first kids' meal toy, the fast food industry wrestled with a history of American optimism that devolved into, in too many cases, scam franchising that tarnished the sector. When the era of the kids' meal was in full swing, and these premiums were being produced for many restaurants, countless toy designers, factories, media companies, and corporate executives swarmed the process in an attempt to make cheap, engaging, and safe toys that brought as many new customers as possible to both the food counter and the toy store. These participants in the physical process of making a kids' meal toy, likely by virtue of working on such tight schedules, often produced so much concept material incredibly quickly that much of it is still being found, remnants of promotions as old as three decades ago, hurriedly shoved into filing cabinet coffins unlikely to see the light of day ever again. This is understandable; the job of these drafts had been done. A promotion that either resembled or rejected them emerged, and, once that happened, parents, kids, and collectors became the final judge in the matter of their success. They defined that success on two fronts: sales in restaurants, and crossover interest in whichever licensed property was being promoted, if there was one. As we see in the above case studies, this consumer reaction helped put wind in the sails of profits, crash waves against quarterly reports, and, in some cases, spur lawsuits by businesspeople who were that rare but potent blend of angry and litigious. For all of this, it cannot be argued that kids' meal toys have no meaning, no impact, and no relevance. They are, rather, at the center of a history treated as small as the toys themselves, but should instead be unboxed just as the premiums are. Historical narrative is only part of the story. These toys interact with communities, demographics, social norms, and cultures for which much theory has already been developed. As there has been very little work done at the intersection of that theory and these toys, the upcoming chapters will explore more deeply if and how they align. It is us in those little kids' meal toy bags, at least to the extent that we are the ones motivating marketers, fast food corporations, media conglomerates, and toy makers to come together and produce a short-term product on a massive scale. Therefore, it is worth our while to academically evaluate the big ideas in these smallest of objects. I believe we have a near-limitless wealth to extract.

CHAPTER 2

Molding Race

The Kids' Meal Toy's Role
in Fast Food's Relationship to Blackness

"Come join us for the fun inside!"
—Kid Vid, Burger King Kids Club mascot

"They want our rhythm, but not our blues."
—Popular saying regarding
white consumption of Black culture

On December 21, 1968, Herman Petty became the first Black franchisee of a McDonald's restaurant. Located in the Woodlawn neighborhood of Chicago, the store cost $125,000, or $1,066,081.18 in 2023's money. According to Ronald Jones, one of McDonald's first Black executives and their first Black field consultant, "Not one piece of equipment in his store was in proper working order—if it worked at all. There was no air conditioning. There was no freezer. Inside and outside, the store looked like it was ready for the wrecking ball" (Berfield). The degree to which McDonald's intentionally gave Black franchisees like Petty run-down stores would eventually be debated in Court, but, at the time, this operator had to figure out how to make this dilapidated location profitable. After all, it was not only Petty's money at stake but also that of his two partners, white men who, like many others, were an unfortunate prerequisite for a Black man attempting to get a loan in the late 1960s. But McDonald's wanted this venture to work, too. For the corporation, the success of Black-owned franchises meant that McDonald's could maintain a foothold in the "urban core" despite the uprisings of the day that were fueled by countless examples of inequity, inequality, and the shattering assassination of Dr. Martin Luther King, Jr., which occurred just eight months prior to Petty opening his restaurant. Ultimately, Petty was able to buy out his partners and earn a profit operating his franchise, leading McDonald's to honor his achievement, and their own staying power in Black communities, with a plaque on the restaurant that is still affixed to it as of this writing.

If this was a win, it was a nebulous one. Yes, Petty was able to grow his wealth as a Black man owning his own fast food franchise in 1968. This was a feat, and Petty's ability to weather it should be celebrated. But the plaque cemented onto Petty's store is also a metaphor for the way in which McDonald's clamped onto the Black community to ends that have not always been so positive. In 2023, fast food chains, largely companies whose upper echelons are dominated by white executives, have disproportionately populated Black and Brown neighborhoods, offering them an influx of cheap, but food that may offer employment to community members on the lower and middle rungs, but still make upward mobility beyond that a difficult climb. This also crowds streets where Black-owned small businesses sometimes struggle for space between corporate giants with real estate spending power that outmatches mom-and-pop shops. The result of this is a lengthy history that has undeniably intertwined Black history and the legacy of fast food chains, for better and for worse, leading to a present moment where scholars look at this corporate/community relationship as a way to analyze big ideas like Civil Rights and Blackness in the American economy.

Kids' meal toys tend to be omitted from this analysis. In some ways, this is understandable. Kids' meal toys are not typically made with the primary purpose of representing historical or social realities. They are playthings that are sometimes disposable, sometimes memorable, and are designed with the intent of being a mealtime distraction that provides a certain, often inconsistent, level of fun. However, this chapter wonders if kids' meal toys can, to some extent, apply to this broader conversation about fast food's role in the Black community. To better understand this, I turn to Marcia Chatelain's seminal work on the fast food presence in Black neighborhoods, as well as specific kids' meal premiums that show how said franchises represent this clearly targeted demographic. While many if not most toys are built around movie and TV premieres that fast food corporations have little control over, some, as mentioned in the last chapter, are in-house mascots created entirely by these restaurants and their affiliated marketing agencies. Through those, these toys become a purer representation of the company, as they are unconstrained by a production studio's narrative, and can be crafted to do whatever McDonald's, Burger King, Taco Bell, or any other company needs them to. In many cases, fast food chains forego human-looking mascot characters in favor of fantasy animals like McDonald's Birdie or Taco Bell's Nacho and Dog, which do not reflect back one specific demographic of customer, but appeal more broadly by being a new creation to which many—regardless of race, class, gender, religion, or ethnicity—can relate. However, one fast food company, Burger King, veered from this trend and created, for the 1990s, a team of animated multi-racial human children mascots called the Burger King Kids Club, whose many promotions offer a point of entry into this larger conversation about race and corporate quick eats.

But in order to get to that '90s toy-centered discussion, one needs firmer grounding in the ways fast food interacts with Black communities more broadly. In her book *Franchise*, Marcia Chatelain writes, "Fast food is a prism for understanding race, shifts in the movement for civil rights, the dissemination of black culture, and racial capitalism—the deep connections between the development of modern capitalism and racist subjugation and oppression—since the 1960s" (Chatelain 4). The example of Herman Petty is but one beam of fractured light refracted by this prism. It allows us to talk about ways corporations invade Black spaces for their own profit-making, and how that can establish a ceiling for those said companies partly elevate. The case of *Herbert L. Washington v. McDonald's Corp.* raises further questions along these lines. This 2021 complaint argued that Herbert "Herb" Washington, a former Major League baseball player and once the owner of the most McDonald's locations of any Black franchisee, was discriminated against by the parent company when it "purposely steered Mr. Washington into stores in distressed, predominantly Black neighborhoods, which—as McDonald's well knew—yield considerably less profit than stores in more affluent communities" (*Herbert L. Washington v. McDonald's* 1). Washington alleged McDonald's did this over the course of decades, across all of his assigned restaurant locations. McDonald's ultimately settled the lawsuit for $33.5 million and Washington's exit from the McDonald's system, but this case still enlarged what Herman Petty witnessed in his location to the bigger issue of redlining, or the real estate practice of illegally keeping Black buyers out of white-dominated communities (Rogers). It is a part of what Chatelain refers to as "racial capitalism," in that Washington and Petty both participated in capitalist enterprises, but still had to do so within the racist framework whose economics provided free labor to white landowners on the backs of Black enslaved people, and then continued increase white wealth through Jim Crow laws and Black dehumanization that allowed, and in many ways still allows, for the devaluing of a Black workforce with the same expectation of white profit. As Chatelain points out, both fast food corporations and the U.S. government opened the door to Black-owned franchises in the 1960s and '70s through entities like the Small Business Administration, the Office of Minority Business Enterprise, and the Minority Business Development Agency, all of which facilitated a world where loans given to prospective Black franchisees could funnel fast food into their communities, thereby giving the corporations profit from their new stores and the fees paid to open them, plus a foothold in areas that might not be conventionally receptive, as well as offering franchise owners limited growth if they could successfully operate stores that were, per Petty and Washington, in many ways built to fail (Chatelain 15). The communities themselves, though, frequently receive the least in this model, experiencing little investment in their prosperity beyond the restaurant itself, getting food that interacts more with dopamine than health, and grappling with feelings of exploitation as top corporate executives reap massive profits with no significant trickle-down effect. It is the prevalence of this food in Black communities that, says Chatelain, "is often identified as the culprit among the research on high rates of obesity, diabetes, and hypertension among blacks," yet those reports, often lacking an understanding of how fast food giants came into Black communities, also erroneously and stereotypically equate this consumption to an innate and disproportionate enjoyment of these restaurants among community members (Chatelain 4). In other words, it is not that Black people, as a whole, simply like fast food more than other racial groups, but that decades worth of franchising and policy making have clustered these restaurants in Black neighborhoods, frequently edging out other options in the process. It is tempting for writing around this aspect of the fast food industry to paint these companies as either wholly positive, offering jobs and growth to members of Black communities, or entirely negative, working toward Black economic and bodily detriment. Chatelain, though, describes a more complete "push-and-pull era" opened by post–1968 Black franchising where Black franchisees could benefit from their investment, but communities were also given cause to voice concerns over how corporations who were mostly white at the highest tier made money off of their neighborhoods (Chatelain 16). This creates a world where united opposition to fast food corporations is made difficult by real-world examples of select individual opulence.

It is here that a discussion of Black representation in kids' meal toys can be helpful, not in pursuit of some binary judgment for or against fast food chains, but to think critically about how an industry so historically connected to Blackness constructs it. There are many ways in which fast food chains interact with Black communities, cultures, and bodies beyond the employee and franchisee worlds. Television commercials, print advertisements, corporate jingles, catchphrases, radio announcements, community events, support for non-profits, and myriad other avenues provide plenty to analyze in this regard, and contain more complexity than one book chapter could ever handle.

To scratch the surface of this, in the 1970s and '80s, McDonald's hired a separate advertising firm to sell product specifically to Black customers. Cultural critic Ellen Seiter provides a nuanced discussion of this relationship between advertising and race in her book *Sold Separately: Parents and Children in Consumer Culture.* Seiter uses as examples two specific McDonald's commercials, "Report Card"* and "Big Dreams," both from 1988 to 1989. These commercials feature groups of children congregating inside McDonald's to celebrate successes and ponder the future. She mentions that, in both, the Black kids are glossed over, not given speaking parts, and only briefly shown in the commercials. She is right about this, but I note, additionally, that, despite Happy Meal promotions being in full swing by 1988, the commercials do not attempt to sell them, though they feature children, albeit somewhat older. In fact, the commercials do not attempt to sell any specific product. Instead, it is as though they vouch for McDonald's as a kids' "third place," or a place where they can convene that isn't home or school, to talk about their common woes or strategize about their futures. This makes the implications of Seiter's analysis all the worse: it isn't just that children of color aren't engaging with McDonald's products, they are a minimized part of the McDonald's environment. In Seiter's words, "McDonald's commercials portray the largest number of children of color, but the leads are still reserved for the white children" (Seiter 139). That, though, is not the full story.

The aforementioned commercials were products of Leo Burnett, an advertising company hired by McDonald's in 1981 in a surprising shift away from Needham, Harper, and Steers, the firm who crafted the McDonaldland characters and much of the corporation's presence in the decade prior (Dougherty). Seiter takes interest in McDonald's ads created by the Burrell Agency in Chicago, a different firm brought in to speak to Black customers, as this was the advertiser's specialty. While Seiter zooms in on the 1988/'89 Burrell Agency ads, it is important to note the company's longer relationship with McDonald's. The fast food giant had been working with Burrell since the early '70s.

---

*The commercial titled "Report Card" aired in 1988, and it featured kids recovering in a McDonald's from the stress of receiving their report cards at school. Years later, in 2007, the Campaign for Commercial-Free Childhood complained that McDonald's unethically used Florida report cards to advertise their business (Chief Marketer Staff). These incidents illustrate the line McDonald's walks with its advertising. The public at large does not react as negatively to the corporation's inclusion of kids in the ads as compared to when they are perceived as marketing directly to them. Kids, therefore, can be messengers, but not, in the eyes of some, recipients.

Chapter 2. Molding Race

During this time, Burrell McDonald's ads appeared in Black-centered magazines like *Ebony*. These ads often featured Black people enjoying McDonald's food accompanied by a caption that today reads as at best code-switching and at worst stereotype. The start of the text below says, "When your time is tight and you've gotta keep on steppin', McDonald's is right there." White scholars need not be too critical of this, as Tom Burrell, the founder of the Burrell Agency, is Black, and known for making corporations understand that "Black people are not dark-skinned white people," an appreciation of demographic difference revolutionary in business at the time. While perhaps today the dropped Gs and slang of the ad might read as pandering now, and maybe it did to some in

1975 as well, Burrell's intentions were surely to speak to his own community, and indeed McDonald's hired him for exactly that purpose.*

Seiter carries this forward by looking at three Burrell commercials from the '80s: "Joey" (1982), "First Glasses" (1986), and "Special Delivery" (1987). These commercials provided a deep, loving, nuanced view of Black family life, never attempting to falsely equate the concerns of such a unit to

A 1975 McDonald's print advertisement that ran in *Ebony* magazine.

---

*It should be noted that while we sometimes see such blatant appeals to a specific community as pandering, the softer touch of McDonald's "I'm Lovin' It" campaign decades after these ads was objectively, massively successful.

their more privileged white counterparts. Instead, the ads acknowledged that Black life in the United States was unique, not only in its struggles but in the ways it thrives too. Of course, tacked onto that was the notion that McDonald's could adequately serve Black communities, but such a pitch is not out of place in media that is explicitly advertising. Seiter takes no issue with these ads, but indicates that they, like the Burrell print ad mentioned above, circulated not on national Saturday morning cartoon blocks like the Burnett commercials did, but in small areas with large Black demographics. Thus it is possible that Black families may recall these ads easily, while white people may never have known they existed. This echoes a complaint heard in McDonald's Civil Rights lawsuits: that white franchisees could essentially set up shop anywhere, while Black operators were limited to communities of racial similarity. For the McDonald's side, though, it should be said that Seiter's ads are limited to the 1980s, as her book was published in 1995. It is a snapshot in time. There are no publicly available data to suggest

This 1993 McDonald's promotional cassette is the second volume of their "African-American Heritage Series," evidence that Black lives have been present in the chain's premiums alongside nuanced discussion of community impact.

how McDonald's ads land now, but, in 2021, Leo Burnett made the "Fancy a McDonald's" commercial for its U.K. market, and featured a vast array of racial diversity one would expect to see in Great Britain, all with fairly even prominence. Transposed atop the '80s work that Seiter analyzes, it would seem this campaign is a step forward. That, however, is not to suggest McDonald's has somehow "fixed" its racial missteps—in fact, the company still has Civil Rights litigation pending—only to attempt to present a small update to Seiter's work.* It is also to establish the complexity of the backdrop in front of which any kids' meal race analysis occurs. There is a long history of imagery that carries through print, radio, television, film, and internet media messaging about how Blackness fits into the narrative of fast food spaces.

Kids' meal toys, though, are unique in that they are physical representations of characters, sometimes Black characters, given to the general public for the primary purposes of play, collecting, re-selling, or trading. These toys are supported by inserts, meal bags and boxes, television advertising, and other scaffolding used to contextualize the object received. Often, these items will be paired with a major motion picture or TV series, as noted in the previous chapter's discussion of licensing, in which case the toy's paratextual nature is clear, and its source text provides the main source of context that informs the directed play around the prize. But whether licensed or not, these toys are always fairly cheap, mass-produced, and quite abundant, qualities that link them, in the largest sense, to the history of the racist toy trinkets of the past. Henry Jenkins cites the work of Patricia Turner and Kenneth W. Goings to show how racist toys and toy-like artifacts such as the Little Black Sambo doll were "cheap, mass-produced, and much more likely to be sold in discount variety stores than in department stores, which catered to the middle and upper classes" (Jenkins). Kids' meal toys, too, occupy a space similar to the discount variety story. Fast food chains, too, exist to sell items cheaply and quickly,

---

*To be clear, "Civil Rights litigation" is a broad term that includes many cases, some of which reflect matters in this chapter, others, like *American Alliance for Equal Rights v. McDonald's Corporation*, which argued that the chain's HACER scholarship violated the law by offering scholarships only to Hispanic recipients, are less relevant, here.

and so use all the tools at their disposal to achieve this end. Goings adds that these toys needed to fall back on stereotype because there was little room for detail or nuance. While not nearly the same, one might suggest the Burrell ad presented earlier, with its quick short-hand for Black slang, moves in a similar direction due to the limited space it has to use and the speed with which it must connect with a reader. The same is true, as I will show, of certain kids' meal toys, and the work of Turner and Goings can help one understand how such toys, like the Confederate flag-bearing General Lee food box in the 1982 regional McDonald's *Dukes of Hazzard* Happy Meal, could appear in places that have no real interest in interacting with the history of such imagery. It is speed and simplicity, rather than explicit racist intent, that open up opportunities for unintentional and/or perceived missteps concerning race, and can also explain positive moves toward portraying racial equity like the 2022 McDonald's *Black Panther Wakanda Forever* Happy Meal which featured a series of 10 toys that all represent characters of color.

The importance of this representation is magnified by the fact that kids' meals provide toys at minimal cost to those who purchase them. That intersects with Black communities in that, due to many institutional and national failures, 21 percent of Black Americans live below the poverty line, making an average of 10 cents on the dollar when compared with white earners ("Homelessness and Black History"). This combined with the presence of fast food restaurants in Black neighborhoods means that those affected by poverty seeking a less expensive way to provide their children with toys of which their more privileged peers have in abundance may use kids' meals as an option. According to Ellen Seiter, "One dimension of [the complaint that commercials sell kids toys and food] is the painful experience of working class parents who must repeatedly deny their own children the goodies that surround them in stores and that other children seem to have so many of. But the growth of children's consumer culture has made some things cheap enough that poor parents can provide them, at least occasionally: the two-dollar McDonald's Happy Meal with its Barbie or Hot Wheels toy, the four-dollar Ninja Turtle" (Seiter 38). For Seiter, the kids' meal provides some relief in the storm of commercials* that advertise the many pricey playthings a child could have. It is up to the consumer to decide whether the potential bodily and/or societal cost of fast food flooding Black communities is worth the access to toys, but, either way, Seiter's point that the substantial increase in child-targeted marketing in the 1980s and '90s diversified the price points at which parents could buy in remains true. Kids' meal toys may represent one of the lowest cost tiers, but have the potential to wind up in the hands of those who do not have much else. For this reason, considering the bodies those hands are attached to becomes especially urgent for corporate decisionmakers who choose the ways in which they would like to represent the demographics they serve.

In pursuit of giving, here, the depth of analysis to said corporate decision-making, let us consider the Burger King Kids Club, an in-house cast of characters made by the fast food giant in the late 1980s, brought to prominence at the turn of the decade into the '90s, as a case study in the relationship between race and kids' meal toys. Though Burger King started child-focused advertising early, using animated advertisements for "the Burger King" starting in the late 1960s, with a plethora of in-store exclusives to follow, they got into the kids' meal game late, taking until 1990 to get kids' meals national and consistent, over a full decade after McDonald's went national with the Happy Meal. From a distribution perspective, this delay makes sense. It is one thing to give away, or sell for a nominal fee, exclusive items. If a store does not receive a shipment of those, there may be disappointment, but the meals will remain intact. If a restaurant chooses to start pairing toys with kids' meals, though, the supply chain of those items all of a sudden needs to be much more consistent. Should a kids' meal come without the advertised toy, the integrity of that menu item is compromised, creating a more significant problem for the store. Perhaps this is why, in 1987 and 1988, Burger King ramped up its in-store, non-kids' meal exclusives like the DC Super Powers cup holders, which were available for $1.27 "with any soft drink purchase."

---

*Or, now, social media influencers and viral content.

Free with Every Kids' Meal

Once the chain found it could regularly supply customers with these add-ons, they began their kids email promotions with Beetlejuice toys in April of the new decade's first year. Burger King's second kids' meal materialized cars containing the characters of the Burger King Kids Club, an internal band of mascots meant to appeal to kids.

Running from 1990 to 1999, the original Burger King Kids Club contained seven original members with a light mix of race and disability representation: Kid Vid (a blonde, white, visor-wearing cool kid who leads the group), Boomer (a white redhead hockey enthusiast coded as a tomboy), I.Q. (a white, also red-haired bespectacled boy clearly offered as the nerd of the group), Snaps (a white, blonde photographer who embodies Western feminine beauty norms more conventionally than Boomer), Wheels (a brown-haired, white disabled engineer who soups up his wheelchair), J.D. (a dog not owned by any one particular member of the group, but more a meta-mascot of the team), and Jaws (a Black explorer who is often seen eating a hamburger, and who will be the focus of this section moving forward). Later, Burger King added Lingo, a bi-lingual Hispanic artist coded masculine, in 1990, and, in 1997, Jazz, a musician who resembles a female musician of unspecified Asian American heritage. This group, in whole or in part, would be featured in Burger King TV and VHS tape commercials, restaurant magazine comics, all throughout materials for the Burger King Kids Club, which, in addition to being the name of this unit of characters, was also an actual organization children who frequented Burger King could join via a membership application, and in toys found in the kids' meals. Of the kids' meal promotions Burger King ran during the '90s, fourteen of them featured Burger King Kids Club characters as either figurines or images on cardboard paper goods. This produced no shortage of collectibles related to this team.

Therefore, to include, among others, Jaws, a Black character, meant that Burger King would materially represent Blackness in their mass produced toys just five years after Yla Eason created Sun Man as a response to He-Man's predominantly white, or white-coded, toy line. This meant that a Black figurine would be in the hands of random Burger King guests as, due to the "surprise" nature of the kids' meal, Jaws would not need to be "chosen" as he might off the peg of a

Chapter 2. Molding Race

In this concept art for a Burger King birthday party invitation, we see Jaws, second from the right, in essentially his finished look. Most of the others appeared in the Burger King Kids Club as shown, with the exception of Wheels, the disabled character, who underwent minor changes after this draftwork.

toy store display, but distributed alone for a length of time uniform to the other characters in each promotion. And this would happen many, many times between 1990 and 1999. Of the 14 aforementioned waves of Burger King kids' meals that featured Kids Club characters, Jaws appeared in thirteen of them. Jaws was omitted from only the 1991 Burger King Kids Club Water Mates line, which, notably, also left out team leader Kid Vid, focusing instead on Wheels, I.Q., Snaps, and the newly-added Lingo in either seaworthy vessels, or, in I.Q.'s case, atop a dolphin inexplicably wearing glasses.

In the years the Burger King Kids Club was active, Jaws appears in the following promotions, listed here with the year of its release and Jaws' toy in the line:

- Burger King Kids Club Transporters (1990): Jaws rides in a hamburger-shaped car drinking a soda and eating a burger of his own.

- Burger King Kids Club Worldwide Treasure Hunt (1990): Jaws appears in various comics that accompanied Crayola coloring supplies.
- Burger King Kids Club Action Figures (1991): Jaws gets a posable action figure that uses his most frequently-seen likeness.
- Burger King Kids Club Water Mates (1991): Jaws does not get a toy in this line.
- Burger King Kids Club Wild Spinning Tops (1992): A Jaws figurine sits atop a green spinning top.
- Burger King Kids Club It's Magic Kids' Meal (1992): Jaws' image is on his "Disappearing Food" trick, which involves a small red box that makes cardboard food POGs "disappear."
- Burger King Kids Club Save the Animals Albums (1993): Jaws is a trading card, as are the other Kids Club characters, all appearing in their typical likenesses.
- Burger King Kids Club Glow-in-the-Dark Trolls (1993): One toy is a Jaws/troll hybrid.
- Burger King Kids Club Sports All Stars (1994): The Jaws figurine comes with a large football it can throw. Jaws appears in football gear in certain TV commercials.
- Burger King Kids Club Pranksters (1994): Jaws is on the air pump that connects to a fake spider. The air pump makes it move such that it appears "alive."
- Burger King Kids Club Coolers (1995): Jaws is a green water bottle. Jaws' main outfit color is green, generally.
- Burger King Kids Club Glo Force (1996): Jaws is glow-in-the-dark figurine around which a deep sea diver outfit snaps.
- Burger King Kids Club Planet Patrol (1997): The Jaws figurine features a robotic-looking body in a flight pose with two parallel wheels in the midsection.
- Burger King Kids Club Bug Riders (1998): Jaws rides atop a purple spider, the second time the character is connected to an arachnid.

In the toys where Jaws is more than his usual tall, green-shirted self, one can read a few character traits, such as they are. Most notably, there are two promotions, the Transporters and It's Magic!, where Jaws is in some way connected to food. In the first issue of *Burger King Kids Club Adventures*, the free promotional magazine for the group offered in stores, Jaws is defined as Burger King's "taste-tester," likely the reason for his name, in reference to the part of the body that chews food (*Burger King Kids Club Adventures*). This, however, is not explained via any of the toys nor is it ever referred to again past the premiere issue of *Adventures*, so the name "Jaws" is left to trigger the two far more common associations: the bloodthirsty shark, or the James Bond villain. While Burger King's Jaws resembles neither, Black characters in Western media, especially in the 1990s, came pre-loaded with negative associations. In the words of Diane Levin and Nancy Carlsson-Paige in "Marketing Violence: The Special Toll on Young Children of Color," "children are more likely to associate positive characteristics with white characters on television and negative characteristics with minority characters," written in reference to a 1998 Children Now report (Levin 429). This is not a reflection of life as it is, but rather a media ecosystem that has cranked out narrative after narrative with whiteness at its heroic center while antagonizing Blackness. Should one obtain the *Burger King Kids Club Adventures* magazine issues, it is clear that Jaws is a soft-spoken environmentalist with a penchant for Burger King food, but one can safely assume far more consumers only knew him through the toy, which frequently only presented his name. Given that name shares space with two antagonists, and Levin and Carlsson-Paige's assessment of Black vilification in media, Jaws is given more to overcome initially than the other Kids Club members.

The 1991 Burger King Kids Club action figures give consumers the best deeper looks at all of the characters, allowing their fully articulated bodies to be rendered in three dimensions. Here, Jaws' Blackness becomes a contrast to Kid-Vid's hipsterism. Kid-Vid is clearly the group's leader, as he is the one conducting the action in Burger King's kids' meal TV commercials, using his magical remote to zap kids away from the boredom of adults and into the children's utopia of the fast food restaurant. Kid-Vid is white, but his look is a stone's throw from Kool Moe Dee's 1980s hip hop persona. Kid-Vid wears large, reflective glasses, a backwards (or to-the-side) baseball cap, red gloves with the fingers cut off, a blue T-shirt and jeans surrounded by a sash that holds his various cyber-magical devices. The basic elements of this—the visor, the cap—evoke fashion trends in Black culture in the years just prior to the emergence of the Kids Club, with rappers of the 1980s and the character of Will on *The Fresh Prince of Bel-Air* giving the style its cool.

To some extent, the placement of Black style upon a white body is not surprising. In his *Civil Rights in the White Literary Imagination*, Jonathan W. Gray* critiques Norman Mailer's "The White Negro," pointing out, "Mailer claims that 'the source of the Hip is the Negro' (340) and that one might avoid the conformist traps of 1950s America by 'absorb[ing] the existential synapses of the Negro (341)" (Gray 64). Gray's take on Mailer probes the way the marginalization of Black people gave the author a unique outsider perspective on white mainstream society that emphasized courage in the face of policies designed to do harm. Mailer, in "The White Negro," advocates for the white hipster's adoption of this lens, but doing so ignores the oppression faced by the Black community that kindled the fires of civil rights protest which necessitated this approach in the first place. Essentially, white hipsters have much to gain by taking on the outsider perspective that originated from within Black culture, but doing so also risks stripping that outlook of its roots in persecution and exile. For Kid-Vid, any Black culture he literally wears turns to appropriation as it appears on a white body elevated above his group to the role of leader. He benefits from the "cool factor" of his outfit, but has no need for the racial justice heritage of an appearance designed for Black empowerment against racist institutions and social norms. By contrast, Jaws, as he is presented in Burger King Kids Club paratexts, possesses none of these design elements, instead becoming a body detached from any sort of historical reference.

Though, Kid-Vid aside, in avoiding assigning Jaws accessories of Black 1980s hip hop, Burger King also dodges stereotype. Instead,

---

*The author of this text, Jonathan W. Gray, is not to be confused with Jonathan Gray, the media scholar, who is cited elsewhere in this book.

Jaws' look allows for a bit more complexity. He sports a flattop hair-cut, easily identifiable as a young Black male style of the early '90s, and ever-popular Chuck Taylors with a green short-sleeve button-down cardigan with a blue T-shirt and shorts underneath. He is assigned qualities like an interest in environmental science that show consumers possibilities other media presenting Black characters did not. Here, one returns to the earlier discussion of fast food's overall role in Black communities, assessing both individual success and cultural exploitation.

As the Burger King Kids Club characters moved into the mid-'90s, their default likenesses became redundant. Therefore, the kids' meal started to feature more creative mash-ups of the team. In two instances, this capitalized on the glow-in-the-dark trend that seems to burn hot in the toy world at least once a generation. The first made Jaws into a troll, of the "troll dolls" that have existed in some form since 1959, with their untamed hair and, sometimes, good luck jewel on the belly. The second cast Jaws in glow-in-the-dark plastic while accessorizing him with a snap-on heavy gear deep sea diver suit. In both cases, this removes Jaws' race from his skin entirely, as he becomes the same color as the other Kids Club members. This decision was most likely a practical one: the plastic that glows in the dark is conventionally one color, and, unless one opts for glow-in-the-dark paint apps on a more realistic-looking figure, that is the color that the produced toys will be. However, in this discussion of race, I cannot help but see this iridescent color as a slightly green hued close neighbor of whiteness, and quite a distance away from Jaws' brown skin tone. This does not come up in any of the contextualizing materials for these glow-in-the-dark figures, and, from a certain perspective, one might wonder why it should. After all, the gimmick is the thing, and all the toys in these lines perform it well. But if one is not only playing with their toys but also reading them through a racial lens, these promotions reveal a limitation of fast food toys created from in-house mascots. Toys like these, as opposed to those with multi-million dollar two-hour films backing them, have only so much space in a 15-second commercial or a rarely read in-store magazine. In that minuscule pocket of time, marketing agencies will choose, time and again, to focus on directed play, or how the toys work, and establish the most basic level of connection with the viewer. That is not to say the deeper racial questions asked by products like these should not be answered, but that, if the goal is Capitalistic pursuit of profit, they have no room to be. Fast food corporations move so quickly and imply through the process of converting intellectual property into toys that academic discussions of their choices can really only happen after the fact.

A similar quandary is faced in the comics medium. Typically, a comic book has roughly 22 pages to convince a reader to buy the next one. While many comics have probed race to varying degrees of success, there is often, especially in comics of the 1990s and before, a sense that more could be explored, but doing so would require holding space for realities the privileged may find uncomfortable. As Robert Jones, Jr., said, "The mainstream comic book industry is afraid to tackle the notion of what a truly radicalized black person with superpowers would actually look like and what they would do with those powers" (Jones). This refers to the way Marvel comics head Stan Lee was, as Sean Howe puts it in *Marvel Comics: The Untold Story*, "the master of the middle ground," for which honest portrayals of superheroic Blackness, which may include revolution through powers capable of destroying racist institutions would move the needle too far away from the center, and, in the minds of some executives, may create concerns that potentially alienated readers will not help break sales records. This is why, as Howe further said, "The presence of blackness did not equate to an unambiguous antiracist stance from Marvel" (Howe). How could it? Showing readers a Black person and truly investigating how that Black person might exist in the world empowered both literally and figuratively are, under the umbrella of white Capitalist products, two separate things.

Likewise, kids' meal toys walk the middle ground as though it is a tightrope. They will not intentionally step meaningfully into social commentary any more than they will desire to move into bland irrelevance. As such, even though the glow-in-the-dark Burger King kids' meal toys present a Jaws whose Blackness has been erased and exchanged for near-whiteness, the textual scaffolding around that conundrum will not explore what an actual "truly radicalized" Black person might do in that situation any more than Robert Jones, Jr.'s, comics would. Scholarship is one way it is possible to zoom in on these kids' meal toys and view them from the angles not afforded to them in their brief advertisements, plugging them into larger conversations of, in this case, race, extrapolating three-dimensional selves from plastic bodies often thought of as disposable.

This also allows, in the example of Jaws from the Burger King Kids Club, the exploration of how a Black body changes throughout its different iterations across years. In 1997, almost at the end of the Burger King Kids Club's tenure, Jaws goes cyborg. In the Planet Patrol promotion, a high-tech red and yellow suit encases Jaws, with only his head visible. The torso of his body has two wheels embedded in it. These are positioned so that the toy can roll across the floor, mimicking a person in "flight," much like Superman races between buildings. The human/vehicle hybrid is awkward, with its head much smaller than the rest of the body, which is presumably bigger so as to hold the wheels. Of the team represented in this promotion, Jaws is the only one whose body is fused with wheels. Three of the others are in vehicles, and Kid-Vid has a propeller atop his head, Inspector Gadget style. The "Planet Patrol" moniker adds an element of the superheroic to this group, making them protectors of Earth who use their enhancements or vehicles for defense in the most general sense. There is, of course, precedent for Black bodies turned superhuman via technological enhancements to their strength. Robert Jones, Jr., in his critique of this trope, highlights Cyborg, the DC superhero, who, like Jaws, has a body largely made up of metal that is capable of forming a range of accessories. For Jones, part of Cyborg's problem is that his body often becomes a tool that facilitates the success of the white characters around him. That is not so much the case with Jaws, if only by virtue of there not being enough supporting material to say, but he nevertheless does visually represent this trend. By equipping Jaws with technological enhancements that increase his physical abilities, the character begins to drift toward a history of Black bodies only treated as valuable when their bodily strength proves useful to white Capitalism. As Jones Jr. says, "So, of course [Cyborg] is an athlete; of course he plays football. White supremacy must always find some 'productive' use in black bodies, must always be able to capitalize off of our labor" (Jones). It should be noted that, in the 1994 Sports All Stars promotion, Jaws, too, plays football, his figure in that line accompanied by an oversized football for him to toss. That is not necessarily to say that Jaws, or any other Black character, "cannot" like football, or become a cyborg, but that such traits have been made to serve what Jones calls a "white supremacist framework" that often paints those elements onto Black people at the expense of explicit antiracist work through intentional call-outs of stereotypes.

However, to complexify this: Jaws was given non-stereotypical qualities in his earliest iterations. The comics that debuted his character give readers, as mentioned earlier, a soft-spoken environmentalist who often floats above the antics of the group. He wants to be a scientific explorer. He is, in his introductory framings, what one today might consider a "Blerd," or Black nerd, which, in the mainstream white-centered culture of 1990, was an uncommon pop culture representation of the way plenty of Black scientists were moving through the world. It is also true that Jaws' height—readers of the *Burger King Kids Club Magazine* learn he is the tallest of the group— is emphasized, thus moving him closer again to the stereotyping Robert Jones, Jr., finds in Cyborg, but at the very least there is some character building that runs counter to this. But because these traits are not intentionally and thoughtfully maintained, and other more stereotypical qualities are brought in, the deeper aspects of Jaws' Black representation potential go untapped.

And this potential could have been quite tapped. A recently-discovered early internal drawing of the character that would eventually become Jaws tells a very different story even from what would eventually appear in the *Burger King Kids Club Magazine*.* The full-color sketch produced by Alcone Marketing Group for, according to the label on the art, the first "[Kids Club] Nat'l Logo & Character

---

*The art for this character was found in an old filing cabinet inside an office building once owned by Alcone. The building was about to be torn down when the contents of the filing cabinet were saved. This concept art now resides in the author's personal collection.

Revision" presents the character of Calvin. Calvin shares some similarities with Jaws. He is a young Black man with not quite a flattop, but close to it. Calvin, though, sports a green, white, and blue striped button-down, sneakers, eye glasses, suspenders *with* a belt, and cargo pants. Both the belt and his pockets are filled with scientific equipment, and he has a telescope slung over one arm. If one imagines Norman Rockwell painting a portrait of a more dignified Steve Urkel, they would have a solid vision of this drawing. Calvin also holds a toy space shuttle, and, on a sticky note at the bottom of the drawing, someone, presumably from Alcone, has written, "Tuskegee Airman" and has suggested, in another Post-It, that Calvin might wear a "flight jacket over a Goretex parka." The reference to the Tuskegee Airmen, an all–Black group of fighter pilots who fought during the Second World War, stands out. It grounds the character in a specific image from Black history, and, had Burger King run with the idea, one assumes lessons might be built around Calvin's idolization of these Black pilots of the past. That is not to suggest that Jaws' persona was somehow empirically worse, but it did very much exist in the '90s, with no interest in evoking the past. Jaws, like the rest of the team, was a kid in a vacuum, although, as the previous discussion of Black character tropes in white mainstream media illustrates, not really. Without an explicit investment in Black historical heroes, and a lack of true understanding of Black joy and empowerment in the 1990s, Jaws was left to be filled in by a focus on the easiest possible character traits: his height, his football playing, his physical strength. In and of themselves, these traits are legitimate, but, as writers like Robert Jones, Jr., have pointed out, when applied to Black characters without specific intentionality by white corporations, they intersect with a racist legacy that then also exists within the new fictional body. This highlights the need for the empowerment of Black creatives within corporate spaces, as their compensated input can ensure thoughtful clapbacks against stereotype, and meaningful representations of Blackness such that the thousands of little plastic bodies may, in the end, be disposable, but the message behind them is not.

I cannot speak from experience on the influence of Jaws, or the possible impact of Calvin. As a white consumer, I do not know, personally, whether seeing Jaws in a kids' meal for the first time, as a kid, would be uplifting. I hope there are kids and adults who found his inclusion meaningful. The best I can do is plug Jaws into the legacy of fast food's intersections with Blackness, the largest of which has been through franchises in Black communities. In those cases, Chatelain's "push-and-pull" is clear; there is a push toward individual wealth and some Black empowerment, and a pull to get stores that are equal to those in white communities, as well as broader community growth from the presence of largely white-owned corporations. That seems to be true of Jaws kids' meal toys, too. There is an undeniable presentation of a Black body, there, and the slightest

Left: Early, unused concept art for the Burger King Kids Club character "Calvin," who was later reworked into the character "Jaws." *Right:* In contrast, here again is Jaws' official "look," as it appeared on near-final concept art for a Burger King Kids Club entrance sign.

counterstereotypical traits within him, too, so long as one digs for them. As Dwayne McDuffie said, "In comics, there's two kinds of Black people: there's Shaft, and there's Sydney Poitier" (*White Scripts and Black Supermen*). In many ways, Jaws manages to be both. Some toys and character traits stress his physical ability, while others his soft-spoken gentleness. This may have been novel enough to provide Black empowerment on an individual basis, but the deeper community possibilities, as unlocked by a moment where a fast food corporation took the opportunity to prove that they really saw the neighborhoods they were so happy to take money from, still feel unrealized. Maybe the best metaphor for this entire relationship lies in a 1990 Burger King Kids Club commercial that appeared on select VHS tapes of the animated *Teenage Mutant Ninja Turtles* episodes. It opens on a live-action white man drawing the Kids Club characters. Soon, the characters come alive and steal the hamburger the man was eating. This causes the entire commercial to transform into a film reel, which the human artist leaps out of, in pursuit of his food. As this mayhem ensues, we push back further to see another real-life human, the commercial's white director, reach into the reel and yank out the hamburger for himself ("Burger King Kids Club Commercial"). Instead of seeing human kids interact with the cartoon Kids Club, as was typical, this commercial focuses on a power structure that places its most diverse group on the lowest rung. Further up the latter sits a chain of white management whose middle rung may be vulnerable, but whose top always gets the hamburger. Black franchisees, likewise, could grow to lower mid-level advancement, but often found movement higher to be extremely difficult if not impossible. Jaws, too, was able to permeate material culture as a toy, but was halted at turns in his story that would have moved him away from white-generated Black stereotypes. If there is always a bigger hand reaching into frame after the hamburger, however, it may, as of this writing, be production studios like Disney and Pixar, who have largely made obsolete food company-developed mascots like the Burger King Kids Club, which became defunct at the turn of the 21st century, as did most other fast food-specific characters (though, McDonaldland is slowly making a comeback as of 2023). With these studios becoming more invested in Black stories, the likelihood of finding a Black character in a kids' meal in 2023 is far higher than in 1990. Pixar's first Black protagonist, Joe Gardner, found his way into a McDonald's Happy Meal in 2020. Afro-Latino superhero Miles Morales, as Spider-Man, slung Burger King Kids' Meals in 2023. And, in 2022, *Black Panther: Wakanda Forever* gave way to a Happy Meal that featured only characters of color. However, Disney can only influence kids' meals, not fast food corporate racial fairness in franchisee growth. That change is ultimately an internal one, less obvious to the general public than a new line-up of kids' meal toys. Through the work of writers like Marcia Chatelain, and court cases such as that of Herb Washington, though, one hopes to hasten the day where all affiliated Black hands have an equitable opportunity to be where the burger ultimately stops.

CHAPTER 3

Plastic Bodies
A *Fat Studies* Approach
to Health Messaging in Kids' Meal Toys

"McDonald's latest tactic was to hire Mayor Beame's campaign public-relations adviser, Howard J. Rubenstein, to represent them in New York and, undoubtedly, put in a good word at City Hall. That move is apparently paying off since the only response to an 11,000-name anti–McDonald's petition delivered to the mayor's office by the Friends of the 66th Street was a routine we'll-look-into-it reply."
—Mimi Sheraton, "The Burger That's Eating New York," 1974 *New York* magazine article about New York City neighborhoods' efforts to keep McDonald's out

"Q: What kind of fruit can put out a fire?
A: Watermelon!"
—1992 McDonald's Food Fundamental Happy Meal bag

There is little question that fast food consumption has risen steadily since the 1950s. As Mark Jekanowski, et al., indicate in their "Convenience, Accessibility, and the Demand for Fast Food," of those who ate food prepared outside the home in 1967, 14.3 percent went to a fast food chain. By 1999, that number reached 35.5 percent, according to the U.S. Department of Agriculture (Jekanowski 58). As of this writing in 2023, the Centers for Disease Control's National Center for Health Statistics reports that percentage is higher still, with 36.6 percent of American adults consuming fast food per day ("Fast Food Statistics"). Of course, a lot has changed since 1967, most notably the number of fast food chains and franchises. As these locations permeate the United States more and more, statistics marking

83

an increase in those taking advantage of this availability read as logical.

Alongside this, the CDC also notes an increase in obesity among adults and children, with childhood obesity statistics provided by the National Institute of Health trending upward from around 5 percent in 1971 to approximately 19 percent in 2021, with general spikes occurring in 2003 and 2007 ("Overweight and Obesity Statistics"). Because of this parallel rise in fast food and childhood obesity, much scholarship has been devoted to the question of whether these statistics show causation or correlation. While the data portrays a more complicated picture, local laws and groups have, in certain cases, leapt to the conclusion that fast food is to blame. This assumption has left the kids' meal toy as the material embodiment of fast food's "seduction of the innocent," insidiously acting as the gateway to childhood obesity by being the object that lures kids toward fried food and grease.

However, obesity is much more complicated than this, and that proposes the possibility that the kids' meal toy is, too. This chapter will dissect the advent of children as modern consumers, fat studies scholarship around obesity, and writing about the influential role of the kids' meal toy in childhood decision making to argue that these fast food prizes are scapegoated by those who may be well-meaning in their health advocacy, but unaware of the larger framework in which these items exist. Rather than unpack the ways in which obesity is discussed culturally, or process the reasons why Black and Hispanic consumers experience obesity at a higher rate than average, actions like legislative bans on kids' meal toys for certain food provide a more direct, concise way to feel as though a problem has been addressed, when in fact its underlying causes remain. While general data does provide an overall rise in both fast food chains and childhood obesity, local statistics that should show drops in obesity after such bans do not quite live up to expectation. That, plus the inclusion of fat studies academics in this conversation of obesity, provides a sort of restorative scholarship that challenges some assumptions upon which prior writing builds its theses.

The history of the relationship between health-questionable

food manufacturers, toys, and children goes back over a century. As discussed in the introduction to this book, Cracker Jack boxes housed not just sugary popcorn and nuts, but small toy prizes, starting in 1912, often cited as one of the earliest examples of a food company pairing with mass-produced toys in order to entice kids. Around this time, cereal companies like Kellogg's began upping their sugar content and their children's promotions to capture the same market. However, as Scott Bruce has shown in his many visual guides on the subject, by the 1950s, this type of marketing was in full swing with both licensed and in-house premiums found in cereals. Some of these popular promotions included:

- Cardboard models for "Sgt. Preston's Yukon Trail" based on the "Challenge of the Yukon" radio Program: Quaker Puffed Rice, 1950
- Walt Disney Fun Masks: Wheaties, 1950–1951
- Hopalong Cassidy Western badges: Post's Raisin Bran, 1950–1951
- Captain Video Space Men figurines: Post's Raisin Bran, 1953
- Superman "Stereo-Pix" cut-outs: Sugar Frosted Flakes, 1954
- Atomic Submarine miniature baking powder-fueled vessel: Kellogg's Rice Krispies, 1954–1955
- Superman belt buckle: Kellogg's Corn Flakes, 1955
- Mouseketeer cut-out records: Wheaties: 1956
- Sky King "statuettes" (figurines): Nabisco Rice Honeys, 1956
- Lone Ranger figurines: Cheerios, 1957
- Thunderbird model car: Post Sugar Rice Krinkles, 1959

And these only barely scratch the surface of cereal box toys available throughout the '50s. Aside from providing a concise summary of the decade's popular interests (Westerns, the atomic age, Disney, and cars), these are also all examples of food companies building relationships with media producers to increase kid demand for their sugared cereals. While a bowl of cereal will likely contain fewer calories than the roughly 405 that are in a Chicken McNuggets Happy Meal, stray from the recommended one-cup serving size (as many do), and the gap begins to close. Furthermore, the types of toys used in kids' meals and the aforementioned cereal premiums do not differ immensely. McDonald's offered die-cast miniature Hot Wheels cars comparable to the Sugar Rice Krinkles 1959 Thunderbird in 1983, 1988, 1990, 1991, and at least once a year thereafter until 2020. Figurines from popular movies and TV series echoing Captain Video and Sky King of the '50s can be found scattered across multiple fast food kids' meals such as 2020's *She-Ra and the Princesses of Power* Sonic Wacky Pack and the multiple Burger King and Subway promotions for *The Simpsons* released in the '90s and '00s. McDonald's would even offer a paper record similar to the Mouseketeer Wheaties 1956 promotion for not a Happy Meal but a 1988 Million Dollar Menu giveaway game. Pre-kids' meal in-store fast food promotions of the 1960s, as mentioned in Chapter 1, also resembled these cereal prizes. The Burger Chef Family Circus licensed pins circa 1965, for instance, could have just as easily come from a 1953 box of Grape Nuts which contained one in a series of Roy Rogers pin backs. If Bob Bernstein insists his inspiration for McDonald's Happy Meal promotions came from cereal boxes, these examples support a similarity between the two.

These commonalities highlight the one major contrast even more starkly: cereal box toys of the 1950s did not, and do not, receive the same degree of scrutiny for obesity as kids' meal premiums of the late 1970s, '80s, '90s, and '00s do. There are a few reasons for this, the primary of which ultimately interrogates cultural attacks on fatness as always health-motivated. In the 1950s, marketing by Sugar Information, Inc. led the public to perceive sugar as a healthy additive that would aid weight loss. This was entirely in response to then-new research stating the opposite: that high sugar products did not in fact possess healthful qualities or cause weight reduction. Pro-sugar advertising won awards and cultural favor, keeping their message front-and-center until the next wave of less flattering research started to overtake it in the 1980s ("Misleading Vintage Ads About"). Parallel to this, weight advertisements in the 1950s often targeted adult women, as opposed to children, and, while many of them, like those for the drug "Ayds," sold snake oils on anti-fat fearmongering, others, like those for Ironized Yeast, promoted weight gain, creating a nebulous not-too-thin-not-too-fat scale range for women to achieve in pursuit of the "domestic goddess" myth, or the idea that women were expected to pivot their mental and physical existences toward heteronormative marriage and homemaking. Of course, that is not to say this marketing accepted fatness. The women featured were all straight-sized, even in the "after" photos of weight gain ads, and often celebrities, as well as, at least as far as mainstream publications were concerned, white. This plus the well-funded Sugar Information, Inc.'s campaign to embrace the key ingredient in many of the previously mentioned kid-centered cereals as healthy, meant that child obesity as it pertained to sugar was not as common a research priority of the '50s, and those conducting studies in the 1970s and '80s, rather than go back and reevaluate the work and lives of those three decades prior, instead focused on fast food and its newly-accelerated, standardized appeal to children.

But the children of the 1950s were the parents of the 1980s, and ignoring their body diversity cuts out a key variable in measuring the impact of fast food, and kids' meal toys, on child obesity of the latter decade. Instead, however, the U.S. government, through the U.S. Senate Select Committee on Health and Human Needs published two rounds of dietary guidelines for Americans in 1977 and 1980, both advocating a reduction in fat intake, leading to the popularization of lean meat and low-fat and skim milk. As in the "fat free" craze of the 1990s, this did not result in fewer fat people according to studies conducted throughout these decades (Temple). Still, this concern pivoted to children with the deregulation of the Federal Communications Commission (FCC) in 1984, which made kids programming on television prime real estate for commercials meant to sell children foods seen as in-conflict with the low-fat trend of the time. This undoubtedly helped the pace of kids' meal toy advertising quicken, as fast food chains had much more latitude on how frequently they popped up during, say, Saturday morning cartoons. Thus, many of the more iconic McDonald's advertisements were products of the mid- to late 1980s, with characters like Grimace, Ronald McDonald, Birdie, and the McNugget Buddies, all mascots for quite a while prior, becoming enshrined in the nostalgia of many children of the era through the repetition and story-building they could do on TV. As Cortney Price writes in "The Real Toy Story: The San Francisco Board of Supervisors Healthy Food Incentives Ordinance," the effects of this change remained felt well into the 1990s, when some regulations on advertising time returned, but commercial content stayed self-regulated by the industry. If the common notion that fat content in food was in fact causing a rise in the number of fat people, these commercials would have no government obstacles to prevent them from marketing that food to children (Price). Alongside this concern, other research built upon a 1974 study conducted by Thomas Robertson and John Rossiter which found that an average first grader has essentially a 50/50 chance of understanding that a commercial is designed to persuade, rather than inform or command. This means that a child in this age range might hear a TV ad say, "Come to your nearest fast food restaurant now!" and not be able to process that as a tactic meant to influence a decision as opposed to a directive they must follow. Robertson and Rossiter also found that commercials using loud music, sound effects, and lively action are best suited to capture a child's attention (Calvert 217–218). By these measures, most popular fast food kids' meal advertisements of the 1980s and '90s would qualify as extremely alluring to children. This, combined with the emphasis on an alleged negative effect of high-fat foods, produced the narrative that fast food chains were targeting kids and creating what became known as the "childhood obesity epidemic." While one may see the appeal in an easy solution to what is constantly presented as a problem, even perhaps going so far as to consider personal experiences that support this answer, modern studies are far more reluctant to name a singular "reason" for fatness, instead noting that body size is motivated by a range of factors.

According to studies promoted by the Centers for Disease Control (CDC) and the National Institutes of Health (NIH), body size variance results from interactions between variables that can be genetic, environmental, and dietary ("Genes and Obesity," Temple). This means that while it may be tempting to explain fatness by pointing to only one's family history, science suggests that genes and their mutations can merely speak to a very small percentage of the population classified as "obese" ("Genes and Obesity"). Furthermore, the NIH has found that foods high in fat and/or sugar also do not provide much in the way of a singular explanation for fatness. That particular study noted that ultra-processed foods provided the most evidence for that category being a key player in fat retention, but also stated that more research was needed in order to establish this fully (Temple). Indeed, further science may be complicated by the fact that what is frequently termed the "obesity epidemic" continues despite popular fast food restaurants discontinuing the use of preservatives and fillers in their beef. McDonald's hamburgers, for instance, are 100 percent beef, of essentially the same or better quality than what one might buy at a supermarket, a claim supported by both the McDonald's website, which is mandated to report all ingredients in its food, and corporate chefs who were involved in hamburger patty production ("Beef and Burgers FAQs" and Haracz). According to that same website, nothing in a McDonald's hamburger uses the artificial preservatives needed to be considered an ultra-processed food with the exception of the pickles. Therefore, if ultra-processed foods are theorized to be a key contributing factor to fatness, and a McDonald's hamburger no longer qualifies as such an item, the logic behind fast food elimination to reduce body weight does not stand.

Fast food toys provide specific evidence that can help show the fallacy in the alleged fast food/fatness causational relationship. In 2010, believing that Happy Meal toys acted as an entry point to foods that cause child obesity, the San Francisco Board of Supervisors voted to limit these premiums to only the meals that abided by health and nutritional standards such as the inclusion of fruit and vegetables and a lower salt content (Price). While this particular study was not published at the time of the ordinance, a 2012 paper would support the idea that kids will select a healthier meal option if it is the only one accompanied by a toy (Hobin, et al.). However, questions remained over whether incentivizing this one choice would truly make an impact in the body sizes of children. Then-San Francisco Mayor Gavin Newsom thought not, and initially vetoed the Board of Supervisors' measure, resulting in a second vote whose majority in favor was large enough to make the rule veto-proof. However, the

Board's own language also doubted its efficacy when it said, "This article is not suggesting that the San Francisco 'Toy Ban' will solve the obesity problem or even make a sizeable dent on a nationwide scale" (Price 348–349). Its goal instead, as stated in the ordinance, was to "raise awareness" and "challenge the restaurant industry" (349). The latter motivation is revealing. It suggests that health, in the form of anti-fatness, is secondary to perpetuating an adversarial relationship between government and fast food, exchanging a deeper conversation around the intersection of body size, healthfulness, race, class, and gender for the assignment of blame on one specific industry. Cortney Price's article offering background for the ordinance cites both a 30-year rise in "obesity among children" and the introduction of the Happy Meal three decades prior as events linked by causation, but never wrestles with the history presented in this book, such as ways fast food chains used premiums to increase children's excitement for their brands prior to the Happy Meal, or the fact that cereal box toys were selling sugar-coated flakes to kids for many years before the late '70s largely without being roped into legislative arguments about childhood fatness. Instead, the San Francisco ordinance relied on a perception of fast food popularized by Morgan Spurlock's 2004 documentary *Super Size Me*, in which the filmmaker consumes McDonald's food for every meal in a month, never allowing himself to turn down the meal size option noted in the film's title. As a result, Spurlock's doctor found a number of growing health concerns at the end of his 30-day period of consumption that were linked back to the ingestion of fast food. To an extent, this was correct: Spurlock only ate McDonald's food, and that did produce valid health-related problems; however, conversations around the atypical nature of the documentarian's eating habits were omitted from evaluations of the film as horror took hold around the alarming nature of his physician's report. But this unusual eating pattern matters, especially if it is assumed that children consume McDonald's at the same rate. The reason Happy Meal commercials utilize so many tactics that appeal to children, and the toys themselves rely on properties with which kids are familiar, is that it is still very hard to get most kids into a McDonald's on a frequent basis. Children do not

90

have the agency to transport themselves to a restaurant, or the financial ability to pay for meals themselves. Fast food corporations know that, as far as kids are concerned, they are mostly benefiting from the once-a-week treat, the occasional impulse buy, or the cave that happens after a significant amount of child pleading. As fat scholar Dr. Anastasia Kidd said, "Nutrition is really about variety and satiety" (Kidd). Children may frequently find both by virtue of the rotation of food their adult caretakers provide them with. When their diets are more homogenous, especially if they are more fast food-filled, it is often not by choice. In those cases, the lack of necessary variety comes from the way fast food corporations edge out supermarkets in underprivileged neighborhoods, replacing them with a handful of items that can be purchased cheaply, but rarely change. This combined with the racial barriers that saddle adults of Black and Brown communities with statistically higher working class hours, less free time, and smaller paychecks creates an environment hostile to even the possibility of food variety. In these cases, the problem is not fast food toys luring kids away from the many healthful options awaiting them, but institutional racism and classism maintained over generations cycling low income families through fast food restaurants that are their only choice.

Perhaps this is why the data do not bear any fruit for the San Francisco Board of Supervisors' kids' meal toy restrictions, but do affirm the need for conversations of race and diet variety to go deeper. San Francisco's ordinance went into effect in 2010, and, in 2012, overall child obesity, as measured by San Francisco's government health data, was at about 38 percent. Five years later, in 2017, this percentage was at approximately 35 percent, with nearly all demographics experiencing a brief, small drop before a rebound and plateau which took the child obesity rate back to nearly what it was at the start of the data. Both African American and Hispanic demographics maintained a higher than average obesity rate across all years measured, and Filipino kids in San Francisco saw a steady rise during this time period, rising from roughly 53 percent in 2012 to 66 percent in 2017 (San Francisco Government Health Data). Another government survey which targeted San Francisco Fifth Graders specifically found the number of those outside the "Healthy Fitness Zone" hovered around 36 percent from 2013 to 2017 (San Francisco Health Improvement Partnership). Therefore, if ordinances like the one enacted by the San Francisco Board of Supervisors are to present kids' meal toys as a gateway to unhealthy eating, the effects of which are to be measured through obesity rates, one should expect their restrictions of such premiums to have a bigger impact on data measuring body size in kids. When the average stays in the mid–30 percent despite these changes, it suggests that Gavin Newsom's position, like the possibility admitted by the ordinance's own context, that such measures do not tend to create meaningful change was correct. All the while, these statistics ask us to have the conversations avoided by putting fatness at the doorstep of kids' meal toys. They consistently show Black and Brown populations have higher obesity rates than white demographics, which could springboard into broader discussions of cultural beauty standards, access to food variety, wage inequality and its impact on time available for home cooking, and acceptance of body diversity—a range of angles that may in some places intersect with fast food corporate practices, but cannot support sole blame being assigned to them. But these influences on culture are less visible than, say, a Happy Meal toy, which has been dealt a role at once innocent *and* suspect, a societal position it must exist within very carefully.

Because of this, kids' meal toys are sometimes used to represent a fast food chain's commitment to health, especially when their cuisine's nutritional content is called into question. A number of kids' meals from a variety of restaurants have emphasized outdoor activity, exercise, and health mindfulness throughout the years. McDonald's gave out beach balls (1986), Beach Fun toys (1987), and yard activity toys (1993) in addition to scores of others, including pedometers (2004) that were offered to adults in their "Go Active!" meal. Additionally, Burger King gave out small Super Soakers in their kids' meals (2011), Subway included an array of sports and dance toys throughout the early '00s (2004, 2005, 2008, et al.), Sonic's Wacky Pack contained Nerf guns (2021) and licensed frisbees for a number of properties including *Teen Titans GO!* (2023),

Chapter 3. Plastic Bodies

This 1994 McDonald's "Super Action Calendar" features the residents of McDonaldland engaged in sports, adding to a corporate narrative that emphasized physical activity.

Wendy's included outdoor toys in many of their 1990s kids' meals (i.e., Summer Fun Sun Gear, 1991; Saurus sports balls, 1993), among myriad more examples. While most kids' meal toys have been figurines or miniatures of some sort, the number of sports toys is substantial. This provided fast food restaurants a way to literally put physical activity on the menu, countering those who would say that these chains can only detract from health. But beyond the many examples of active kids' meal toys, one specific promotion stands out for the way it revised and contradicted its corporation's menu items.

In 1992, McDonald's included the Food Fundamentals line of transformable figurines in one of its Happy Meal promotions. The Food Fundamentals were a group of five anthropomorphic foods. These were:

- Otis the Sandwich: A helmet-clad, rollerskating sandwich whose arms and legs could be extracted from his hollow sandwich body. The sandwich resembled a homemade one, with lettuce leaves peaking out from bread that could be white or whole wheat.
- Milky the Milk Carton: A feminine carton of milk whose pop-out arms held weights for her to presumably exercise with.
- Slugger the Steak: A T-Bone masculine steak whose biceps became evident once his arms were unfolded from his plastic meat body. Sporting a mustache, Slugger resembles a stereotypical bodybuilder who might be found flexing on a California beach.
- Ruby the Apple: A female-coded apple whose hands gripped a tennis ball and racket, thus suggesting her sport of choice.
- Duncan the Corn: This was the line's "Under 3" toy, meaning it was safety tested for kids under three years of age, so it did not transform. Instead, it depicted a muscular corn on the cob character holding a basketball.

Each regular toy came with a booklet created in conjunction with the American Dietetic Association (as advertised prominently on the cover) containing facts about each food, as well as small paper bread slices, milk cartons, steaks, or apples that acted as miniature notepads and fit within the toys' bodies. Each toy directed children toward transformation play, engaging with the "blank" side of the plastic food item as a miniature replica, and then, by rotating the toy so as to reveal its anthropomorphic facial expression, opening the hollow inner portion, and unfolding the limbs contained within, fully realizing a two-inch tall character who was, from one angle, "disguised" as an everyday staple. It was this conversion that most struck me as a child who received and played with these premiums. They spoke to other successful McDonald's Happy Meal toys that transformed from menu items into robots or dinosaurs, for which I already had great fondness. For me, they were not so much characters that integrated into other stories I created using the action figures, dolls, cars, and LEGO minifigures of my toybox as much as they were "trick" objects my child brain delighted in leaving in the family apple bowl, knowing that one of the Red Deliciouses was actually Ruby lying in wait. While surely children and other consumers used these prizes in different ways, they felt, to me, in a class by themselves, a kid's commentary on foods that otherwise failed to stir up much personal excitement.

At least, not as much excitement as a McDonald's meal. This highlights the most glaring truth about the foods on which these toys were modeled: none of them, with the exception of the milk that was added in the late 1980s, were on McDonald's menus in the early '90s U.S. market. Instead, they were stand-ins for what nutrition groups like the co-sponsoring American Dietetic Association *wanted* to see on the menu. In 1991, for example, The *New York Times* reported that McDonald's was in the midst of answering "a growing chorus of criticism of its food," and, in so doing, introduced the "McLean Deluxe," which conformed to the low-fat trend of the decade through a processing method that replaced some of the sandwich's fat content with water (Ramirez). While the McLean Deluxe was indeed marketed as a "healthier" menu item, it was still, at its core, a McDonald's hamburger. It was those very hamburgers that were called into question by, among other sources, a 1986 pamphlet titled "What's Wrong with McDonald's," which was distributed in London by Greenpeace activists. The pamphlet's first complaint was the restaurant's "Promotion of Unhealthy Food," which gave McDonald's' food processing methods as a reason to reject their menu items. While the leaflets were only distributed a few hundred times, McDonald's brought a libel case, since dubbed the "McLibel case," in 1990 against the activists responsible for distributing the aforementioned material. While McDonald's pushed back on the pamphlet's claims, they also took actions, like the creation of the McLean Deluxe, to ensure positive public perception during a time of sluggish growth for the corporation.

I argue that it is this context which gave the 1992 Food Fundamentals Happy Meal its *raison d'être*. Whole foods like apples and corn, and staples associated with nutrition like lean steak, low-fat milk, and a homemade sandwich could never be present, in total, on the McDonald's menu without a significant brand identity crisis. The McLean Deluxe was the corporation's best menu compromise as it walked the line between defending its prior food practices and making just enough adjustments so as to address what it no doubt would deem the public's misperceptions. However, the Happy Meal toy space provided McDonald's with an opportunity no other menu area could. It gave the company the chance to add not only traditionally "healthy" foods, but, by virtue of those foods being plastic, a message, as well. Unlike an edible apple, Ruby could play tennis, advertise the McDonald's/American Dietetic Association partnership, and, best of all, never spoil, thereby ensuring that this statement lasted well past the quickly-approaching termination date for the promotion. While it is unlikely many looked upon this one Happy Meal promotion, a blip in the deluge of toys distributed by the company that year, and, based on that alone, suddenly believed in McDonald's as a bastion of health when, just a month prior, they considered the chain an enemy of nutrition. Taken with the advent of the McLean Deluxe and the corporation's public relations moves, these toys helped tell a story. That story was one of a restaurant that cared about consumers' nutrition, recognized the many facets of health, and went above and beyond to lead in these areas. Today, the Food Fundamentals toys are the surviving debris of this campaign, outliving the McLean Deluxe and its advertising by burying themselves in nostalgia, collections, and antique store dollar bins the nation, and perhaps the world, over. There, these toys exchange messages in support of a "healthy" or "reformed" (or "deceptive," depending on one's perception) fast food corporation for those of childhood playthings lost or kept, items displayed to represent the completeness of a series, and/ or objects in desperate search of an owner. Nevertheless, though, the moment remains.

The early 1990s, and McDonald's' efforts to present itself as the polar opposite of London Greenpeace's 1986 claims, persist in these toys, if a bit more mutedly now, and that opens up yet another role fast food toys play, culturally. As much as kids' meal toys are messengers of our own memories, emotions, obsessions, and selves, they also preserve the aspirations of their corporations of origin at given moments in time. If the late 1980s contained mass media and grass-roots claims of fast food health negligence, the early '90s, with its waves of athletics- and nutrition-conscious kids' meal toys like those noted above, brought those corporations' responses. It is true that fast food chains cannot tell one what to think, but their kids' meal toys can do a lot to influence what one thinks about. Due to the relative permanence of kids' meal toys, and toys in general, it is easy for them to walk with us into our present, but that only emphasizes the role of scholars and historians, who can see past the personal, current love of these objects and contextualize them within their pasts, using them to assess the adequacy of their answers to the questions of their times, and the accuracy of the corporate narratives they were trying to tell.

Additionally, because most kids' meal toys are not the results of in-house marketing companies but licensed intellectual properties, those corporate narratives are not always just those of a fast food company, but the movie-producing powerhouses that use these premiums to promote their latest ventures. On its most superficial level, this means that, say, toys in the 2017 *Despicable Me 3* Happy Meal will paratextually support the story told by their source

In 1999, Marvel Comics poked fun at the unhealthiness of fast food even while the company relied on the industry to distribute premiums in their name.

film. However, deeper than that, kids' meal toys can also describe aspects of their parent media company's brand identity. For example, in 2006, Disney severed its relationship with McDonald's over healthfulness concerns regarding its Happy Meals. While McDonald's partnered with other media companies in the years that followed, Disney, with its consistent blockbuster hits that frequently turned children into fervent consumers, was a major loss. In 2018, McDonald's eliminated the cheeseburger option from Happy Meals, reduced the size of their kids fries, and reevaluated the sugar content of its drinks, thereby more closely aligning their menu with the requests of health advocates (Flager). As a result, Disney returned to McDonald's, willing to repair their broken bond and restore the studio's licensed characters to Happy Meals. In this case, the Happy Meal toy tells not just the story of Disney movies, but of the company's desire to center child health, so much so that they will withhold their intellectual property from a fast food giant until they comply with standards held by the studio. As toys for Disney's *Incredibles 2* found their way into Happy Meals in 2018, so did a message about the shift in food, a health controversy, toys as pawns in the "Health Wars," and who held power in this licensor/licensee agreement. Still, however, these toys have more to say about fast food's connection to its consumers' bodies.

Just as Gavin Newsom, as mayor of San Francisco, doubted the restriction of kids' meal toys would have any effect on childhood fatness—a doubt the numbers seem to support—fat scholars wonder whether fast food "quick fixes" to public relations issues with food quality such as menu toy program alterations miss a larger, more complex problem. As fat scholar Dr. Anastasia Kidd notes, "There is no cause of fatness other than genetic diversity ... [and] our obsession with starvation" (Kidd). Indeed, even the numerous papers that observe the rates of fatness—Kidd indicates the word more commonly used, "obesity," is a mid–20th-century slur that literally translates to "eat oneself to fatness," which acknowledges no other cause for one's body type besides personal choice—per fast food consumption note that their findings are not conclusive. This is not to say that no fat body can be unhealthy, but that "health" and the lack thereof exists across the body size spectrum. As such, when a fast food corporation promises to address health concerns by reducing the size of its french fry portion, and then, culturally, the success of their follow-through is measured by the presence of more thin bodies, all involved have grossly oversimplified the process by which a person becomes "healthy." Instead of making health a multifaceted set of qualities that can include fatness, its prevalence is judged solely or mostly on the elimination of fat people or the perception that this will happen should the course be stayed. As noted previously, the San Francisco kids' meal toy restrictions did not meaningfully alter fatness rates in children, but that did not stop the idea of taking this step to lower "obesity," and therefore increase health, from appealing to many. In this way, the oversimplification of health concerns works to the advantage of the fast food corporation, who can quickly alter their offerings until protests die down instead of assessing the ways in which their very existence reduces the lack of food variety, especially in poor neighborhoods of color, thereby creating supermarket food desserts that are truly a detriment to measures of health that transcend questions of fatness.

Fast food giants will frequently choose the change that can be spun into positive public perception versus that which will implicate their participation in larger toxic systems of racism, fatphobia, and other forms of discrimination. In the previous chapter, the example was given of Black franchisees who were, as Marcia Chatelain explained, included in the McDonald's system only to find further examples of inequality and localized harm. Even as of this writing, in 2023, news of McDonald's' removal of their self-serve drink machines sweeps the online, TV, and radio outlets while word of the corporation's civil rights audit, now materializing as virtual focus groups with franchisees, claims only one lone CNBC article despite both stories emerging on the same day in September. If asked, one is likely to rank "civil rights" higher than "access to drink machines" on a priorities list, and yet the lower item draws more clicks. This is not to present any sort of conspiracy theory about media coverage of these issues, but instead to suggest that the machine pivoting attention toward the (over)simplified restaurant experience solution at the expense of the institutional social crisis is so well-oiled that it can easily be a boon to the fast food industry.

Therefore, kids' meal toys can occupy this space, too. They can distract attention from larger health questions surrounding access to food heterogeneity, affordable health care, leisure, and financial support and refocus it on a minor tweak to adjust a specific body which will, somehow, solve the problem at hand. Except the problem at hand is so often one of perception, not of fact. If this were not the case, both the San Francisco kids' meal toy regulations and the Disney/McDonald's separation would have made some measurable impact on public health. Instead, even the metric of choice by many advocacy organizations, "child obesity," shows little change. However, the public perception of institutions like the San Francisco Board of Supervisors, the Walt Disney Company, and even fast food chains like McDonald's, once they make their menu changes and write the accompanying press releases, can more easily shift toward the better without the aid of fact. Fat scholarship asks for that to never be sufficient.

Though fast food consumption has been on the rise since its eruption in the 1950s, it is still a relatively recent phenomenon. As such, its effect on bodies that ingest it has been treated with an understandable amount of skepticism given its relative novelty. In this, kids' meal toys become multinarrative objects, at once being gateways to poor health, characters of a nutrition-conscious corporation, paratexts of film companies that care about child wellness, and distractions from actual sources of harm. This centers many of the cultural roles within the little plastic bodies that accompany our hamburgers and chicken nuggets around questions of what that food will physically do to consumers. Perhaps this indicates kids' meal toys' power to speak to us where fast food cannot, or maybe it is further evidence of human pareidolia reflecting our bodies, and ourselves, back at us from the bottoms of cardboard food boxes and cartoon restaurant bags.

CHAPTER 4

"Collect 'em all!"

Collection Theory as a Way of Understanding Fast Food Toy Permanence

"A Happy Meal toy reminds people of a sweeter time, a simpler time ... a pre–Kardashian time."
—Max, *2 Broke Girls*

"What a man wants from objects is not the assurance that he can somehow outlive himself, but *the sense that from now on he can live out his life uninterruptedly and in a cyclical mode, and thereby symbolically transcend the realities of an existence before whose irreversibility and contingency he remains powerless.*"
—Jean Baudrillard, "The System of Collecting"

Kids' meal toys are objects to be collected. This language is replicated on advertising translites that read, "Collect All Four." It is on the bags of the McDonald's Disney 50th Anniversary Happy Meal toys, which are numbered 1–50, creating a sequence to be completed. For the 1999 McDonald's *Inspector Gadget* Happy Meal, the toys were not only numbered, but collecting all of them was necessary to build a large figure of Inspector Gadget himself, leaving a piece of this kids' meal toy play only accessible to completist consumers. Furthermore, stories of "hunting" kids' meal toys at assorted restaurant locations were common when I spoke with enthusiasts, collectors, and even casual fans about these items. One collector said that, as a child, her mother would call local McDonald's locations in search of one particular dalmatian in the 1996 *101 Dalmatians* toy promotion, for which 101 distinct, miniature, plastic dogs were produced, making full sets hard to come by. This particular story is personally relatable. For me, the frustration of finding all but a ghostly Lisa Simpson in the Burger King *The Simpsons* Spooky Light-Ups kids' meal was unbearable, eventually resulting in my pleading with the cashier of one particular restaurant to let me have the Lisa they had on display (they wouldn't) and ending in a retreat to eBay, where finding the figure came without the triumphant victory of discovering it, as collectors say, "in the wild." Since then, social media has facilitated trading groups where kids' meal toy hobbyists strategize and trade goods. There, one will notice some collectors rolling the dice and buying the kids' meal without knowing which toy they'll receive, while others go straight to the counter and ask to see the toys available that day, often purchasing the ones they need without the added grease. For these fans, age is not a factor. My friend was a young girl in 1996 when she was trying to catch her *dalmatian d'resistance*. I am a grown adult, communicating with other grown adults on social media groups, comparing kids' meal toy finds. All of us in these groups, however, are participating in a culture of collecting that is created by, and around, kids' meal toys.

In this chapter, I will use Baudrillard, Freud, Benjamin, and others to understand how and why we collect. I then apply this to kids' meal toy collecting, specifically, in order to meaningfully explore what drives collectors to these objects. In this exploration, I show how fundamental collecting impulses combine with corporate direction to hype interest in kids' meal toys. This, then, links with nostalgia to make permanent playthings that were planned as temporary, thereby moving these toys from their intended cultural role as mass-produced, limited-run pieces to artifacts of the past capable of holding far greater meaning.

The Baudrillard and Freud Happy Meal

Within this culture, there are varying degrees to which a collector will go in order to participate in kids' meal toy fandom. The spectrum runs from occasionally collecting the toys that fit their taste, to insisting on finding full sets for all toys, even the promotions that do not necessarily fit with their interests. Collectors toward the latter extreme sometimes go to great lengths to find toys only available in international markets, buy prototypes, and interact with restaurant "insiders" to get information on upcoming promotions ahead of the general public. As someone who has personally exhibited all of this behavior, it is both from introspection and cultural curiosity that I wonder what, exactly, drives this impulse. For Baudrillard, I and collectors like me are not seeking any sort of immortality through our collections. We are not, he would say, hoping our collections outlive us, and, therefore, grant us some sort of notoriety long after our lives have ended. Instead, Baudrillard uses Freud's example of the ball to explain the motive, here, as something more playful, and, more importantly, more cyclical. In *Beyond the Pleasure Principle*, Freud reflects on his grandson shouting "Fort!" ("Gone!") and "Da!" ("There!") while playing with a toy ball. He notes that, for the child, the ball disappears and appears, over and over again, keeping the boy rapt in the cycle of an object's vanishing and rematerialization (Freud). Baudrillard summarizes this by indicating the ball allows the child to "experience the alternating absence and presence of its mother ... the anguish of lack being dispelled by the sustained cycle of re-appearances of the ball" (Baudrillard 17). The theoretical framing of the "cycle" helps address some behaviors that drive fans to fast food counters in search of missing "balls." More specifically, the oscillation between "the anguish of lack" and the "sustained cycle of reappearance" can be routinely observed in kids' meal toy collecting, so much so that restaurants capitalize upon this in order to drive demand.

This demand relies on desire. Consumers, especially kids, must *want* to participate in fast food toy promotions. Cultural critic Marsha Kinder cited Peter Brooks and his work *Reading for the Plot* to expand on the "Fort/Da" game by suggesting that the whole "process is monitored by desire" (Kinder 21). Brooks posits that the appeal of a story like *Arabian Nights* is that the way it prolongs its own narrative "keep[s] desire alive" in its readers by resisting its own end, or death. Kids' meal toys are often marketed in a similar fashion. The pattern is clear: a toy promotion releases, it runs its course, and then is replaced by the next one. There is an expectation that the overall "story" of the kids' meal will continue, which is why even though fans may have promotions they are less enthusiastic about, they still participate in the fandom, understanding that they will have another chance to hear a tale that interests them if they wait out one that does not. This fans the flames of collectors' desire to keep the tradition of the kids' meal toy alive. They do not want one of their favorite stories to end.

Corporations, for their part, have been happy to oblige. Fast food restaurants like Burger King and McDonald's have a history of using ornate displays to showcase every toy in a kids' meal promotion's set. These displays can often be found by cash registers in various sizes, ranging from roughly three feet to five feet in length. Beyond this, translites (or, now, digital menu displays) offer pictures of full sets, advertising the fact that, with enough trips to the store, the consumer could have a collection that looks just like this. The practical purpose is clear: these displays allow kids to develop an attachment to a particular toy, or to the entire set of toys, thus driving their desire to order a kids' meal. However, this is in direct contrast with the actual process of getting a kids' meal, in which *one* toy, most often a random one, is delivered to the consumer secretly, within a bag or box that offers no insight into the object inside. In this moment, the buyer experiences the appearance of the collection, and then the "anguish" of the lack of the full set. That does not mean the experience is necessarily an unhappy one, merely one that provides for outcomes where the toy's receiver is either disappointed by the toy they received, in which case an exchange, trade, or another trip to the store can occur, or satisfied with their plaything, but then, feeling that sense of victory, starts to yearn for the others in the collection that has so rewarded them with what is in their eyes the "best" of the line.

This process is replicated on a larger scale during the time when kids' meal toy promotions switch from one license to another. It was once relatively easy to find information about upcoming kids' meal toy promotions on the websites of various fast food chains. This has recently changed, though, so much so that collectors have had to rely on leaks from insiders to clandestinely learn about upcoming promotions. A recent trip to happymeal.com, for example, revealed a great deal of information about the current toy line offered at McDonald's, but provided no option to learn what will be in the next one, say nothing of an overview of releases for the coming months. This may shift depending on whether one is seeking toy information for the domestic or international market, or if the company should simply decide to offer a preview of the next toy wave, but the fact of intentional absence remains at least a large portion of the time. Here, there is again a sense of disappearance, the ending of one toy line with no knowledge of what is coming next, coupled with the almost immediate appearance of a new line, a process that cyclically repeats previous promotions' ends and starts. "Fort!" "Da!" "Fort!" "Da!"

Even Freud's unsurprisingly Oedipal analysis that the disappearing and reappearing ball stands in for the loss and presence of the mother applies to the way we discuss the role of fast food restaurants, via kids' meals, in some children's lives. Though Freud speaks literally of the mother in much of his work, he also advocates the interpretation of signs and symbols, most notably in *The Interpretation of Dreams*, which allows for a more figurative reading, as later theorists have done.* D.W. Winnicott, in his *Playing and Reality*, establishes the idea of the "good-enough mother." Winnicott writes, "The good-enough 'mother' (not necessarily the infant's own mother) is one who makes active adaptation to the infant's needs, an active adaptation that gradually lessens, according to the infant's growing ability to account for failure of adaptation and to tolerate the results of frustration" (Winnicott 7). Essentially, the good-enough mother, under ideal circumstances, can help an infant develop by intentionally "failing" to constantly provide the highest possible amounts of care. When we study Winnicott's four ways infants might deal with these "maternal failures," we see that a purposeful lack of nourishment can lead to the infant understanding that such absence is temporary, or, to reference Baudrillard, cyclical. These "failings" of maternal love also foster within the infant a "process" for working through the "good-enough" moments, thereby creating "mental

---

*Freud was also a great collector of antiquities, accumulating more than 3,000 by the time he died, so I have no problem interacting with him collector-to-collector, here (Forrester).

stimulation" from forming a response to a lack of the motherly fixture (Winnicott). Nourishment, love, and mental stimulation may be fairly conventional offerings of the socially-normed mother in the United States. The "good-enough mother" knows that one does not need to provide all three "perfectly," and, in fact, that underperforming has value in early childhood development. To carry this forward into this study of kids' meal toys, I contend that Winnicott, by defining the mother as not necessarily the "infant's own," gives license to expand the definition of "mother." While any human being can, theoretically, offer the aforementioned three maternal contributions toward child rearing and then some, and moderate the amounts of them received in any given moment, we must consider that, when it comes to defining their roles in children's lives, fast food restaurants can, and do, too.

Nourishment comes from the food, and the toy contributes mental stimulation, usually in the form of play or entertainment. "Love," or something like it, springs from the immersive, commercial world of fast food mascots like Ronald McDonald or the Burger King Kids Club animated members. One 1997 Burger King kids' meal commercial promoting an M&Ms-based line of toys opens with a boy and girl's mother hiring an elderly, curmudgeonly nanny to babysit them. In a flash, Kid Vid, the cartoon Burger King Kids Club ringleader, uses a magical remote to zap the kids to a Burger King, sans mother or sitter. While they're there, they interact with the Kids Club gang and play with their new toys. In the final beat of the ad, Kid Vid once again uses his remote control to make the Burger King logo slap the nanny hard enough to knock her out of frame, ending with the mantra, "Great food, cool stuff, kids only." Though this is a single example, there are a number of tropes that span numerous kids' meal commercials from that era on. The obliviousness, meanness, or total lack of parents and/or guardians, the presence of a mascot or licensed character as the parental stand-in controlling the fantastical circumstances of a child's world, and the definition of the fast food restaurant as a whimsical place that trumps a kid's daily reality are all repeated in numerous commercials across many chains. The absence, whether physical or mental, of human parents, and their replacement by a corporate mascot issue a double dose of Winnicott's "good-enough mother." By excerpting the child's true guardian from the narrative, the commercial offers the child consumer, now well beyond the infant stage in which Winnicott starts the benefits of the "good enough" behavior, the restaurant promises a place where the mental stimulation the child has gained from filling the intentionally created mother-shaped hole in their early life can grow exponentially. Now, questions of what to eat, how much to eat, when to play, and with whom to play all fall under the child's purview—quite a lot of agency to give to someone who is, in many other circumstances including the real-life version of visiting a fast food restaurant, too young to be granted it. Furthermore, in the aforementioned 1997 commercial, Kid Vid is the ideal "good enough mother." He ensures a safe and fun environment, and that the basic tenets of nourishment, love, and mental stimulation are present, and then by all accounts leaves the kids to it. He reappears at the end to define the space as one exclusively for nourishment ("great food"), mental stimulation ("cool stuff"), and love ("kids only"), and succeeds at being at once like the children in the commercial and different enough to be an authority figure ("Kid" is in his name, though his actual age is unknown, not to mention he exists in an entirely different dimension from the three-dimensional human kids). Commercials like this one hook children into the process of collecting kids' meal toys by showing off the "cool stuff," yes, but also by presenting the space in which that "stuff" is obtained as one that can satisfy growth needs shown by Winnicott to be positive factors in development from infancy and beyond. Given Freud's involvement of the loss and presence of the maternal in the disappearance and reappearance of the ball and Winnicott's definition of the mother as someone intentionally setting an at times low bar for care, fast food chains, through kids' meals, do a good job of offering a similar experience, not just through the cyclical lack and fulfillment of a toy, but also by constructing themselves as motherly, or at least parental, providers, who then withdraw and return that companion in just as circular a manner. This elevates the stakes in some kids' and collectors' interactions with kids' meal toys, stretching their metaphorical and sentimental value beyond the limits of their plastic molding and into the realm of an emotional connection to the whole give-and-take of corporate, Capitalist "mothering" that offered a playful distraction from "death"—perhaps not literal death, but the death of childhood as represented by the increase of responsibilities and aging—sometimes over great spans of time.

This may also help explain some of the discomfort felt when this cycle is interrupted. In 2021, McDonald's announced the company would begin a 90 percent reduction in plastic Happy Meal toys that would be fully realized by 2025. This process would include toys made from, in addition to other non-plastic materials, paper, as seen in the 2022 *Teen Titans GO!* promotion, which featured fold-out paper posters, which offered consumers the chance to color and play games on the character-themed pieces themselves. This inspired a range of negative comments on the Happy Meal Toys Facebook page, which has garnered over 49,000 likes since its inception. Comments like "Paper toys suck," "The last [*Teen Titans GO!*] 'toy' was so boring and thrown away in just an hour," and "Can we have plastic toys back, please?" were 20 of the 101 comments on a post announcing that an upcoming toy line was *not* paper, and virtually all of the 218 comments on the previous post about the toys that were. Concurrently, a new change.org petition holds 1,180 signatures from people who want McDonald's to "continue to offer high-quality [plastic] Happy Meal toys & initiate [a] toy recycling program" ("Continue to offer"). This outrage shows one response to a disruption in the cycle of kids' meal toy collecting. Unlike Freud's grandson and his ball, kids' meal toy collectors know that their toys are not actually disappearing. They have come to expect the reappearance, so long as that reappearance brings back their "ball," as they have come to understand it. In this case, the "ball" is likely to be some form of small, plastic figurine or toy, perhaps with a gimmick or action feature. Deviations from this norm have happened historically (see the 1991 Astronauts Happy Meal, featuring cardboard spacefaring vehicles), but the 2021 announcement asserts that these deviations would become the norm, at least until sustainable, plastic-like materials could become commonplace in kids' meal toys. This now makes the "anguish-laden fact of lack," the lack of the kids' meal toy collection as defined by the bulk of decades' worth of items, final, and that runs contrary to what the cycle of collecting was set up to do. Fans' anger would probably not be couched in Baudrillard's terms, but they still offer cultural critics a way of understanding, in the general sense, what happens when large numbers of enthusiasts push back against a corporate decision meant, at least in this case, to have some benefit for an environment currently suffocating from disposable plastics. It is not a matter of a mob of hyper-obsessed collectors getting upset over a change that, to those outside the fandom, may seem inconsequential; it is a much more universal instance of a cycle interrupted, which, to Baudrillard, holds metaphors for death and mourning without the possibility of an object's "intercession" (Baudrillard 17).

The Benjamin Kids Club

While recognizing that the culture of collecting kids' meal toys contains certain psychological and psychosocial factors that play a role in fostering a desire for these objects, potentially from a very early age, helps establish why these items are ubiquitous in homes, offices, antique stores, and online marketplace pages across the United States, if not the world, it is also important to understand how these toys offer power to their collectors that hooks them into systems of trading, selling, and bartering with kids' meal playthings. Specifically, kids' meal toys achieve value not as art objects, but as the currency of a collector culture network which contains nodes that connect to other fandoms. This is possible because kids' meal toys are mass produced in such volume that McDonald's has become the largest toy distributor in the world, with a Happy Meal toy coming with 20 percent of all sales at the chain's restaurants (Guenette). Production like that stokes the fires of a fan base big enough to fight to get toys early on in the run, find certain characters first, and maintain old collections in mint-in-bag condition for future sale, despite many of those toys winding up in the dollar bins of collectibles stores.

In his essay "The Work of Art in the Age of Mechanical Reproduction," Walter Benjamin notes that this sort of culture is a symptom of the transition from art object to mass produced good. He writes, "For the first time in world history, mechanical reproduction emancipates the work of art from its parasitical dependence on ritual ... instead of being based on ritual, it begins to be based on another practice—politics" (Benjamin). This does not mean "politics" as we might consider it today, but rather a more general politics governing the use of large-scale machines, commerce, employment, and product making. Ritual is a far more intimate practice, involving a limited number of people. Politics, with etymological roots in the "city," needs a much larger footprint. If kids' meal toys halted at their prototype stage, their value may be calculated similar to that of a painted portrait. One might ask questions about the sculptor, the technique used to make the object, and the process behind its creation—the ritual or rituals that gave it origin. From there, the one-of-a-kind prototype might find a seller interested in its uniqueness, the way an art collector might buy a Dale Chihuly piece. However, when that prototype goes into production, that form of valuation becomes obsolete. The molds that make the toys become the most valuable components of the operation, as they, like the negative from which numerous photographic prints are made, become the *sine qua non* of the fast food restaurant's kids' meal profits. As Benjamin states, "From a photographic negative, for example, one can make any number of prints; to ask for the 'authentic' print makes no sense" (Benjamin 6). The process of reproduction makes moot the concept of "authenticity," as one plastic McNugget is as "authentic" as the next; indeed, it is exactly the same. The object holds not nearly as much value as the engine that creates it on a massive scale.

This aligns with Walter Benjamin's collecting habits, which included the acquisition of pre-industrial Russian toys. Writes Benjamin: "To renew the old world—this is the collector's deepest desire when he is driven to acquire things" (Pfeifer 84). This comment ties the purpose of the collector to that of someone who reaches into the past with the intent of pulling forth artifacts so that a culture lost to history can exist again. There is, in this, a need to preserve, as without preservation the objects pulled forward through time would not survive. However, Benjamin's collecting impulse is not entirely preservation-based. "The collector disrupts an existing order by extracting objects from their original context and placing them in a new schema," writes Benjamin (84). Here, Benjamin expresses a need to strip away old context so that the collected objects can exist in a new world with the intention of disrupting norms. In this way, Benjamin favors the collection of non-mass produced goods specifically so they can contradict an industrial age.

This does not blend with the type of collecting fast food corporations ask of their customers, which is entirely focused on the present-tense amassing of their very mass-produced kids' meal offerings, but that is not to say Benjamin's style of collecting has no relevance to a study of such objects. Much current fan discourse around kids' meal toys announces concerns around the fact that the kids' meal toys of the present are not as appealing as those of the past. This sentiment came up often when I spoke with fans for this book, and it almost inevitably echoes every time I mention kids' meal toys casually. Fan nostalgia for the toys of, say, the early 1990s creates a longing for the promotions of the past to the extent that some individuals cannot see any appeal in modern premiums. That does not transform the older toys into the pre-industrial art objects of Benjamin's shelves, but it does make them into pieces of the past collectors pull forth with the intention of disrupting the norm created by present-day offerings. Kids' meal toy collectors share a motive with Benjamin, even if they do not share interests. Though, similarities may extend farther. Benjamin's collection held many toys considered in Annie Pfeifer's book to be "demotic," or "used by ordinary people" (96). However, the German term Benjamin used for these objects was "volkstümliche," which can mean "popular" or "folk," as in hand-made folk art. Either way, though, Benjamin's toy collection contained items like straw dolls formed during a harvest and then dried over time (112). These are hand-made, but by no means expensive. Also, this doll in particular evokes memories of food consumption, as kids' meal toys are, in at least as much as their manufacturers' stamps indicate, always linked to their own roots in sustenance. Both the doll and the kids' meal toy are popular within the context of their times, but only the former is a "folk" object.

Free with Every Kids' Meal

If fast food companies create mass produced toys, there is at least one other connected entity that makes the equivalent of folk art within kids' meal culture: fan communities. For Benjamin, politics overtakes ritual as the driving force behind goods once they are mechanically produced. In fan communities, their politics begin to take ownership of the reproduced art of kids' meal toys and convert them into the currencies of their fandom, and signifiers of their political presence as fans. First, in myriad social media groups devoted to the exchange of kids' meal toys, members not only advertise the sets and/or items they have for trade but also the pieces they want for their own collections, speculations on which toys are more abundant, which restaurants were supplying specific characters, and other news and rumors that surround the collecting hobby. In some groups, members are not allowed to exchange money for kids' meal toys, basing their practice solely on the trade of items. While one may speculate that these groups revolve around only the current lines of kids' meal toys, they actually feature a blend of offerings from both recent and vintage waves. This creates within the groups tiered levels of their membership: those that buy full sets of modern waves primarily to trade for other, more desirable pieces, those with kids who have received doubles of a specific toy and are looking to diversify, those who have a fandom for a restaurant or toy line that reaches far back into previous promotions who are trying to move old stock or trade it for other vintage items, and, finally, usually a banished bunch of group-proclaimed scammers who entered the group and committed offenses such as not upholding their end of a trade.* This alone creates a political culture that uses kids' meal toys as both capital and symbols of specific types (modern, vintage, obsessive, casual) of fandom.

---

*There might be a loose correlation, here, with the way Leicester University's Department of Museum Studies director Susan Pearce divided collecting into three types: systematic, fetishistic, and souvenir collecting (Pearce). Systematic collecting happens with the goal of having a collection prove an ideology. Fetishism in collecting means that one's identity becomes intertwined with the collection. Souvenir hunting "is prized for its power to carry the past into the future" (Windsor). While Pearce was speaking about museums and fine art collectors, it is possible to see those who collect kids' meal toys as representations of a particular fandom or idea, those who collect them as objects representative of themselves, and those who use them as souvenirs of past eras brought into the present at work, here.

These objects also extend farther than representing different ways of being a fan and into different ways of being a person. In these cases, the easily-obtained kids' meal toy becomes a sort of shorthand for one's political body, especially in cases where a particular fandom, translated into fast food promotions, and demographic intersect. One such fandom, *My Little Pony*, has had a strong presence in Queer culture largely due to the message of friendship and acceptance within the modern show and its surrounding media. It is also, as self-proclaimed Brony* and trans author Mitch Kellaway writes, "heavily, unapologetically marked as feminine, indeed with an overt femininity that has become newsworthy for not repulsing otherwise gender-normative men" (Kellaway). For Kellaway, the text itself is Queer, and, by its existence, interrupts socially normed performances of masculinity. This, too, has the power to embrace many people, but certainly men like Kellaway and Non-Binary folks assigned male at birth by portraying a complication of the gender binary in such warm, affectionate, and well-made terms. In addition to the substantial amount of product made to promote *My Little Pony: Friendship Is Magic*, as of 2019, there have been 14 separate waves of *My Little Pony* kids' meal toys in the United States, most of which from McDonald's, with the remainder issued by Burger King. In her essay "The Same Aisle: The Intersection of Resistance and Discipline in Brony Fandom, or Friendship is Mythological," Dr. Tracy Bealer goes back to Benjamin's notion that politics overtakes ritual when art becomes re- or mass-produced. Bealer asserts:

> The art that Bronies produce, as well as the fans' consumption and display of the toys that structure their fandom in safe and sanctioned spaces, *increases* the value of the art object through providing a language and economy that strengthens and perpetuates, and perhaps works to normalize, Brony community and culture and its inherent deconstruction of the gender binary [Bealer].

This suggests that, by taking, say, a Twilight Sparkle Happy Meal toy from McDonald's 2012 offering and displaying that object, a

---

*A Brony is a male or masculine fan of *My Little Pony*.

consumer under the loosely-defined Queer umbrella* not only hoists a flag for their own identity but also gives the object itself value by transferring it from being solely a mass-produced good to an emblem of strength and solidarity for a marginalized identity. Therefore, it serves the Queer collector for this art to be reproduced in Benjamin's terms, as this process opens the object up to hold the value, in the form of meaning, infused into it by its owner. Given that kids' meal toys are an incredibly accessible toy—they are sold at a low price, produced in massively large numbers, and can even be purchased fairly discreetly—they have the power to hold this sort of value many times over, for many different identity groups who may be, as a whole, held back from the kind of power, privilege, and wealth necessary to obtain a more expensive vehicle for their politicized selves. Of course, this should not imply these objects always become emblematic of marginalized identities fighting for equal rights. The toys themselves are neutral vessels, and can just as well hold value as representatives of ideologies that are morally repugnant. This same fandom, *My Little Pony: Friendship Is Magic*, has had to confront the neo–Nazi faction of its base, and it should be noted that these objects provide just as much "language and economy" for them as they do for the Queer fans mentioned previously. If anything, this empty vessel quality of the reproduced objects increases the types of collectors that can exist in their orbit, even while performing the same function as bearers of meaning for all of them.

In cases like these, collecting is not driven solely by the Freudian cycle of absence and replenishment, but a string of meanings that springs from Benjamin's take on reproduced art. Here, the kids' meal toy starts not with the collector, but with the sculptor who makes the original prototype toy. This singular piece exists, at least for a little while, as an art object that represents the decisions of its sculptor. When toy sculptors like Shawn Crosby worked on the 1994 McDonald's *Animaniacs* Happy Meal toys, he crafted the action feature on Dot's ice cream cart, an ice cream cone that bobbed up and down as

*Essentially, here, anyone outside of a cisheteronormative self-definition.

114

the toy was wheeled, from a place that reflected his artistic vision of a fun feature. However, once this piece moved along its line of production, going from Crosby's personal prototype to a mold capable of producing thousands more ice cream carts, it lost what Benjamin would call value based on "ritual" and political value, the value of the product to make money, started to take over. Then, when the toy finally made it into Happy Meals, and into the hands of consumers, they began to fill the toy with a different type of political value: the kind that represents them as collectors and/or human beings. This, of course, would apply more to those who received Dot's ice cream truck and displayed it because they somehow identified with Dot (or her love of ice cream), but, in those cases, the toy would take on a meaning that does not place the object back at Crosby's original artistic values, but within the realm of the consumer's identity, far-flung from anything the prototype could have conceivably held.

Whether Freudian cycle or Benjamin's ritual/political meaning exchange, the impact these motives have on kids' meal toy collecting happen more often in the present and future tenses. In other words, one buys the current kids' meal toy, only for that line to disappear, to then reappear in a form that they also collect, or one watches kids' meal toy lines as they emerge, and before they are released, in order to assess whether that particular run would become representative of a valued piece of their identity. While a portion of the collector community might fit some of these patterns, there is one group that can't be best represented by either of these options: those that view their collections as ways to interact with the past.

Would You Like Nostalgia with That?

While the use of kids' meal toys as fandom currency or identity emblems injects a unique kind of political value into the toy, nostalgia tends to reunite the reproduced art object with ritual. These rituals can occur at the initial point of purchase, a later revisiting of the toy, many years after the object had receded into the shadows of memory, or at all of the aforementioned points. Nostalgic ritual, regardless of the shape it takes, falls under the umbrella ritual of *nostos*, the Homeric word for "homecoming," as it points its participant(s) toward a past experience, identity, or personal truth that is pulled, bittersweetly, to the emotional present. Kids' meal toys are objects capable of triggering emotional, nostalgic ritual.

In her chapter "Death, Memory, and Collecting: Creating the Conditions for Ancestralisation in South London Households," Fiona Parrott uses the example of Anna buying McDonald's Happy Meals with her children as a way of mapping the rituals they assigned to the toys. Per Parrott's record, Anna says, "[My children] weren't allowed to open [the Happy Meal toys] till after they'd finished eating. So there was a little bit of a ritual" (Parrott 299). The ritual referred to here separates kids' meal toys from other toys one might buy at a toy store. Kids' meal toys remove many factors that prevent one from collecting larger toys with the same ritualistic consistency. For one, kids' meal toys are cheap, often advertised as "free" or included in the price of a kids' meal; larger, main-line toys cost much more. Kids' meal toys also come as a bonus alongside food, which satisfies a basic craving, hunger, whereas toy store-bought toys may address desires, but not fundamental needs. Fast food restaurants further remove personal choice from the equation if one opts to simply order the kids' meal without first inquiring which toys are offered. This allows for a fantasy that the kids' meal toy wasn't chosen, but bequeathed unto the child via some mysterious conduit. Certainly there is greater risk that the toy will be unappealing, but the low cost of the toy and the likelihood of getting another one in the near future make this disappointment fairly low-stakes. At a toy store, much more is on the line when price and choice are key players in the product a consumer ultimately picks, and there is no mystery around who picked the item. Additionally, when one has children, as Anna does, trips to a fast food restaurant are convenient, with many scattered across countless cities and towns; toy stores, toy aisles, and toy shopping websites require one to search specifically for that much less abundant, singular category.

And Anna adds one more factor that distinguishes her kids' meal toy collection through Parrott's analysis, "The weekly acquisition and series of characters and themes, often relating to films on release at the same time, gives the collection a temporal structure that makes it, as she says, 'rooted in time'" (Parrott). Kids' meal toys make possible nostalgic ritual by this "root[ing] in time." Anna mentions the rituals she would perform with her kids in later years, when the kids' meal toy collection would be spilled out all over their floor and played with again. For Anna, this process allows her and her children to share memories by sharing the toys, as they recall when each one was obtained, how easy or hard it was to find a specific toy, and where they were when they received it. She contrasts this with her sister, who keeps her belongings out of reach of her children, lamenting that, when this sibling passes away, these possessions will be meaningless to her kids, who never had the chance to fix them to certain points in time through shared, ritualized, nostalgic memory play. Nostalgia, therefore, can create collections where kids' meal toys are worn down, paint-chipped, and played with, but the memories surrounding that wear can be plentiful, and perhaps bittersweet, as they start to represent an era that was happy, but unalterably in the past.

That said, the thought of well-worn toys would activate every shred of anxiety in other nostalgic collectors. Anna, too, mentions that she has a second set of her kids' meal toy collection in her attic, preserved in mint condition in their original bags. Anna admits the second set is for her kids to inherit, though the kids swear they will never sell them off. Therefore, if monetary reward is not the motive for keeping a pristine second set of toys, one must ask what else might be preserved through it.

Time evokes decay. As time moves forward, Anna's memories, children, toys, and Anna herself decay. Bodies and memories can be maintained up to a point, and do not necessarily decay in a linear fashion. Recall and bodily function can go through phases of heightened and weakened performance that can fluctuate over time, but at a certain point, the ultimate decay, death, becomes inescapable. While Baudrillard might say the collecting impulse itself is a way of coping with this, the plastic toys themselves, being on a far slower decay clock than humans,* suggest that their preservation, alongside their completeness, offers a creative way to maintain not just the objects, but the nostalgic memories and histories that the collector aims to also keep in mint condition. This maintenance allows for yet another ritual, that of cleaning and storing the preserved items so as to combat the accumulation of dust and/or light damage. When performed, Anna's kids' meal toys exhibit the height of durability, a quality one cannot ascribe to memory in quite the same way. In seeing the fruits of this labor, a collection well-maintained, one may preserve what Anna calls the "moments of happiness" contained within her kids' meal toys, or, failing that, cope with the contrast human limits present when overlaid atop plastic resilience.

These ways of collecting kids' meal toys further mark these objects as "in-between" items. To the collector of kids' meal toys, their existence as paratexts for a range of intellectual properties is reduced in favor of their role as fast food promotionals. Fans of particular source media like *My Little Pony: Friendship Is Magic*, however, deprioritize kids' meal toys' roles as restaurant industry products in favor of their ability to efficiently symbolize their identities. Kids' meal toy collections will, in many cases, outlive the kids who receive them, but also can contain so many memories those children, or general consumers, create. They are *fort!* and *da!* at once, ever-present and longingly absent. They are complete, but always with more to come; cheap, but full of meaning. Despite the myriad ways kids' meal toys are collected, I'd argue it is this in-between-ness that keeps them collectible. The one-dollar (or less!) kids' meal toy bin may not be the most appealing stop at the flea market or antique shop, but when it becomes an inexpensive portal to one little item from that favorite movie, or a marker of a familiar restaurant, or the last empty spot in an otherwise-complete series, or a mint-in-bag version of the object wrecked by childhood, or a hopeful return to a lost time—what passer-by, much less what collector, could resist?

---

*For proof of this, just ask the eight million metric tons of plastic that entered the ocean in 2010 alone, and is expected to remain there for quite some time ("A Guide to Plastic in the Ocean").

CHAPTER 5

"For all the girls and boys"

Binary Gendered Kids' Meal Toy Promotions and the Queer Consumer

"ARDETH: Say, when do I ever get to race for this club?"
"JACK 'RABBIT' WHEELER: Ardeth, you know girls can't drive for the Hot Wheels!"
—Dialogue from *Hot Wheels* TV series (1967)

"Don't blame me. Blame Mattel. I don't care."
—Weird Barbie, from *Barbie* (2023)

One of my strongest memories as a child was when my mom took me to McDonald's in the early '90s. They were running a Barbie/Hot Wheels Happy Meal promotion, a common offering that would pop up several times throughout the decade, thanks to a collaboration with Mattel. As usual, I ordered the Happy Meal, but, when I sat down and opened it, I found a Barbie waiting for me inside. In what felt like an instant, my mother marched the Barbie toy right back to the cashier and traded it in for a Hot Wheels car, as if my assigned gender hinged on this moment. This was, in all likelihood, a case of an overworked, underpaid cashier either being understandably unable to calculate a binary gender from a child at an age where androgyny is common, or simply grabbing a Happy Meal box pre-stuffed with a toy and quickly filling it with food in an attempt to provide quick service. My mind also occasionally wanders into thoughts of a gender revolutionary McDonald's cashier defiantly announcing that toys have no gender through giving out Barbies and Hot Wheels cars at random, but then I think of the McDonald's I was in, at the time and place I was there, and I get a little more realistic.

Free with Every Kids' Meal

The 1990s' boom in child-centric marketing, escalating from the "80s" rise of the 30-minute television show-mercial, made kids like me into data points. Unbeknownst to us, we were important parts of corporate identities, with executives fighting over who could best represent our preferences and desires. Despite the ever-evolving whims of children, it is these spaces that can be hotbeds for the conventional thinking around who might want a Barbie doll versus a Hot Wheels car. Media scholar Derek Johnson noted, "Long-held beliefs about the 'naturalness' of gendered marketing, for example, gain their power in this ritual space [of corporate executives claiming they have unique access to the insights of kids] from the affinities that adult professionals are able to claim with their child consumers" (Johnson 94). This echoes the movie *Big*, except the literal child-adult played by Tom Hanks is, at best, a costume donned by an executive to persuade conference rooms of corporate decisionmakers that the more traditional, binary-gendered approach is the safest sales bet, and therefore the best. They do not want to riskily rewrite the rules, as Hanks' character does, but instead respond to sales data from years past. I do not argue that the data are wrong. They surely show more girls than boys ask for Barbies, and more boys than girls request Hot Wheels. Furthermore, if that were to shift, the short life of a kids' meal promotion alone would surely not be the platform that causes such a sea change. This is not to say the norm ought to be maintained, only that, in the '90s, my own gender questions bubbling beneath the surface had no chance of breaching in the kids' meal toy production and marketing process.* Because, at this time, a majority ruled out even the possibility my potential wants for gendered toy marketing might be different than what was accepted as "natural," I could only ever process my Happy Meal glitch on a delay.

A 25-year delay. For me, as someone who speaks and thinks through toys, it felt right to validate my gender through searching my plastic memories. It isn't that one's gender needs validation— one is who they say they are—but more so that many of us still seek

---

*Though, as I will address, they would later.

to validate ourselves because that affirmation brings empower-ment and pleasure. I've seen many people of many genders do this through clothing, jewelry, participation in sports, choice in perfume or cologne, and numerous other methods of announcing on the out-side what is so true on the inside. Binary-gendered toys were a fixture of my early childhood. The pink aisles were expressly forbidden. The muscle-y, spring-loaded ones made up the labyrinth I was supposed to successfully navigate. For years, I never questioned this because I never thought one *could* question it. I never longed for anything different because I never knew there was anything else to long for. Social norms worked on me. They wormed their way into my brain and took up residence right next to the parts that knew there was no other gas to breathe but air, and no other liquid to sustain my life but water, and, in sitting beside those immutable facts, they became them. When I let myself get the Barbie Happy Meal in 2019, I felt the waves of validation baptize me.

Today, my collection of mint-in-bag McDonald's Barbies num-bers in the higher double digits. When I perform my solo show, *TOYS 101*, which tracks my Queerness through toys, I open one with the audience and we play with it together. It's a cathartic moment that works best, like a lot of play does, when shared. I argue that my Queer toy scholarship works the same way. It is another form of playing with these kids' meal keepsakes that have transcended their intentions to dive so deeply into my personhood that they can-not help but emerge universal. Through this transformative play, pre-programmed character descriptions offered on cardbacks and minicomics are interrupted by my Queerness reformatting the plas-tic husks into the unrestrained avatars it needs them to be. The toys malfunction in the same way that fateful day at McDonald's mal-functioned, and, in those malfunctions, Queerness thrives.

Understanding how these malfunctions, or "glitches," cre-ate Queer spaces is key to my Queer reading of kids' meal toys. As writer and curator Legacy Russell writes in her book *Glitch Femi-nism: A Manifesto*, "With physical movement often restricted, female-identifying people, queer people, Black people invent ways to create space through rupture. Here, in that disruption, with our collective congregation at that trippy and trip-wired crossroad of gender, race, and sexuality, one finds the power of the glitch" (Russell 15). In other words, with legislative, social, physical, mental, moral, religious, and economic attacks on the bodies Russell mentions, the pathways set out for cisgender, heterosexual, white, male-identifying folks to navigate the world are often either closed or heavily barricaded to those in one or many of the margins. Therefore, if society's default programming does not allow for equitable space-making, the only hope in achieving such is through the glitch, or a refusal to permit the "system" to work as designed. Russell uses the example of when they used online avatars to "explore" and "expand" identities that were not assigned to her. Kids' meal toys can be discussed similarly because, though they are "away-from-the-keyboard," or, as Russell would say, "AFK," items, they, by representing pre-loaded identities the same way virtual avatars can, also offer users a way of inwardly and outwardly holding space for Queerness.

Between 1991 and 2019, the Barbie/Hot Wheels binary has appeared at U.S. McDonald's restaurants 24 times. If one counts not just Barbie/Hot Wheels joint promotions, but all Happy Meals where two toys were offered at once along an either implicit or explicit gender binary, that number jumps to 125 within that same time frame.* At first, the two toy lines in these promotions broke down into pretty much what Simone de Beauvoir might expect–"active" toys marketed toward boys spun off from legacy lines and "passive" dolls representing key pink aisle mainstays: Tonka trucks (boys) and Cabbage Patch Kids (girls), Transformers (boys) and Littlest Pet Shop (girls), Fingerboards (boys) and Hello Kitty toys (girls), Digi Sports games (boys) and Hello Kitty watches (girls). However, as we go deeper into the '00s, glitches start to occur in this binary. In 2005, a Happy Meal promotion for *Power Rangers* ran with one for *W.I.T.C.H.* Both source texts were about teams of young people who were given superpowers

---

*The normalization of "girl's toy"/"boy's toy" Happy Meals really starts in 1991, as there is only one toy offering that predates this, 1985's *Transformers/My Little Pony* Happy Meal, which is an outlier, and a regional (instead of national) Happy Meal, in the rapid succession of binary-gendered Happy Meal toys in the '90s and then even more so in the '00s.

to fend off antagonists. Though all of the *Power Rangers* characters offered were male (from a variety of generations of the long-running franchise), and all of the *W.I.T.C.H.* characters were female, the purpose of each team was essentially the same, to actively ward off the forces of evil. One of 2012's binary promotions was the *Pokémon: Black and White* and *Zoobles* sets, two toy lines that both featured cute, plastic creatures that would be almost indiscernible to someone unfamiliar with either property. The toys' physical differences mainly boil down to color schemes (*Zoobles* have a bright pastel palette, *Pokémon* are a little darker) and body shape (*Pokémon* tend to be a bit more angular and rigid than *Zoobles*), though, even so, the Pokémon toy Oshawott would fit right in at a Zoobles party. The two properties were, no doubt, segregated due to the demographics they were marketed toward and more popular with, but on a fundamental level, the appearance of these two lines disrupts the active (masculine)/passive (feminine) binary reinforced by other lines (the Digi Sports games and the Hello Kitty watches, for instance) by sharing similar basic traits.

Moving forward, this disruption becomes even more striking. In 2014, McDonald's offered an *Adventure Time*/Paul Frank Happy Meal. The *Adventure Time* toys, advertised against a blue backdrop, drew ire for removing the female characters from its offerings in exchange for having the monkey-based Paul Frank items step in as the "girl's" product (Woerner). Here, McDonald's took *Adventure Time*—a source text popular not just with boys, but girls and Non-Binary kids, too—and used previously-established cues like the blue background in a binary toy set, to establish it as the appropriate Happy Meal prize for male children. This sparked outcry in online fan communities. Gizmodo's Meredith Woerner called this a "huge mistake" that was "an affront to everything *Adventure Time* represents" (Woerner). To be sure, the show establishes, time and again, the embrace of gender play and fluidity as character gender presentations challenge norms and even switch from episode to episode. On the Paul Frank side, there is also nothing to indicate that the character of Julius the Monkey is intended for any specific gender. Through this Happy Meal, one sees that McDonald's time-tested paradigm of "boys' toy" = "blue," "girls' toy" = "pink" could not integrate proper-ties whose content opposed or operated beyond it. Therein lies the glitch. One is led to expect, by the long line of McDonald's Happy Meal toys gendered along binary lines, that the *Adventure Time*/Paul Frank Happy Meal will be a logical next step in the boys'/girls' toy pattern, but instead the toys disrupt the pattern partly because of their source contexts, and partly because of their contrast with the pink/blue template into which they are forced. Through fan criti-cism, the toys' queerness finds a home in this glitch, this in-between space carved into the once seamless transition between binary gen-dering and toy products.

It is perhaps no coincidence that, around this time, McDonald's was also changing its official language around the toys. Corporate guidance trained employees to distance themselves from the "girls' toy"/ "boys' toy" language and move toward asking guests which of the two offered toy properties they would prefer. Despite this move, however, customers still reported that the binary gendered language was still present in their experiences at restaurants. In 2008, Anto-nia Rose Ayres-Brown, the 11-year-old daughter of law professor Ian Ayres, wrote a letter to McDonald's corporate protesting the fact that she was constantly asked, in McDonald's Drive-Thrus, whether the Happy Meal was for a girl or boy. She voiced concern that this could reinforce harmful stereotypes about these two genders. The next year, she received a response stating that McDonald's trained employees to ask which of the two brands of toys a child might want, as opposed to inquiring about gender. The father-and-daughter duo then performed an unscientific study in which they visited 10 New Haven, Connecticut-area McDonald's restaurants a total of 13 times and ordered Happy Meals. Those restaurants asked for toy pref-erence in non-gendered terms only 15.9 percent of the time. In all other cases, they were asked if the toy was "for a boy or a girl" or if a "boys' toy or girls' toy" was desired. Later, the team conducted a sec-ond study of 15 McDonald's locations in which 42.8 percent of stores visited would not allow a child to have the toy that did not match their perceived gender presentation. While the sample size in both cases is small, Ayres confirmed through online interviews with other consumers that his and his daughter's experiences were not outliers; in fact, they were typical. It certainly aligns with my personal experience, in which McDonald's employees asked me whether I wanted a "girls' toy" or "boys' toy" during Happy Meal toy purchases I made as recently as 2021.* This supports what Legacy Russell writes in *Glitch Feminism* about the gender binary, "To exist within a binary system one must assume ourselves to be unchangeable, that how we are read in the world must be chosen for us, rather than for us to define—and choose—for ourselves" (Russell 14–15). The binary resists change. When it is consistently reinforced via a Happy Meal format repeated 125 times, the paradigm shift requires more than a corporate policy memo. It needs to come with a larger acceptance that the ritual of receiving a Happy Meal toy was never a ritual in the truest sense, a preordained practice centered in the spiritual or supernatural. Instead, the Happy Meal toy allows for some element of customer choice, at least within the range of available products—a fact that decades of commercials downplayed in favor of the "magic" of surprise.† Therefore, even with McDonald's attempt at changing language around the dual-toy Happy Meals, the binary persists, and the moments of queer flourishing must still rely on the glitches.

The good news is there are glitches abound in Happy Meals, even beyond the gendered, dual-toy promotions. Film scholar Becca Harrison studies glitches throughout the Star Wars film franchise. Her work utilizes Glitch Theory, as outlined by Legacy Russell and others, to posit that, because it took decades before Queer content was included in canon and even endorsed non-canon Star Wars storytelling, the glitches in the film, as seen through, for instance, moments of unintended interruption in Princess Leia's holographic plea for help, create bubbles in the text that resist the

---

*To the credit of one of my friendly neighborhood McDonald's restaurants, one cashier asked me whether I wanted a toy "for a girl or boy," and was promptly corrected by their manager to use brand-specific terminology instead.

†Because of this, I want to make explicit that individual cashiers should shoulder absolutely zero of the blame and burden, here. They are underpaid, overworked, and should in no way be expected to burst queer joy out of glitch space and protect it as it thrives in the fertile open ranges of pop culture. I charge the far more privileged with that task.

patriarchal desire for flawlessness and grow implicit Queerness that rebels against even the films' creators. As Harrison writes in her paper "Star Cistems Will Slip through Your Fingers: Glitches, Malfunctions, and Errors as Queer Resistance in Star Wars," "I propose that glitches provide a mode of queer resistance…. Situating the material history of glitches in Star Wars within queer theory and histories of trans-oriented media, I read errors and malfunctions as defying patriarchal logic and as reminders that queerness cannot be erased" (Harrison). The "patriarchal logic" Harrison alludes to includes the attempts to smooth out filmmaking glitches such as matte lines in later releases of movies in the Star Wars saga, which she associates with the patriarchy as such perfectionism is built around appeasing the scrutiny of the most privileged tier of viewers. Because not all glitches can be erased from the Star Wars franchise, as some, like Leia's hologram, are woven into the narrative feel and mood of scenes, the Queerness that Glitch Theory affords them becomes just as permanent. Happy Meals further this conversation in two ways.

First, McDonald's Happy Meal promotions have included the Star Wars saga eight times, as of April 2025. In 2008, the August–September Happy Meal offered toys from *Star Wars: The Clone Wars*. These toys were bobble-headed figurines molded into ships that would correspond to the character represented. While the toys were promoted within McDonald's restaurants encased inside a display framed with CGI character art from the hit TV show. However, of the actual toys offered, only some were from *The Clone Wars*, specifically. Others, like Darth Vader in his modified TIE Fighter and the famously off-limits Han Solo in the Millennium Falcon came from the live-action films, a possibility never announced by the advertising material around the toys, which simply referred to *The Clone Wars*. While entirely understandable that McDonald's would want to feature some of the franchise's most popular characters, this introduces a glitch into the expectations established by this Happy Meal promotion. Given that all of these toys were presented under the banner of *Star Wars: The Clone Wars*, one may view the presence of anachronous characters, like Han Solo, as a mistake, an error, or a glitch, akin to the confusion some had after seeing the non-glitch presence of aliens resembling the one from *E.T.* in *Star Wars: Episode I The Phantom Menace.* This presence gives one pause.

These toys are also glitches in that they come with no accessories, a glitch-creating norm established by the mainline action figures. The absence of accessories is necessitated by their role as kids' meal toys, as such add-ons would make the toys more expensive to produce. However, regardless of the reason, this separates Star Wars Happy Meal toys from the expectation that a "real" toy from the franchise by Hasbro would contain a lightsaber, blaster, or other accoutrement. This tradition itself created a glitch in the toys' relationship to the source films and TV shows. In many cases, Kenner and later Kenner/Hasbro packaged Star Wars action figures with weaponry even when their characters never carried any. Jonathan Gray discusses this through Dan Fleming's work when he writes, "Fleming sees the toys as variously able to strengthen or weaken established meanings in the [Star Wars] films." Fleming goes on to state that the toys do this through their accessories, which provide play "versatility" that cannot be supported by either the figures' limited articulation or, in some cases, their on-screen versions' lack of active participation in the narrative (Gray 178–179). To be sure, Star Wars action figures like Hammerhead and IG-88, to focus on two upon which Fleming reflects, were packaged with laser guns even though they are not seen using these weapons in the original Star Wars trilogy films. This allows kids and other collectors to create new text out of these paratexts, which add more to the characters through these accessories so that those who own them have more play options. The kids' meal toy must often also offer children a reason for engagement, but, because of their need for a lower price tag, they frequently are required to do this without the help of accessories. Because this means these toys exist as a glitch within the realm of Star Wars action figures, fast food companies in turn craft their premiums with other glitches: bigger heads, sounds that may or may not perfectly replicate those onscreen, new "close enough" products, and a selection that sometimes does not align with that of the source material. That places these products into the fringes of many toyboxes that are filled with mountains of mainline action figures and their accessories, giving pause to those who attempt to fit them into storytelling in which all other toys are stylistically uniform. One reaches for an explanation, whimsical acceptance, or outright rejection.

This process is similar to the one often felt by Queer people when they are present in many cisheteronormative spaces, in which they are burdened with the emotional labor of either justifying their identities, or stealthily existing within a crowd forcing this character from another movie into its own, a feeling that costs the crowd nothing, but can create dysphoria for the individual who must now hold their actual self alongside the person they are assumed to be. While this dysphoria can be metaphorically likened to the presence of Han Solo in the 2008 *Star Wars: The Clone Wars* Happy Meal, that is not where Glitch Theory asks us to land. Glitch Theory, per Harrison and Russell, demands we consider the effect of a Han Solo toy in this prequel promotion. My reaction to the Han Solo toy, which I believe to be a fairly common one, was joy. I was happy to have such an iconic character, and immediately used my imagination to integrate this piece into the stories I could make using the other *Clone Wars* toys. Maybe the smuggler gets to play quick-draw with General Grievous (also in the promotion). Perhaps Han decides to take Anakin under his wing and avoid the whole "turn to the Dark Side" all together. Or possibly he's made into a Jedi by Ahsoka. All of these and an infinitude more are possibilities created by the glitch. This type of imaginative adaptation is praiseworthy, and often instinctive, in children.* This, then, pulls us back to the hypothetical group situation described above, in which a Queer person is othered in a cisheteronormative space. Glitch Theory wants Queer joy to thrive, and that can translate into real-world scenarios via the same integration one uses to incorporate the Darth Vader toy. Yes, the toy, like the Queer body, is not one that "rules" would, strictly interpreted, allow for, but the glitch has allowed for its presence, and our imaginations allow for inclusion. In this way, the glitch becomes beneficial, beautiful,

---

*See Vivian Gussin Paley's *The Boy Who Would Be a Helicopter* for one in-depth case study in support of this.

and adds to the narrative possibility of the text as-experienced, versus as-intended.

The second way Happy Meals, and, more broadly, kids' meals, intersect with Glitch Theory revolves around malfunctions of individual toys. For the 2008 McDonald's *Star Wars: The Clone Wars* Happy Meal, YouTube reviewer FastFoodToyReviews made a video evaluating each of the toys offered in the promotion. In the video, he demonstrates the electronic features of some of the toys, all of which serve to illuminate lightsabers held by certain characters for whom such an accessory would be canonically acceptable. When FastFood-ToyReviews gets to the Asajj Ventress toy, however, he discovers her lightsaber does not illuminate, even after the appropriate button is pressed. He makes a couple of attempts, and assumes the battery has "petered out" (2008 MCDONALD'S STAR WARS...). In this case, FastFoodToyReviews has stumbled across an error, or glitch. The toy, for whatever reason, does not function as advertised. The difficulty of deconstructing the toy to examine the battery inside means this glitch will likely be permanent, as there is no easily accessible compartment where one might remove and replace a dead power source. On top of this, the solid construction of the piece makes it hard to establish the root cause of the glitch at all. It may be the battery, but it may also be the lightsaber's bulb, or something else entirely. In the quest to create a toy that is both cheap and not a choking hazard, McDonald's has also ensured its inner workings will stay hidden to consumers. The permanence of this glitch reminds me of the permanent glitches Becca Harrison identifies in the Star Wars films. There, the persistence of on-screen glitches affix Legacy Russell's Glitch Feminism to the text from the get-go, and throughout its many revisions. By analyzing the presence of these glitches in Star Wars Happy Meal toys, one establishes that Glitch Theory and its Queerness are not only qualities of the films but the merchandise, too. Like Harrison notes with the films, these glitches also appear from the start of the Star Wars franchise, on through this 2008 example, and will likely continue throughout the saga's lifespan. After all, Star Wars toys began with a glitch. Given that Kenner could not produce action figures for 1977's *Star Wars* by Christmas of that year, they opted to sell a coupon which would promise buyers an "Early Bird" box of figures as soon as they were available, a few months post-holidays. This sales tactic was an extreme departure from the way toys were sold, and was necessitated by the physical impossibility of getting new toys on shelves by one of the biggest buying days of the year. It was an industry malfunction, an error in timing, a glitch in the toy world, and it launched a toy line that still produces a robust catalog of new figures each year, some 45 years later. Even after the release of the Early Bird action figures, vinyl capes on Jawas were swapped for cloth ones, Snaggletooth was blue and out-of-scale with his on-screen counterpart, lightsabers had two telescoping pieces before being reduced to one solid piece, the prototype of Boba Fett's original action figure fired a rocket, before that was deemed unsafe and glued in place—the list goes on and on. In light of these much more significant, wide-sweeping glitches, one malfunctioning Asajj Ventress in a single Happy Meal seems small. However, every glitch, no matter the scope, furthers the idea that ways in which we analyze on-screen media can also be utilized to read the paratextual merchandise made to promote them. Since Glitch Theory places upon glitches the importance of Queer rebellion, the existence of those glitches far and wide, horizontally, across text and paratext, allows one to overwhelm anti–Queer media with readings that make space for such Queerness to thrive from inception to the now, in every body—celluloid, paper, or plastic—built for the modern franchise empire.

While this expansion of Glitch Theory into new pockets of media opens up non-traditional texts and paratexts (like kids' meal toys) to literary and Queer analysis, the unique errors sometimes tragically present in toys complicate such readings. In film, there is a limit to the harm that can be inflicted by glitches on-screen. Matte lines may frustrate a certain type of cinephile, but they are unlikely to kill them. Strobe effects and rapidly flashing lights can induce seizures, but these are often not errors, as evidenced by the warnings that now precede many episodes that contain such moments. In kids' meal toys, which are meant to be offered without the need for prior evaluation to kids of many different ages, glitches can be deadly. In

Chapter 5. *"For all the girls and boys"*

1999, Burger King offered a *Pokémon* promotion that featured 52 different toys encased in a Pokéball that separated into two halves. The error, as Burger King would quickly learn, was that one half of the sphere could fit airtight around the nose and mouth of a 1- or 2-year-old child. I will go into this case in greater detail in Chapter 7, but, for now, it is important to know that this malfunction proved fatal, as a child suffocated to death in this manner. While cases in which kids' meal toys cause death are rare, the fact of them forces me to consider the viability of literary analysis against something with such heavy real-world consequences. Some may attempt to fold this into Glitch Theory, arguing that, in many instances, glitches are deadly, and that they use countless means to erase bodies all the time. What I see, however, is a limitation, and one that Legacy Russell's Glitch Feminism recognizes. Glitches are helpful in talking about the Queerness of avatars—definitely online ones, and, in my view, also those molded in plastic. In Glitch Feminism, the human form is only relevant in relation to its avatar. The glitch is, as Russell writes, "anti-body" (Russel 69). It maintains that the personas we claim in online spaces represent re-imagined bodies that make room for Queer identities cisheteronormativity edges out. Given this, I am not willing to co-opt deaths like these to further my interest in the textuality of toys. Instead, I would rather posit that these heartbreaking moments create a line that separates the study of toys from other, more traditional media studies. They are a reminder that toys produce an intimate experience that is fundamentally different from the ones produced by books, movies, and songs. In those cases, the viewer's relationship to such art happens in between the object and the audience. One ponders a message, absorbs an image, projects back thoughts and feelings in response. Toys can produce a similar interaction, but they add chemicals, small parts, fragments, shards, accessories, mechanical features, electricity in close proximity, and other dangers that threaten physical existence in ways a novel does not. Because of this, the study of toys creates glitches within literary theory, even Glitch Theory, where the two, theory and text, cannot merge seamlessly. The result is an object, the kids' meal toy, that must exist in an in-between space, neither fully literary text nor meaningless object. Thus, the kids' meal toy is suspended between recipients who are, at least some of the time, interested in reading the plaything as a text or paratext, locating it within a broader cultural tapestry, and creators, for whom practical issues of cost, design, and safety far outweigh questions of the end product's sociocultural meaning.

While the toys themselves contain glitches that lend themselves to Queer reading, other times, the glitch occurs due to unforeseeable and ultimately mysterious collisions of Queerness and toxic masculinity within the home. My friend, the poet Rajiv Mohabir, recounted for me his childhood experience with the 1988 McDonald's *Bambi* Happy Meal toys. Rajiv loved the movie, and was thrilled to receive a toy from it with his meal. Upon taking the toy home, however, he learned, rather spontaneously, from his father that these toys were forbidden. As a result, Rajiv's father discarded his *Bambi* Happy Meal toy, leaving Rajiv to solve the mystery of why. Because Rajiv is gay, and says this was evident even in childhood, he figures that his father's homophobia was the motive. *Bambi*, in the eyes of Rajiv's father, was not a text that embraced a certain brand of cisgender, heterosexual masculinity that emphasized an active, dominant male presence in society, and, therefore, could only instill in his son traits that he perceived to be feminine, passive, Queer, and/or gay. The toys, as not just representations but vessels of these traits, were seen as too great a risk. However, Rajiv recalls having other Happy Meal toys, like Ursula from the 1989 *The Little Mermaid* promotion, that did not draw such ire from his father, despite allowing for a similar Queer reading. Therefore, Rajiv can only speculate as to why his father's homophobia applied so strongly to one Happy Meal toy and not another. It could be that the toy's presence in the home was seen by Rajiv's father as a glitch, an error, and, once that one error was eliminated, the possibility of a second became inconceivable to a man who had, presumably, bought into some version of patriarchal perfection, where smoothness and uniformity were assumed to be given circumstances. Still, this form of implicit homophobia remains shrouded in as much mystery as the fathers of many such households.

A certain type of father does not, and perhaps cannot, ever let his son see his entire self. In his meditation on the intersection of paper and plastic bodies, i.e., paper dolls and action figures as well as his own drawings, and masculinity titled "The Fantastic Paper Man: Heroic Proportion, the Ideal Body and Me," Richard Harrison sums up the appeal of Robert Bly's argument in his book *Iron John: A Book About Men* by stating that the reason lies in the claim that fathers become mysteries to their children because of their work. They are gone during the day, and, when they come home in the evening, there is no real knowledge of what this type of father had done with his day. Because this mystery is repeatedly established through a set schedule, other mysteries such as reactions, disciplinary measures, and rules are given a free pass to exist without critical pushback. Harrison adds to Bly's argument with his own experience, though, when he writes, "But, for me, even when Dad was at work, he was a *presence* in our house.... But what could *never* come back in life, what had to exist in my imagination alone, was the man that he had been" (Harrison 119). Work did not remove Harrison's father from the house, at least not figuratively. Instead, the obfuscation was a result of his dad's history as an athlete and serviceman in World War II, a life wrapped up prior to Harrison's birth and since shrouded in casual secrecy. So when Harrison started drawing superheroic male forms, and his father almost instantly disapproved, this young boy's imagination had to take over in order to explain the response. Like Mohabir, Harrison also came to the conclusion that the reason must lie in his dad's past, but the details can ever only be as certain as the history itself.

That does not invalidate the conclusions. Mohabir is surely right that his dad's response to the *Bambi* toys stemmed from homophobia. However, because of the general mystery of the father, as shown through Harrison, the exact engine that drives that homophobia, rooted in upbringings and experiences sons in queerphobic households may never hear from the stoic, silent mouths of their dads, will remain a factual secret, placing the burden of emotional labor upon the imagination of the Queer child. In these cases, the same imagination that could give rise to myriad play scenarios with the *Bambi* figurines these children received with lunch becomes darkened by the shadows of their fathers' pasts, lit only by the dim bulbs their kids have struggled to place along a thin timeline to shed comforting light on presumed logic for their dads' spontaneous, personal, and sometimes contradictory anger.

Kids' meal toys are perhaps best suited to disrupt, or glitch, these sorts of environments because of their often unplanned and unchosen arrival. When I received a Barbie instead of the Hot Wheels car my assigned gender presumably wrote me a prescription for, lunch became a battlefield. Marsha Kinder's notion that it is commercials which gender toys, not experience, suddenly became real-world (Kinder 50). Marketer intent conflicted with consumer experience. This advertising created a need for a conversation around what my assigned gender allowed me to do, and what was off-limits. It included shock and outrage. I was baffled. The flow of a meal, even a meal operating under the general status quo of a McDonald's restaurant, was disrupted, and the answer to that disruption was a violent lurch back toward binary gender stereotypes. Furthermore, the practice of binary-gendered kids' meals cannot help but glitch. In 2009 and 2014 , McDonald's offered American Girl Happy Meals. Since the American Girl doll is marketed to the demographic it is named after, McDonald's paired each promotion with a toy they felt could appeal to boys. The 2009 Happy Meal, then, offered LEGO as its other choice, a famously gender-blind toy.* In the latter promotion, American Girl items were released alongside PokémonXY toys. Even if one accepts both of those second options as "boys' toys," there is still a glitch at play. American Girl dolls have gone to great lengths to tell diverse stories of girlhood.† Their dolls are learning tools by which anyone can see a swath of the spectrum available to those who are girls and women. Neither LEGO race cars nor PokémonXY can complement this. In fact, I am hard-pressed to think of a mainstream toy marketed to boys that does for that gender what American Girl does for its. My experience of boyhood was one in which a spectrum

---

*It should be said that this promotion centered around LEGO race cars, which one could fairly perceive as a boy-marketed item.

†See *Dolls of Our Lives: Why We Can't Quit* by Mary Mahoney and Allison Horrocks for more on the ways the American Girl doll materializes diverse femininities.

of masculinity did not exist. There was one "right" way to go about it, although no one seemed to agree on all of its qualities. While practicality dictates that McDonald's' choices in either Happy Meal were merely an attempt to include another popular property, and that is true, it is hard for me not to see in these selections a failing not of the fast food giant or toy companies, but in social presentations of boyhood. Given this failing, the glitches of masculinity feel all the more enticing to me.

In Glitch Theory, we can embrace the glitch and accept its potential for discovery. In his introduction to *Glitch Art in Theory and Practice*, Michael Betancourt quotes a 2011 *IDN* magazine article that described music artists' responses to glitches by saying, "'Instead of holding their hands up in horror and crying: 'Oh, oh, we have a glitch!' the artists featured in this article say 'Whoopee! We have a glitch!—and proceed to make the most of it'" (Betancourt 2). From this, one can extrapolate the creative power of glitches to take a piece of art in a sudden, spontaneous, unique direction, as if coming sui generis from the art itself. Kids' meal toys provide a similar lesson. Perhaps the best teacher is the 1999 Ronald Scholars premiums. The entire promotion was a glitch, only featuring two toys taken from the 4-toy set released previously as "Food Foolers, instead of seven or eight new items, per Happy Meal norm. One was a cell phone that looked like a container of french fries, and the other was a miniature computer shaped like a Happy Meal box. Given Glitch Theory's use of computer avatars and imaging, the Happy Meal Box Computer is most relevant, here. On the outside, this plastic toy looks like a red Happy Meal box, arches for handles, and a yellow smile horizontally yawning across one side. At the push of a button, the box springs open, and a faux keyboard pops up, the top of the Happy Meal box now acting as a "monitor" for this computer. Into the monitor, one loads one of three double-sided rectangular pieces of cardboard, each of which looks like a 3.5-inch floppy disk. Each "disk" contains a McDonald's character—Ronald, Grimace, Hamburglar, and/or Birdie—pointing to or looking at a field of red static. The static looks like a glitch one might see on a television with a bad cable connection or wonky antenna. It is crimson snow, fuzz. Beneath it, an image is barely visible, covered, as a TV picture is, by the glitch overlaid on top of it. However, when the disk is placed into the red "monitor" of the Happy Meal Box Computer, the red static fades away, and the image becomes clear. This toy, like the artists in the aforementioned *IDN* article, not only contains what is commonly experienced as a glitch—TV static—but also intentionally uses the glitch as a tool for fun. In the context of this Happy Meal toy, the glitch is acknowledged, and given purpose. Its user is not meant to lament this glitch, but embrace it and play with it. The toy takes the computer, the site of so much of Legacy Russell's work with avatars, Glitch Feminism, and true identities, and, with the push of a button, renders its glitches friendly vessels of whimsy. The toy computer, with its immovable QWERTY-ish keyboard and lack of any electronic components, cannot be used in the practical sense, but can be read through Glitch Theory as a guide for embracing and playing with the glitch. The Ronald Scholar's promotion was surrounded with academic language, even going so far as to offer the possibility of a $25,000 scholarship with the toy. There is no reason why academic language cannot continue to define the premiums.

The Happy Meal Box Computer toy came out no more than three years after my Barbie toy glitch, but my experiences of them could not be farther apart. Now, after coming out as Non-Binary, I look to that Happy Meal Box Computer for a reminder on how to center the glitch, how to hug it, how to weave my glitches into my past, present, and future, and how to finally play with disruption. Arthur Applebee, as stated in *The Child's Concept of Story: Ages Two to Seventeen*, writes, "As children mature, they do not pass out of one mode of response into another, but integrate their older structures into a new and more systematic representation of experience" (Kinder 7). This is meant to say that, as kids grow, they do not give up "childish" ways all together. Instead, they build a methodology for existence and decide where and how those younger ways of being apply. This is not stated as commentary on queerness of any sort,* but it applies, nonetheless. If a facet of growth is integration,

---

*Or kids' meal toys, for that matter.

as opposed to the leaving of one way of being for another, maturity is a "non-binary" experience. It springs not from a series of choices that, once made, wipe clean the mind of its previous experiences, but from reprocessing old ways of moving through the world so that they may be defined anew within the self one *is*, as opposed to the way one *was*. It is in this that I hear from my childhood kids' meal toys, who meant nothing as queer objects to me when I first received them so many years ago, but have now integrated into the system I currently use to navigate my experience of self. Henry Jenkins quotes D.W. Winnicott to describe toys as "transitional objects," at once "me" and "not me" (Jenkins 145). If this is true of toys in general, it is especially true of kids' meal toys, which are not necessarily acquired by the demand of its consumer. Instead, the kids' meal toy will sometimes land, randomly, in the lap of a kid who never considered they might have the object now in front of them. Then, it is up to the toy's new owner to discover meaning, or not, after the receipt of the plaything, not before, when desire builds a narrative and purpose for what will eventually be acquired. The kids' meal toy itself, therefore, is "non-binary," not necessarily in the gendered sense, but in the way it occupies this space between meaning and meaninglessness. In the 1990s, my McDonald's Barbie meant a transgression, danger, for the masculine body that held it.* Today, it tells me a little about the queerness within, becoming a source of validation. If I have projected Glitch Theory onto my Happy Meal Box Computer toy, that makes physical what Arthur Applebee discusses as an emotional transition into adulthood that brings with it past events. I, too, bring with me the material objects of my past, and I integrate them now into the structure I have built for my experience. It is my hope that other collectors have done the same, as it is a joy to feel that the toys you seek, seek you, too.

---

*Had my body been feminine, this meaning might have been radically transformed into something acceptable or mundane.

CHAPTER 6

Appetite for Destruction

Finding Meaning in the Ways Kids' Meals Direct Their Own Disposability

Successful engagement with a kids' meal relies on one's destruction of it. Destruction uniquely shapes the entire experience. Disposable comics and games coat the sides of many meal boxes which sometimes even have built into them cardboard punch-out "racetracks" or "tunnels" that urge kids to remove them for added fun. The food within, naturally, is destined for the destructive break-down of digestion. And the toy, with its low price and simplistic construction, endures only by happenstance attachment to nostalgia, and, even then, attains its permanence against a backdrop of many similar playthings lost, tossed, or relegated to the dollar bins of history.

This is all part of the plan. Consumers are meant to move through kids' meals quickly, so as to get to the next one. However, Capitalistic intentions aside, I argue that destruction plugs these meals and their toys into a larger conversation about the ways in which growth and play are themselves built on wreckage. Though the ways in which one "destroys" a kids' meal, through devourings both physical and playful, are specific to the experience, the fact of their destruction allows them to align seamlessly with the desires and patterns present in the lives of their young demographics.

This chapter explores ways in which kids' meals prompt their own destruction. Included is a look at the type of art used on select boxes and the ways that visually evoke "disposable" media, and how destructibility is sometimes a kids' meal toy asset. I will then read this through the lens of literary play to offer that the way in which

138

kids' meals use destruction plugs them into a history that reaches much farther back than their own. Finally, I will discuss the importance of kids' meal nostalgia and what it means for some toys and boxes to survive their planned demise.

Kids' Meal Boxes and Zines

The University of Texas Libraries' LibGuide defines a zine as "most commonly a small circulation publication of original or appropriated texts or images ... [or] any self-published unique work of minority interest, usually reproduced by photocopier" ("What is a Zine?"). This evokes the black-and-white hand-made Trekkie fan magazines circulated at Star Trek conventions I attended, often appearing to be the product of one person's liberation of an office Xerox machine. These texts contained art, comics, articles, fanfic, slash fic, and myriad other musings that might exist on the fringes of the fandom using "appropriated," unauthorized material that puts consumers in the gray area between fair use and copyright infringement. They resembled the collections produced by friends in political activism and rebellious art school circles. I imagine the joy in collecting and reading zines stems at least in part from a feeling of participating in a grassroots effort, producing and consuming work that we identified with because it was at once connected to a larger fandom or sphere of which we were a part *and* plugged into the smaller niche aspects of our personalities, sometimes intersecting with queerness, race, gender, sexuality, or other building blocks of our selves. While I never mistake kids' meal boxes for home-spun, artisanal efforts, I do often find myself reflecting on a zine-like aesthetic when reading my examples of these containers from the 1970s, '80s, and '90s. This begs me to define the stylistic crossover and ponder its reasons for being. Much more than simply accepting vintage kids' meal toy boxes as de-clawed, G-rated zine imitations, I want to unlock what, exactly, zines provide the medium and how zine scholarship might aid our readings of these food vessels.

In their slapdash, aggressively "unofficial" styles, zines capture a disposability similar to that of graffiti or protest. They proceed with the knowledge that they are, due to both a lack of funds to sustain their creation and litigious media corporations potentially eager to stop their spread should they get too popular, essentially on borrowed time. Zines, like what Luca Visconti (et al.) calls "public art," inch closely to the definition of dirt often attributed to Mary Douglas: "matter out of place" (Visconti 3). They are not the glossy magazines of a bookstore. They are not the "authorized" media of a giant publishing house. The zine, like dirt and graffiti, is unclassified but for the community that, in categorizing them, validates and contextualizes their existence. This ties the zine's heartbeat to small communities who make the life of the medium both meaningful and fragile. The dry-up of readership becomes yet another threat to the life of the zine, but the presence of it serves as an exciting testament to collective action, anti-corporate protest, and the public's ability to construct the narratives it consumes. In this context, the ways in which zines live on the verge of their own destruction provides them with a sort of underdog narrative that supporters want to root for. This, and the popularity of the zine in the 1960s and '70s for which many of the corporate artists of the 1970s and '80s would have been present, places within the zine an "in-between" quality executives and creatives alike would have wanted to appropriate (or perhaps more generously, "return," given the zine's initial parody for the purposes of commentary) for "official" media such as kids' meal boxes. Another reading of this, however, could argue that the qualities of the zine—unclassifiable, unofficial, reproducible, cheap—direct their destruction by, like graffiti, making themselves dirt-like temporary objects that are both not intended for long-term use and incapable of it. Such directed use is helpful for kids' meals, too, as it helps the fast food corporation for consumers to dispose of these offerings quickly so as to focus on the next promotion which is never far behind. In other words, it is not McDonald's intent for consumers to buy one Happy Meal and then, understanding its contents to be permanent, stop in satisfaction, but to continue to replace, collect, build, and destroy so that more can take the place of what was. The visual language of zines help allow consumers to feel they have a presence in this process, just as they would have a role in zine creation, but in fact do not, as the decisions made in most kids' meal creation happen at a corporate executive level, well beyond the realm of the average customer.

Perhaps no Happy Meal box did this better than their first licensed one. As discussed in Chapter 1, McDonald's released the Star Trek Meal in 1979 in an attempt to compete with the Star Wars–based promotions of Burger King and Burger Chef in the years prior. In addition to being a successful TV and soon-to-be movie franchise, *Star Trek* had a robust zine-making community, with its first, *Spockanalia*, dating back to 1967. One zine popular in the 1970s and '80s, *Menagerie*, combined irreverent humor, fan art, slash, and analysis to form "irregularly published" woman-led effort. For example, the August 1977 issue, its 12th, contained work that meshed impressionistic character comix and games.

Here, we see a representation of *Star Trek* aliens like Klingons, Orions, Andorians, Vulcans, and Romulans mediated by a lone Terran, along with a humorous caption and a game that plays with Klingon translation (*Menagerie* 23). While the art styles presented in Star Trek fanzines vary wildly, there is often a strong showing of "underground" comix played for laughs, as shown by the above. The unlicensed parody says the quiet part of *Star Trek* out loud: if an average Earthling found themself in the middle of the intergalactic drama, they would not know how to make heads or tails of it. It was the job of "official" *Star Trek* producers to build a serious sci-fi world of tomorrow; it was zines' job to destroy it with humor. As such, *Menagerie* 12 began with the disclaimer "MENAGERIE is an irregularly published fanzine, which is probably best demonstrated that number 13 was printed two weeks ago" (*Menagerie* 1). Even the zine itself was upfront about its haphazard production that generated copies on 8.5-by-11-inch copy paper, hand stapled, on an uneven schedule. Additionally, if a subscriber completed the games inside their zines, like the fill-in-the-blank prompts above, they would be contributing to the destruction, or at least defacing, of their once pristine issue by the prompting of the text itself. Though some readers, like the one I purchased my *Star Trek* zine collection from, did preserve their issues for posterity, one could not be blamed for disposing of them

More and more Terrans are touring the galaxy these days, destroying the balance of trade and creating interplanetary incidents as they go. Hopeful of restoring the former and, through intimidation, minimizing the latter, the Federation Chamber of Commerce, in co-operation with TransWorlds Airlesslines, has issued for the edification, not to mention bailing out, of befuddled Earthlings everywhere...

The Tommy Tourist Handy- Dandy Galactic Phrase Book

by' Påúlā Şmïth   ært bÿ Léslïè Fïşh

In Klingoni

ON THE STREET
Hello.
Achtung.
My name is _____.
Me yclept _____.
Please take your knife away from my throat.
Nasty-nasty gillette-um.
Please take your boot off my face.
Nasty-nasty fifteen des.
I don't have 10,000 credits.
Nogot dough.
Help!
Kamarad!
I said, help!
Pinki square.

AT THE SPACEPORT
Where is the spaceport?

Wicky wacky woo?
Oh? When was it burned / exploded / atomized?
Brennt Paris?
When is the next starship to _____?
Wann kommt der Zug an _____?
Isn't there anything a little sooner than next year?
Jojo Tojo nogo logo?
How much are first / second / cattle accomodations?
Mastercharge?
I don't have 10,000 credits.
Nogot bucks.

EATING
Waiter, there's a communicator in my soup.
Honi soit qui mal y panse.
What is this I'm eating?
Wuzie slop?
Do you have anything other than raw gleph's eyes?
Tryit, yullykit.

23

A page from the August 1977 issue of the Star Trek fanzine *Menagerie*. containing a humorous representation of franchise aliens and a Klingon translation activity.

after they had gotten from it the satirical fun they desired. After all, another issue may well have been on its way before the current one's last page had even been read.

Much of what we observe in the previous excerpt from *Menagerie* tracks onto the McDonald's Star Trek: The Motion Picture Meal of 1979. Across six unique meal boxes (advertised as five, though two are similar but for a few variant characteristics), McDonald's used comics, humor, and games to provide kids with an engaging experience as they ate and played with whichever *Star Trek* premium they received. While zines are certainly not the only medium that contain these elements (cereal boxes, notably, do, too), the at times off-kilter parody of *Star Trek* through jokes and the intersection of those with serious comics and quirky games provide tonal shifts reminiscent of the property's fanzines which also capture the same effect. For instance, the below Happy Meal box contains everything from a burping Enterprise to a connect-the-dots game to a dramatic profile of the Federation.

Much like the zine, if one uses the box as directed and completes

A 1979 McDonald's Star Trek Meal box containing a humorous representation of franchise elements and activities.

the games, they will contribute to its destruction, much in the same way completing a zine's games disposes of a part of it. If the zine comes with its destruction already in progress through quick, sometimes shoddy construction, the fast food box, too, arrives eaten away by the grease of the food within. Though none of the six possible boxes replicates the Klingon translation game presented in the aforementioned zine excerpt, the McDonald's Star Trek Meal commercial notably does. In said advertisement, a Klingon barks lines at the camera that sound like, "Duuu wuv McDonald's..." while a voiceover translates, "For you parents who don't speak Klingonese, he's saying, 'People of Earth, unite and bring your kids to McDonald's for a Star Trek Meal.... Take it from a father who knows...'" ("Star Trek–Klingon Happy Meal"). What we hear of the Klingon's language does not align with the "official" alien vocabulary as established by the show, but a humorous faux pidgin that resembles enthusiasm for McDonald's. Likewise, the Klingon language game in the previously cited *Menagerie* issue does the same. It, for example, jokingly claims the "Klingoni" for "What is this I'm eating?" is *"Wuzis slop?"* So, on top of imagining a brutish Klingon to be saying out-of-character sentences, both the zine and the promotion have fun with the language itself to subversively interact with an established and fairly rigid intellectual property universe.

While the Star Trek Meal box is ultimately too corporate, too "official," to be a zine, it abides by Alison Piepmeier's expansive definition of the medium. In "Why Zines Matter: Materiality and Creation of Embodied Community," Piepmeier writes, "Zines are quirky, individualized booklets, filled with diatribes, reworkings of pop culture iconography, and all variety of personal and political narratives" (Piepmeier 214). I contend that, above, we see McDonald's employing the same tactics on their Star Trek Meal box. The games and humorously "burping" Enterprise makes the box "quirky," and its embodiment of a uniquely Star Trek container featuring a toy and food somewhat tailored to its consumer individualizes it enough to at least sit on the fringes of the domain Piepmeier assigns to zines. The belching starship joke also serves to "rework" the instantly recognizable science fiction icon. Although there are no conventionally personal or political narratives on the food container, it does contain branding and references that make it distinctly McDonald's. Thus while it is not personal in the way a zine is, it does establish itself as authored by an entity making a new narrative out of an established one. The key difference, of course, is that where a zine expresses "personal and political narratives" unique to an individual or community, typically with the intention of resisting a Capitalist institution, the Star Trek Meal box cannot and need not escape the corporate story placed upon it by McDonald's with the profit-making goal of selling as many of them as possible.

Both narratives, however, can inspire destruction. Political storytelling hopes the reader will put down the zine in order to perform actions that instigate change, and the corporate version desires its consumer to move on, as quickly as possible, to the next item for sale. Because of the former, Piepmeier recognizes the zine as a disposable medium when she writes, "zines themselves are seen by some as disposable (so much so that some zine makers have expressed surprise that zines are being archived in library collections)...," expanding on this to say that the preservation of objects that surround zines, like the envelopes they came in, is even more shocking (Piepmeier 232). Likewise, I have experienced that same incredulity by those who have seen not only my collection of kids' meal boxes but also the wrappers of the food that came within them. Perhaps this is a feat, as, by the 1990s, some boxes even more explicitly demanded their own destruction, like the 1992 McDonald's Streex Happy Meal, whose box came with punch-out sections that allowed consumers to construct a "tunnel" for their air-powered car to race through at the expense of the games printed on the container.

On the box, the perforated section cuts right through the "laser beam" game that asks consumers to complete lines "targeting" specific cars. The food vessel maintains many of the jokes, games, and motifs seen on the 1979 Star Trek Meal box, however, showing the zine-like aesthetics continuing mostly unchanged, adapted to a different property over a decade after the sci-fi movie's promotion. If anything, the 1992 box found ways to layer destruction on top of destruction in pursuit of fun, if brief, engagement, and this type of destruction and

A 1992 McDonald's *Streex* Happy Meal box containing activities and a "punch-out" feature that allows one to make the container into a "tunnel" through which Streex cars can race.

disposability may be best read through the lens of zine scholarship. Of course, zines are not the only way to analyze literary destruction. This is thematically unpacked in more mainstream texts, too.

While the zine and the kids' meal toy box may have disposability in common, they do not share the same amount of what Piepmeier calls "personal narrative." The heart of the zine is in its intimacy. One knows they are reading the work of a person or small team of people, and they are one of only a few who are doing so. That contrasts with the kids' meal toy box, which is distributed to many consumers without the feeling it was tailored specifically for them. However, such a feeling is replicated in the disposable media of kids' meal toy fan conventions and the zine-like newsletters that surround them. For example, McDonald's fan Meredith Williams created a

Chapter 6. Appetite for Destruction

C O L L E C T I N G   T I P S   N E W S L E T T E R -- January -- 1989

Tips for collecting memorabilia from fast food restaurants.

In this issue information is given about items that are collectible from McDonald's restaurants. Many other items can be collected and they will be reviewed in future issues. Subjects covered in this issue are: (A) Advertising (B) Calender/Coloring book (C) Fun Times (D) Happy Meals (E) McKids (F) Olympic Cups (G) Retail Items (H) Valentines.

A. A D V E R T I S I N G --

HOLOGRAPHIC AD APPEARS ON BACK OF DECEMBER '88 NATIONAL GEOGRAPHIC

If you collect McDonald's print advertising you won't want to miss the December 1988, National Geographic magazine. On the back cover is a holographic ad. A hologram is a three dimensional photo etched with microscopic ridges (20,000 per square inch) on rolls of clear plastic. This is a super looking hologram of a McDonald's restaurant. You certainly will want this ad in your collection.

PRINT ADS APPEARED IN SEVERAL MAGAZINES DURING 1988

McDonald's carried print ads in the following magazines during 1988: Time, Newsweek, U.S. News, People, Sports Illustrated, Parents, Family Circle, Good Housekeeping, Better Homes, Women's Day, Working Mother, Life and Readers Digest. Seven different ads were put out by McDonald's last year.
The McD.L.T. 'grabber ad', printed on heavy paper with five holes for your five fingers, appeared in the July editions of Time, People, Sports Illustrated, and Family Circle. This was a very unusual ad and attracted alot of attention.

B. C A L E N D E R / C O L O R I N G   B O O K - 1 9 8 9 ---------------------------------

The 1989 calender/coloring book is being sold in some stores. The book includes food coupons for stores in that local area. Many stores do not sell the calenders anymore. The 1989 calender/coloring books I have seen have Ronald on the front with faces of the four seasons (summer, winter, fall, spring).

C. F U N   T I M E S - The February/March issue is out --------------------

The McDonaldland Fun Times (a comic/coloring book type piece) for Feb/Mar '89 is being given out in stores. It is Vol. Eleven, No. I and features "Adventures with the McNugget Buddies." Not all stores carry the Fun Times and those who do sometimes run out quickly. Some stores have them out where you can see them and some do not. If you don't see them - ask if they carry the Fun Times.

D. H A P P Y   M E A L S ---

McNugget Buddies - The big Happy Meal for the end of December and all

Here is the first page of Williams' January 1989 _Collecting Tips Newsletter,_ a zine-like fan project for McDonald's collectors.

long-running, self-produced newsletter which was mailed to other collectors as a catalog of items the fast food giant had released monthly.* In some of these newsletters, readers learned a little about

---

*In one issue, Williams notes that he works as a teacher, and one wonders if the early tabloids were not the product of late nights in the school's copy room.

Williams' life, though not nearly on the level of a writer sharing deeply private thoughts in a zine. Still, having read early issues of Williams' work, to me it is clear that these cheaply-made, disposable fan creations contained him within, primarily through his meticulous love of all products McDonald's, but secondarily through the tidbits of his day-to-day one could glean from its pages. These newsletters also plugged fans into one another, so much so that an annual convention sprung up and ran for over a decade, an entirely grass-roots effort spearheaded by McDonald's art director Rich Seidelman and others. These conventions featured fan-made exclusive items traded only by the small community that knew of their existence. Here is where what Henry Jenkins would call the "participatory culture" of the kids' meal collector community exists. The meal boxes, like any mass-produced item, struggles to include this, instead relying on "passive media spectatorship" for their audience (Jenkins 3). At conventions and by answering ads in fan-made newsletters, collectors converge and interact with others around their media, thereby creating a personal investment, like the one that exists in a zine, which raises the stakes of their roles within the fandom compared to casually consuming corporate narratives. If the kids' meal box cannot satisfy Piepmeier's definition of the zine as a place of personal narrative, and it cannot beyond the awkward, somewhat soulless inclusion of the corporate identity, these conventions and the fan media crafted by their attendees can. This, though, does not alter its disposability, as, today, these products are not commonly known, and the newsletters have not frequently been saved.* If the destruction of the kids' meal toy box is a part of its fun, the disappearance of this zine-like media, made by collectors who are aging into their golden years, feels like a loss. Perhaps, though, that feeling, like the feeling created by fanzines who spoke to those who may have felt alone in their fandom but for the voices that came irregularly through their mailboxes, might evolve into action that

---

*My collection of them, which contains most of Williams' first four years writing the newsletters, came from someone who had assumed they were McDonald's corporate documents and not fan-made creations.

maintains the heart of fast food collector culture for generations to come.

Destroying Kids' Meal Toys

Today, I often reflect on my preservation of kids' meal toys. Prototypes sit enshrined in clear plastic display cases. Paper matter rests flat in organized filing systems. Toys rest in bins mint-in-bag. Kids' meal translites, that wonderful translucent signage secured into menu boards of the 1980s and '90s to lure kids into begging for the offering of the month, rotate thoughtfully through frames above my dining room table, a different set for each time of year. I have restored more than one Happy Meal toy display. However, when I close my eyes and see my childhood self interacting with kids' meal toys, the carnage is real. I destroyed those things. Not all, to be sure. Some, many of those presented in this book, were treated with reverence, coming from a parent text for which I cared deeply. Others, though, especially those from source material to which I was indifferent, suffered greatly, in myriad, creative ways.

In this section, I aim to try myself for my crimes. I want to establish not just motive, but meaning. After all, some might say the media environment lent itself to destruction. According to Beverle Houston, TV "reopens the gap of desire" by "shattering the imaginary possibility over and over" (Houston). In other words, television presents a narrative that comes with a set of rules. It then uses cliffhangers and clever story tricks to make viewers want to know what the storytellers will imagine for them next, thereby opening a "desire gap" by making audiences surrender to the creators' narratives instead of their own. It does not encourage its audience to imagine their shows' endings. Disney, FOX, Sunbow, or any of the other production houses past, present, and future will tell those who tuned in, perhaps next week or the week after, what the events of an episode all mean. This, for Houston, "shatters" one's ability to think beyond what is presented to them. One could, perhaps, read kids' meal toys in a similar fashion. They are, like the episodes of a show, there one week, potentially gone the next. The result, then, is the consumer wondering which next toy promotion they will be given, not what toy their imagination might conjure without corporate interference. It drives such collectors back to fast food restaurants in the same way it might corral a TV show's audience back at the same bat-time, on the same bat-channel. While it is no revelation to posit that kids' meal toys serve the corporations that make them, I do not believe that Houston's "shattering" of "the imaginary possibility" is the only way to read them, much as I do not think this is the only way to analyze television. Yes, the toys, like story chapters, serve a certain narrative, but one must not discount fan ownership. For television, this looks like the creation of "head canon," or fan-made stories seen by subgroups as perfectly valid, despite its point of creation being outside the endorsed creators. In kids' meal toys, the triggering of the imagination is even more clear. Owners use their toys to imagine stories entirely unrelated to the text from which they sprang. Anecdotally, my own 1995 Burger King Governor Ratcliffe figure, from the animated film *Pocahontas*, was not the Governor Ratcliffe of the movie. In fact, I never even saw the movie, and still have not as of this writing. Instead, Governor Ratcliffe was the figure that decided my Han Solo should wind up in Carbonite. Nonsensical, yes, but imaginative. While I have no data to suggest how many kids play with kids' meal toys this way, I can confidently say I was not alone. At after school hangouts and sleepovers, this type of imaginary kids' meal toy play was common, perhaps because, often times, we did not achieve a full set of toys, and maybe the kids' meal toy in question was the only piece of transmedia we had from a given property. As such, it was treated as a plastic "lost soul," in search of a world, and all we had to invent that world with were other toys from assorted lines. From this, a new play narrative was created. Text out of paratext. So while the 1990s did its best to "shatter" the imaginary through an onslaught of kids fare designed to clearly spell out the laws of their particular lands, the recipients of the massive amount of transmedia from that programming also built many imaginary worlds entirely disconnected from their corporate borders. To that end, Houston's "shattering," which I read as a synonym for destruction, is only part of the story.

Chapter 6. Appetite for Destruction

It does not fully capture what came next for Governor Ratcliffe, either. Since he, in my playscape, was responsible for Han Solo's encasement in Carbonite, child me decreed that he should be frozen next. Lacking Carbonite, I did the next best thing: I placed my Burger King Ratcliffe figure in a glass of water, and then I put that glass of water in the freezer. The next day, I could just make out Ratcliffe's purple outfit through the foggy ice that had formed within the glass. However, this Ratcliffe figurine could not be trusted once thawed, I decided. It was then that I mercilessly smashed the toy into shards, and he was never seen again, a demise perhaps rivaled only by the fate of the real Ratcliffe. Vanessa Smith studies an older form of this destruction in her *Toy Stories: Analyzing the Child in 19th Century Literature*. There, Smith posits that "over the course of the nineteenth century, and across the variety of genres through which that century represented its children, we find example after example of infantile rage, shame, and distress made manifest through the brutalized toy" (Smith xi). Essentially, literary works of the 1800s are full of kids dispatching their own versions of my Burger King *Pocahontas* Governor Ratcliffe figurines. To Smith, this emerges from places of anxiety, anger, and frustration. Certainly, one can imagine violence stemming from these emotions. However, during the time Smith works with, toys, especially new, complex toys, had much higher price tags than their modern fast food versions. Thus the destruction of a Victorian toy, a toy which likely replicated not a licensed property but a social norm such as masculine activity (outdoor toys, for instance) or feminine caretaking (dolls), may require motivations located deep within the psyche. By the 1990s, the prevalence of kids' meal toys, attained and made cheaply and replaced generally with ease, meant destruction could happen simply for fun. My little Governor Ratcliffe "died" somewhere around 1997, and I spent exactly zero time in mourning in the years since. The disposability of the toy in fact meant my imagination could be the more valuable item. It now had a way to physically manifest the story it created in my mind, and it did so with glee. So while toy destruction dates back centuries, I do not believe kids' meal toy disposability can be explained using the same thoughts linked to the more costly toys of the 1800s. That does not, though, mean more contemporary literary theory cannot be applied.

Free with Every Kids' Meal

If Henry Jenkins is my judge, I might escape conviction for my slaughter of Governor Ratcliffe. That is ironic, as my vindication will stem from the man who proclaimed kids' meal toys "pretty lame and easily forgotten" (Jenkins 107). I believe that thousands of collectors in many online communities, a history of kids' meal toy-specific conventions, the rise of fast food premium nostalgia, and the existence of this book help show these objects are not, in fact, "easily forgotten," though each participant in this culture surely can name certain promotions as forgettable. And while I do not pretend to know which items excite Jenkins and what he might class as "lame," I would ask anyone who would apply this adjective to kids' meal toys to observe the highly-articulated 2003 McDonald's *He-Man and the Masters of the Universe* Happy Meal promotion, the transformable, dynamic McDonald's Changeables toys of the '80s and '90s that represented both robots and dinosaurs, or the 2001 Quick (a Franco-Belgian chain) DC Super Hero and Villain premiums that were essentially mainline action figures for the property, only to name a few, and still use the term. That said, Jenkins may be using the term "lame" because kids' meal toys are products of cross-corporation synergy that happens specifically and solely to sell more product. While that is to an extent true, I offer that such rapid, spreadable production also increases the points at which these products may intersect with events outside the design to memorable, or at least interesting, results. A kids' meal toy may spark a moral panic, like the McDonald's *Batman Returns* promotion did, and create an unintended and therefore noteworthy historical moment. Or, as mentioned throughout this section, a toy might be removed from its context all together and used as a villain in some entirely imagined narrative, like the former Governor Ratcliffe.

This is where Jenkins is helpful. When he analyzes Seth's comic "Nothing Lasts, Part 2," Henry Jenkins links destruction to a coming-of-age moment. The aforementioned comic features a central character who destroys his childhood toys in two ways: (1) he crams them into a drawer and lets them get smashed to bits over time as more and more are shoved in and attempts to close the overstuffed carrier shred the plastic inside, and (2) he hangs them from a tree and shoots them. The two types of toy destruction are different. The former is passive, the toys simply break over time out of neglect, while the latter is actively violent. The main character remarks that the shooting represented both *not* a "meaningful act" and an "event to signify the end of [his] childhood" (Jenkins 114). In a way, the destruction of the toys does the same by both being utterly mundane and representing the putting away of childish things; it is the intentionality that is different. It is in this middle space, the area between the mundane and the meaningful, where kids' meal toys thrive. Due to their abundance and cheapness, they blend in with the everyday. As such, the destruction of one would not be notable. In fact, it could be easily reversible, as even if the fast food restaurant had moved on from the promotion that gave rise to the destroyed toy, another one could surely be purchased easily second hand. However, because of their abundance, they are also present for events that, perhaps beyond the realm of Seth's comic, would be seen as important, such as the conclusion of a childhood and a move toward adulthood. In 1997, I was eleven. My family had just gotten the internet. I had an email address. In the coming year, I would get swept up in the Pokémon fad and wonder how to hide my enthusiasm for fear it would not be read as in-step with my expected maturation process. Given all of this, I accept the possibility that Jenkins' reading of Seth has relevance in my mutilation of Governor Ratcliffe. In fact, there were a number of instances of kids' meal toy destruction in the ensuing years, all during a time when I was both embarrassed by and longing for the arrested child within. To read my destruction as a way of processing my desire to end childhood, while still very much being in it, helps me see more clearly a truth I could not express at the time. In that case, I am grateful to the kids' meal toy for being so generic as to not attract attention. The last thing I would have wanted would surely have been to be exposed as attempting to move through deep feelings of anxiety, as the destruction of a 19th-century toy might have given away. Such vulnerability would not have worked in my favor in my school or home communities, though thankfully later therapy has assisted with that particular facet of my upbringing. If Jenkins' understanding of Seth's comic represents a broader, real world experience, as it certainly applies to mine, this type of analysis can offer a great deal as one tries to culturally read the impact of kids' meal toys and other such mundane yet important mass produced objects. It also makes these toys into accessible tools that could assist with constructive destruction, or the destruction out of which maturation can rise, and increased awareness of what might be at stake with this sort of play in which the stakes of the toy are low (its loss is affordable) but the stakes of development are potentially high. To simplify, Brian Sutton-Smith deploys the great *Alias the Cat!* quote to understand the role toys like these can play in human growth: "Hey! It ain't no toy, see! This here is an artifact!" (Jenkins 145).

Perhaps this is where one might explain the popularity of intentionally mangled or destroyed toys. Jenkins mentions the example of *Action League Now!*, a series of shorts in which stop-motion toys protect their world from evil. The toys are misfits, with one being essentially an entirely melted soldier named "Meltman." The idea here, as Jenkins notes, is that these toys have arrived in this condition due to "inappropriate play" (Jenkins 151–152). This combines with my prior analysis of kids' meal toy destruction in that the only way one could obtain replicas of the *Action League Now!* crew was through a 1998 Burger King Nickel-O-Zone kids' meal promotion. With the toys packaged this way, one could easily find cause to heap more destruction on top of their narrative-built deformity due to, as mentioned earlier, their accessibility and low cost. Of course, despite their status as pre-destroyed kids' meal toys, it is remarkable that this particular set of premiums tends to sell, according to recent eBay sold listings, for around $20.00, double (or more) the price for a standard vintage, sealed toy from another popular promotion. And this is not the only example of deformed toys having appeal. Beyond kids' meal toys, playthings such as Cabbage Patch Kids and their "gross" parodies the Garbage Pail Kids, Fuggler, My Pet Monster, and Japanese "Super Deformed" figures (which can be varying degrees of mangled, from merely having an enlarged head to being a contorted monster, depending on the line) have taken hold at various times as fad items. While it would be untrue to suggest Jenkins' reading of Seth motivates all of their popularity, as after all such boundary-pushing taboo is fun and empowering for a kid who on some level suspects adults disapprove of their choice, the act of toy destruction as understood by Jenkins can show these objects, and kids' destructive play with them, as working toward an eventual refusal experienced by many as they mature. That said, others may experience not so much a violent break from their toys, but an evolving relationship in which they collect, study, and even write books about their childhood obsessions. These collectors sometimes experience destruction in a different way. When kids' meal toys change, as they have most recently when McDonald's shifted their Happy Meal toys so that many promotions relied on cardboard play elements instead of plastic, collectors located their destruction in nostalgia, finding the ways in which they played, and at times destroyed, now broken by a corporate shift that does not align with their expectations. As these responses all live on a spectrum, I should also include a nod to the number of parents I have spoken to who have been happy with the shift to paper goods in kids' meal toys, because, as one said, they can simply throw away the premium when their child is done using it. In these cases, destruction is a welcome element for the parent, who views these objects as so commonplace as to be clutter, and directed disposal helps them maintain a tidy home.

However one interacts with kids' meal toys, destruction remains a low-stakes, multifaceted option. It may represent a personal shift. It may be a product of imaginary narrative-building. It may be a necessary part of the clean-up process. With destruction being such a temptation, one should consider the consequences of that disposal: environmental impact, the display of anxiety, and the attack on a nostalgic ideal being among them. Better understanding of what these forms of destruction mean can result in a more accurate appreciation of ourselves and our needs, and kids' meal toys, ever-present and inherently disposable, can be a great tool in these readings.

CHAPTER 7

"Maximum 10 per visit"

Kids' Meal Toys
as Corridors to Trend Access

"You can make a lot of money with a good cat."
—Ty Warner

Kids' meals come with toys. With the exception of the stray book, bucket, or cassette tape, this is generally true. However, because kids' meals also, at times, so effectively combine with the zeitgeist, they end up offering something else, too: access. When kids' meals walk in lock step with fads, they can be points of access to trends that are made unobtainable by the throngs of people competing to acquire the cultural capital that comes with such crazes. Here, I will analyze the points where such fads intersect with kids' meals in order to study how such product mania raises the profile of their tie-in fast food counterparts. This can, as I will show, elevate an otherwise disposable meal to an essential gateway into an important moment of material culture. Finally, I will demonstrate that this relationship does not only move from the fad to the kids' meal. Kids' meals have informed a key toy fad of today, too. This bond, however, has been strengthened by decades of fast food fad tie-ins perhaps best exemplified by their link to '90s toy crazes.

In 1997, at the height of the Beanie Baby craze, McDonald's offered smaller versions of the Ty plushes in their Happy Meals. Called "Teenie Beanies," these editions of Patti the Platypus or Goldie the goldfish could have been the baby stages of the fully-grown products that were drained from pharmacy displays and poured into personal collections and eBay listings at breakneck pace. The result was that the pandemonium hitting retail outlets for Beanie Babies then slammed McDonald's restaurants as collectors swept various locations stocking up on Teenie Beanies. The phenomenon was unique. This Happy Meal promotion did not seek to get audiences to a movie or in front of a particular TV show, as was typical of '90s kids' meal toys. It also was not hyping McDonaldland characters, as the McNuggets and various Ronald McDonald toys did. This Happy Meal was built around a toy that had just emerged and leapt almost overnight to fad status.

The confluence of Ty Beanie Babies, Ty Warner's knack for salesmanship, and the rise of eBay all burned the Beanie fire white hot. The toys were, as will be discussed later, a departure from plush convention, and they were backed by the most obsessive salesman they could get. Their creator, Ty Warner, was constantly tweaking the products, causing under-produced initial versions to escalate in secondary market value, much like the infamous Peanut the elephant, whose color was changed to baby blue after only a relative few royal blues were made. This resale value was largely seen on eBay, a fairly new marketing platform at the time that allowed, and continues to allow, individuals to sell or auction goods second-hand. As the fervor over Beanie Babies boiled over, so did the news segments, articles, and editorials, like the 1997 piece from The New York Times titled, "Goodbye, Tickle Me Elmo; Hello, Beanie Babies," in which writer Joseph Berger knights the new plushes the "it" toy of the year. In the article, Berger reports on three young girls who own a substantial amount of Beanie Babies, which also seems to be typical of their social circles. The first, an 8-year-old, faked sick so she could double back to a toy store she saw on the bus ride to school that advertised a new shipment of Beanies. Others, says Berger, were swept into the fad by friends and family who bought them one Beanie Baby, and then watched as they fell into the economy of collecting, trading, and re-selling. With this culture solidly in place around Beanie Babies by 1997, McDonald's was primed to offer another concept in their Happy Meals: entrance into a world whose "Sold Out" signs and high resale prices provided impassable barriers to the in-demand product that was Beanie Babies.

Free with Every Kids' Meal

By joining with Ty, McDonald's made its restaurants gateways into the most popular toy craze of its day. McDonald's, then, became the first large corporation to break through, largely because, as Bissonnette notes, Warner liked the restaurant's menu. This relationship sparked a new level of accessibility for the Beanie Babies trend. It meant, at last, that these toys could be found, in a special size and capacity, at locations that existed on numerous streets within many cities throughout the United States. Any fast food corporation would have desired a deal like this, but the attention McDonald's got for their Teenie Beanie Babies promotion was unprecedented.

When studying kids' meal toys, one notices that some promotions, like the 1997 Teenie Beanie Babies Happy Meal from McDonald's, create mass interest of historic proportions, while others, like Burger King's 2013 Cut the Rope kids' meal, are barely noticed when they debut, and then fall into obscurity as time goes by. Simply looking at the properties "hot" kids' meal toys are tied to reveals some of their success. Many of them are linked to mainstream toys, movies, or TV shows that have already generated a fervent fan base. Beanie Babies, Furby, Power Rangers, Tamagotchi, and Pokémon all achieved a level of rapid popularity at which they might appropriately be considered a "fad," and all made for successful kids' meals.

According to Gary Marx and Douglas McAdam, five criteria qualify fads: they must be "strikingly new," "non-essential," "short-lived," engaging beyond the seemingly "intrinsic or 'common-sense' worth of the activity," and quick-spreading. Beanie Babies cleanly check off each of these boxes. Though created in 1993, Beanie Babies became what journalist Zac Bissonnette labels an Internet phenomenon that "comprised 10 percent of all sales" on eBay (Bissonnette). They were "strikingly new," not just in the way they were resold, but in how they were made. Whereas many prior plushes were rigid, filled mostly with stuffing, Beanie Babies were intentionally understuffed, and utilized PVC pellets in place of synthetic fiber in the toys' bodies. This created a floppy, posable toy where most plushes could only hold one position. On each was a stand-out heart-shaped tag bearing the name of the Beanie Babies' company and creator: Ty. A short poem adorned the insides of these tags by which consumers could get to know the character they just purchased. Micro-adjustments made to each Beanie Baby by Ty Warner as production went on also created variants that caused certain, specific types of a character to surge in resale value. All of these elements combined to make a toy that departed from the traditional plush toy in exciting ways that fostered collectability and play. Because of their function as a play item or collectible, they also established themselves as "non-essential," a term that reflects the luxury nature of the good. While Beanie Babies were, for many, fun and happy toys, they were not, as proven by their eventual downfall, necessary for life. This is not a dig at the plushes; it is good that non-essential items can be breakout hits upon release and then fade away, while the essentials have longer staying power. I do not want to live in a world where antibiotics are "so last year." But pop culture's three-year flirtation with Beanie Baby speculation is, regardless of how one feels about the objects, easier to digest. Though Ty products are still around as of this writing, Beanie Babies' worth has plummeted. Zac Bissonnette reflects on a 2010 Kimballs auction of approximately 500 Beanie Babies, which sold for "less than one-hundred dollars, probably well below 2 percent of its value at the height of the Beanie Baby market," which, Bissonnette notes, is also the apex of the Internet stock bubble (Bissonnette 5). This "short-lived" nature of the product further deepens Beanie Babies' status as a Marx and McAdam "fad." Within that time frame, though, Beanie Babies reached far beyond their "intrinsic" value as plush toys. Had they been confined to their "common-sense" use, these toys would stop at being children's playthings. A conventional plush toy accompanies a child to sleep, engages them in play, and comforts them in times of need. While Beanie Babies may have done this for some, perhaps many, kids, they also enticed adults into starting a substantial online resale market for the items, thus upping their collectability. Furthermore, given the scarcity and price tag of certain Beanie Babies, owning specific ones became something of a status symbol. In his

Free with Every Kids' Meal

"Whatever Happened to Those Princess Diana Beanie Babies?," author Hayden Manders named the purple Princess Diana bear as a status symbol due to "inventory restrictions" around the toy (only 12 could be sold at a time) and its link to the death of the plush's namesake royalty. Thus, this bear performed two functions beyond the parameters of a typical plush toy: it was a sign of status, and a commemoration of a beloved public figure. By limiting quantities of Beanie Babies and increasing their social functions (toys, status symbols, commemorations, collectibles), Ty stoked the fires of a fad as validated by the cottage industries that sprung up to create tag protectors and price guides that cemented consumers' investments. At the time, Beanie Babies cost five dollars, but, given the culture of collectability around them, many believed they could transform that small expenditure into a massive return overnight. eBay, internet message boards, and collector-specific websites were emerging with the Beanie Baby, and they spread awareness of the plushes at speeds previous fads could have only dreamed of. This created for the Beanie Baby the "quick spread" that Marx and McAdam hold as their final criterion for a fad.

With Beanie Babies firmly defined as a fad, one wonders how the 1997 McDonald's Teenie Beanie Babies Happy Meal, and subsequent similar promotions, fit into the fervor. To be sure, the deal was novel. Ty Warner had previously avoided many mass market avenues for the sale of his company's Beanie Babies, skipping the shelves of Toys R Us and Target for displays in smaller drug stores. Warner was also vehemently against TV programming or films produced for the Beanie Babies license. Thus, when Beanie Babies came to McDonald's, the world's largest fast food chain and toy distributor, it was a philosophical sea change for Ty, a shift he made because, according to Zac Bissonnette, he simply liked the menu. The effect was felt immediately. The Street notes that the 100 million Teenie Beanie Babies minted for the Happy Meal sold out within two weeks, with collectors and kids clamoring for the toys (Button). A 1998 issue of the *Orlando Sentinel* reported on the capture of an 18-year-old McDonald's employee who stole $6,000 worth of Teenie Beanie Babies, selling 300 of them to a coworker ("McDonald's

Worker Stole...."). As a McDonald's collector at the time, I recall many trips to my local Knoxville, Tennessee, McDonald's in which employees insisted on a one-Happy-Meal-per-person policy in order to ration the Teenie Beanie Babies. On a good day, I was a Beanie Baby agnostic, but initially I was besieged by feelings that they represented misplaced priorities that elevated floppy plush toys over, say, the highly articulated *Power Rangers* action figures that I, at the time, advocated for full-throatedly. And yet, even I eventually got a Teenie Patti, and worse: I liked it.

Because my Beanie resistance was broken by a Happy Meal toy, I wonder whether kids' meals are uniquely situated to bring in consumers who might otherwise not partake in a fad. In my case, I grew up in an incredibly gendered play environment. While Beanie Babies are not marketed toward any specific gender, they were still not a toy played with by those in my circle who were socialized as boys. As a result, I felt that asking for a Beanie Baby would "other" me within a masculine group to which I, at the time, very much wanted to belong. However, the Happy Meal brought plausible deniability. I did not get a Beanie Baby; I got lunch. Lunch just so happened to come *with* a Beanie Baby, and one that I happened to secretly desire. Patti was a unique animal, a platypus, whose lush purple color contrasted elegantly with her yellow bill. She stood out to me, and, as my thoughts went from "I will never participate in this fad" to "But what if I *did* participate...," Patti became the toy I would choose if I "had to." Once that door was opened, I imagined partaking in a cultural moment that was bigger than me, and bigger than my friend group. It was a movement that would, in my dramatic kid brain, plug me into something national, or even global. That was attractive. But with the full-sized Patti out-of-reach for not only gender but also inventory reasons, the Teenie version presented an accessible alternative that also satisfied my itch for the toy. While many came to the Happy Meal promotion as Beanie Baby collectors, I arrived as a McDonald's consumer who was Beanie-curious. Kids like me may have, because of this Happy Meal, found themselves at the gateway of Beanie Baby mania, and some, such as myself, entered not long after that. It was just a matter of months before I obtained my first full-size Beanie Baby: Mel the Koala.

While my experience can only be anecdotal in the broader sense, scholarship around fads and crazes help unlock how white-hot promotions like the Teenie Beanie Babies function. Jaap Van Ginnekin researched the origins of fads and delved, specifically, into lapel pins handed out at the Paris Roland-Garros tournament by companies like Ray Ban and Lacoste which set off a French lapel pin fad in the late 1980s and early 1990s. Van Ginnekin writes, "The In-Crowd took to ostensibly wearing these pins throughout the rest of the season to show that they had been 'part of the action' there" (Van Ginnekin 132). This means that, for Van Ginnekin, the private "insider" knowledge shown by participation in a fad outweighs the public's ability to perceive and reward one for partaking. If one is wearing, say, a Lacoste pin from an early '90s French Open tournament while walking around the streets of Paris at the time, another person, perhaps one who was also at the event, might recognize this passerby as in the same metaphorical "club" as them. It is not just that both people, in that moment, would understand the pin as shorthand to mean they share an interest in tennis, but that their fandom cuts deep enough to recognize the unspoken agreement that lapel pins be worn as a tribute to the significance of the tournament and the audience present. However, this feeling is secondary to the personal boost the pin-wearer gets just by owning and displaying the specific object that sums up the colossal magnitude of something like the French Open in a single piece of metal no bigger than a quarter (or perhaps a Franc), whether others see the pin or not. When I reflect on the Beanie Babies fad personally, some of this bears itself out. Above, I stated that, at a certain point, my participation in the fad trumped the potential blowback I might receive from my friend group because it felt like the larger event, the "French Open" of plush toys, would be a boost bigger than any possible criticism. This indicates a private narrative happening in my mind fueled by the construct of the fad. The story of the Beanie Baby, in this moment in time (1997), at this place (McDonald's), felt important to commemorate. Perhaps that is why Beanie Babies worked so well as commemorative objects in general: each one already commemorated the fad which represented a specific time and setting that, by virtue of being temporal, can only eventually fade. However, a kids' meal toy like the Teenie Beanie Baby must be recognized as fundamentally different from a lapel pin. The pin is made for adults, and constructed around an adult event. The kids' meal toy, and toy fads more broadly, are engineered to hook children, and are often backed by media powerhouses, Internet fame, classroom and playground politics, and other factors that contribute to what today one might call "virality." Therefore, I suggest that fads aimed at children do not operate in the same private way that Van Ginnekin attributes to lapel pins. While kids may internally participate in the narrative of the fad by feeling validation from simply possessing the trendy object, there is, for many, an outward-facing element to fad participation that is rooted in the public spaces children occupy and the ways in which peer pressure and social capital function in those arenas. Beanie Babies, Teenie or otherwise, did not make me cool, but they made *some* kids cool, most notably those within circles that focused on the minutiae of collecting. This may be at least partly because an in-depth knowledge of Beanie Babies could offer kids a level of expertise that would overtake even that of most adults. Even my childhood basic familiarity with Mel the koala and Patti the platypus, the latter earned through the Happy Meal's prominence in my life, outpaced what my parents and teachers knew of these plushes. With that kind of knowledge, the sort that one-ups the adults, kids could gain a level of power in knowing what evaded those who seemed to know everything, or at least who seemed to know *more.* In this way, the Beanie Baby fad let collectors of all ages, but most meaningfully children, have an awareness that was future-facing. By knowing, intimately, the ins and outs of Beanie Baby collecting, collectors could foresee, either allegedly or actually, which downstream releases would be valuable, as well as assess the value of trend items in the present, reading errors on tags, the presence of stars on labels, and misprints with such shorthand some might find their vocabulary akin to speaking in tongues. With Van Ginnekin's lapel pins, the action of fad participation is primarily about remembering a past event that only comes around once a year. For the Beanie Baby fad, commemoration played a role in participation, too, but the power wielded by those who rode the waves of continuously produced product, decoding value both ahead of and in real time, cannot be ignored. Furthermore, because of Beanie Babies' ubiquitous and unlimited spread—which contrasts with lapel pins tied to a specific event—the Teenie Beanie Babies Happy Meal illustrates how kids' meal promotions act as an injector of fads into the playspaces of those who might not otherwise participate, in the best of cases, for Ty at least, being a gateway to collecting or at least buying the mainline product.

It is these sorts of fad fast food promotions that stoke the fires of excitement that lure newcomers into the fad. This is a step Van Ginnekin recognizes as important in his description of how "collective behavior," or the actions of a large group versus individuals, maintains a fad. He writes that, first, a previous fad's grip must be loosened such that a new one may take hold. When that happens, the novelty of the new fad brings with it a level of initial exhilaration as ground-floor consumers buy in. Those foundational fad participants carve out a new "psychosocial pattern" that becomes more validated as its following grows. As the fad assimilates more people, its population growth becomes exponential when people once on the fringes join in simply for fear of missing out (Van Ginnekin 135). This is where fast food chains and their toys come in. People on the outskirts of a fad may not populate the places at the center of the craze. These folks may not search eBay for a Beanie Baby, and they may not go to a drug store and take note of the display, but they might order a Happy Meal for their kids, not because it contains a Teenie Beanie Baby, but because it is a consistent and affordable option for lunch. No matter the motive, though, this person has participated in the collective behavior driving a fad: they bought the trend item. Once they've bought in, they might feel a level of unanticipated excitement at their spontaneous participation in the fad, or they may be unmoved. If they feel the latter, the fad likely still remains, as fads are typically dependent on a minority population anyway. As Rolf Meyersohn and Elihu Katz state in their "Notes on a Natural History of Fads," "Most fads are of a minority or subculture," but, as they also note, this is not to diminish their significance, as "minorities provide material to majorities," and "are also an integral part of the total system" (Meyersohn 596–598). Essentially, even at its height, Beanie Babies will not consume *most* of the population, but they will hook a significant fraction that is either (a) predisposed to the generic plush market or (b) susceptible to the excitement created by collective behavior. Those in Group A will rush to almost any place that offers a manifestation of the fad, but those in Group B will go about their routine, and, when the fad by happenstance occurs within that regimen, they will be presented with a decision to join in or move along. Invariably, some will join. Because fast food chains appeal to both the devoted fan and the person in the midst of a routine meal, they are uniquely situated to feed fads a stream of newcomers while maintaining the excitement of their most invested devotees. While Teenie Beanie Babies took me out of my routine and into the fad, another kids' meal promotion serviced the subculture in which I was already a member, and, in that case, the fast food chain performed a much different function.

At the risk of overindulging in my own experience, I cannot help but reflect on the late '90s fad in which I was, unlike Beanie Babies, an eager participant: Pokémon. Released in 1996, Pokémon achieved fad status in the United States by 1998. The Pokémon universe spread out primarily over games, cartoons, and trading cards to create a narrative in which consumers collected or "caught" monsters of various shapes, sizes, and styles that they could then use in "battles" with those of others. When one "caught 'em all," as Pokémon's trademark motto commanded players do for the 151 monsters originally made catchable, and defeated each of the programmed "trainers" or bosses in the video game, they won. In 1998, the *Daily News* reported that Nintendo pumped $25 million into the promotion of Pokémon ("Nintendo Putting 25M"). This resulted in the quick spread of Pokémon video games, cartoons, movies, game cards, figurines, toys, plushes, clothing, collectibles, and, of course, kids' meal toys. While Beanie Babies operated in a space I did not occupy, filling the displays of drug stores I could not wait to get out of, Pokémon hit me right where I lived. The cartoon landed in the Saturday morning kids programming block to which I was already attached, sometimes allowing multiple episodes to run for hours in what was advertised as Pokémon's "Pokéthon." The collectible cards were cheap, an easy ask from parents on trips to the mall, and they promised big returns as the fad escalated. Nightly news reports delved into the resale value of certain cards, like the coveted Charizard, but the actual value for a friend group like mine, in which all 5–6 kids were disciples of the Pokéfad, was social. Rank within the circle was built on who pulled which card, or whose collection was larger. Through card trades, bonds were strengthened or tested. Of course, the Gameboy video games played a prominent role in this, too. By the time we were 13, everyone I ran with owned either Pokémon Blue or Red, with the former given to me that year as a birthday present, along with a Gameboy Color, from a friend who I could only assume had the wealth of an investment banker and the generosity of a saint. If you had beat the game, which involved trades via a cable connecting one Gameboy system to another, you were as good as made within my friend circle.

With this built-out structure around Pokémon, I, along with most of my friends and many kids across the United States, took fervent interest in the 1999 Burger King Big Kids' Meal Pokémon promotion. Unlike the Teenie Beanie Babies, which were gateways into a fad I resisted, these toys acted like a new translation of a text to which I was devoted. While the Pokémon card game allowed consumers to collect characters in waxed cardboard form, and the video game made for great digital collections, these Burger King toys gave fans the ability to own 57 (59 if one counts the "talking" Pikachu as three different toys, as each repeated one of three different phrases) three-dimensional iterations of the famed 151 "pocket monsters" along with Pokéballs (containers for Pokémon in-universe) and exclusive cards. Each toy also contained an additional play feature, being made as either a key chain, water squirter, beanbag, Rev-Top, light-up, launcher, or, in the case of the aforementioned Pikachu, a talking plush. The toys came in "blind bags," or opaque white and red baggies that made it impossible to know which Pokémon rattled around inside unless one could crack the numerical code printed in the lower left hand corner of the plastic. This, combined with the sheer number of possible contents, replicated, as much as one could reasonably expect, the experience of Ash Ketchum, the fictional lead Pokémon collector of the game, traversing the wilds, encountering various surprise monsters as he goes. Fast food chains are uniquely situated to make immersive the fantasy worlds of kids media fads. Their commercials, which often populate the breaks in children's programming, combine, as Burger King's 1999 Pokémon promotion ads did, visuals of real kids enjoying the toys that come with their meals and animated moments from the featured cartoon, thereby dismantling the separation between the fun consumers will have and the adventure experienced by the fictional characters of Saturday morning fantasy. Additionally, fast food chains use banners, standees, window clings, and other display elements to alter stores in such a way that they become representations of fantasy media. Most recently, Burger King radically changed the exteriors of some stores to resemble the colorful animated style of the film *Spider-Man: Across the Spider-Verse*, for which they ran a 2023 kids' meal promotion. The indoor playgrounds more commonly found in these restaurants during the 1990s and prior facilitated this immersive adventure within these stylized environments even further. The toys themselves, then, become tokens of this experience. Perhaps Teenie Beanie Babies, with their intentionally vague fantasy world, couldn't represent this as well as Burger King's Pokémon promotion could, as the latter text has a far more built-out fictional landscape to draw from. But in this way, kids' meal toys better approach Van Ginnekin's French Open lapel pins, commemorating not a single sporting event, but a jaunt through Pallet Town or Cerulean City, lands once thought restricted to the screens and cards of Pokémon, but now, through Burger King's total sensory immersion, made manifest enough for kids' imaginations to fill in the gaps and count the experience as significant as a trip to the beach or a family outing to a local park. So, in addition to any social capital earned

Free with Every Kids' Meal

by possessing the fad kids' meal toy, and whatever private satisfaction one may gain from reflecting on their find, such objects can also become mementos of trips through worlds beyond one's typical reach, places made all the more urgent by their backdropping of fads.

It is here, however, that I would be remiss to ignore the tragedy surrounding that 1999 Burger King Pokémon promotion. Each toy came with a plastic "Pokéball" that could contain the plastic character it was bagged with. This sphere would separate in half and seal around the toy put inside. Because neither of the halves possessed a hole to vent air, and one half in particular featured a divot around its edge that could bridge over an infant's nose, these Pokéballs proved deadly for a 13-month-old in Sonora, California, who suffocated when a container half suctioned over the lower half of her face, preventing the intake of oxygen ("Burger King recalling"). About a week later, another baby almost suffered the same death if not for the quick actions of her father, who removed the stuck-on Pokéball before injury could occur. A recall occurred days later, with Burger King ceasing distribution of these toys, and offering a free small fries in exchange for surrendered Pokéballs. The loss of life is painful in any context. Per this chapter, it is also a reminder of the unique position in which fad fast food promotions find themselves. Because these specific restaurant toys are made cheaply, quickly, and in significant bulk, there is no differentiation between the fad fan who will put the item on a shelf or the grab-and-go eater who will toss it on the floor at home. Fast food toys equalize these groups, and this presents a design problem: how does one make a toy that both preserves fan appeal and can sell to a disinterested passer-by? As a Pokémon fan, the Pokéballs were deeply attractive to me. I would fling the orbs at the wall, bursting them open on impact in a rough translation of their function on TV and in the video game. However, the fantastic realism it brought me came at the expense of others who were tragically impacted by the design of this toy. When fast food chains make fads public, they make them truly *public*. The toys they produce can land in bedrooms of 13-year-olds and cribs of 13-month-olds alike. Their presence in homes can be intentional or spontaneous. While some go to fast food chains as they go to toy stores, invested in a particular promotion, others enter to select a meal, accepting whatever item that accompanies it without much thought for what it is. It is this aspect of fast food chains' cultural role that makes McDonald's the world's top toy distributor: a portion of those they are distributing to receive their toys without the same level of intentionality a fan purchases a specific collectible. Because of this, these restaurants are poised to make fad material culture public in a powerful way, and one that, as seen in the Burger King Pokémon example, must be performed responsibly.

Though fast food restaurants, despite the private nature of their businesses, are long-established places accessible to the public, fads rely on speedy cultural permeation in order to be considered such. Going back to Meyersohn and Katz in their "Notes on a Natural History of Fads," one must not only name a fad to qualify it as such, but it must also be made public (Meyersohn 599). Beanie Babies remained more or less dormant for a few years after their introduction in 1993 until word of mouth, including online chatter, birthed the fad of "Beanie Babie Mania" in 1997, the same year McDonald's Teenie Beanie Babies promotion emerged. By comparison, Pokémon, supported by its fully developed video games, cartoons, and cards, took just half the time—two years—to move from new product to "Pokémania" fad, the height of which can be marked by Burger King's 1999 promotion. The apex of a fad can be measured a number of ways: through sales of fad items, fan attendance at conventions, social media engagement, among other metrics. Because fast food chains are able to not just sell fad items, but alter their layouts and experiences through in-store events and displays and advertising-based hype, they, too, act as one of these metrics by which one may gauge the height of a fad, with one caveat: the promotion in question should be the initial wave.

While Meyersohn and Katz state that fads, unlike social movements, generally do not "leave stable organizations in their wake," which, I would add, is a good thing: society should lend more permanence to institutions built around, say, Civil Rights than Beanie

Free with Every Kids' Meal

Babies (594). Fast food chains tend to enter into contracts that keep promoting fads even after interest in the craze has dissolved. Both Beanie Babies at McDonald's and Pokémon at Burger King had further waves of toys, none of which garnered anywhere near the same amount of popularity. By the time those promotions emerged, their parent fads had simmered, leaving only the die-hard fans to chase after them. It is these core fans that, as Meyerson notes, "operate" the fad and maintain it past its peak, using the same infrastructure to communicate about the craze items. In this way, fast food chains become part of that infrastructure. They facilitate communication among fans by being public spaces that disperse fad and former fad tokens to those who congregate either in restaurants, online spaces, or conventions to engage with this material culture. It was easy for a non-fan to get swept up in the 1997 Teenie Beanie Baby promotion at McDonald's. After all, the fad was on the news, in newspapers, online, and spreading via word-of-mouth. But McDonald's did nine subsequent Teenie Beanie Babies promotions, none of which received the hype that the original got. Therefore, one has to think that those eagerly consuming the 2009 Teenie Beanie Babies plushes were devotees of the brand.

Or, they were devoted to Happy Meal toys. According to the scholarship around fads used above, kids' meal toys cannot, in and of themselves, be a fad. They are not named as such, they did not go through a quick initial period of popularity followed by a fizzle, and, due to the long history of toy-with-food promotions, they were not "strikingly new." But they do have their collector base. That base, though, typically functions as any other toy collector community would. They chase rare items across multiple properties, look to obtain international exclusives, find promotions of nostalgic or otherwise personal interest, and buy and sell items over long swaths of time. Those base collectors items that are kids' meal toys sometimes integrate into fads, benefiting from their success sometimes at the price of continuing to push the craze past its prime. This adds to scholarship around fads as it shows how they impact items that, like kids' meal toys, maintain a much more steady, consistent presence in material culture.

Because kids' meal toys have this stability built upon afford-ability, convenience, and availability, they do not just sell consum-ers a toy, but admission into a de facto society of trendy consumers. In October 2022, McDonald's offered an "adult" Happy Meal in conjunction with style brand Cactus Plant Flea Market, classified as such because it featured premiums that appealed to older cus-tomers. The toys included were non-articulated figurines of Ham-burglar, Birdie, Grimace, and the Cactus Plant Flea Market mascot, all in the company's signature primitive style with each character bearing four eyes instead of two. The collectibles were offered with a Big Mac or 10-piece Chicken McNuggets, as opposed to the more kid-friendly smaller portions of the typical Happy Meal. The Cac-tus Plant Flea Market figurines were offered in opaque white bags, preventing the item from being seen prior to opening. There were no action features associated with these figurines. They were, in the words of one toy designer I spoke with, "not fun." However, I contend that fun wasn't what McDonald's was selling in the first place, here. Given that Cactus Plant Flea Market routinely sells fashion wear whose price point is out of reach for many aside from the celebrities who have been spotted in their exclusive clothing, these McDonald's collectibles sold access. Through these meals, which were still priced higher than most menu items, but signifi-cantly less than most other Cactus Plant Flea Market products, adults could purchase entrance into a fad that included only a select number of wealthy consumers. The Cactus Plant Flea Mar-ket toys also offer a window into how social media impacts fads, as the brand's online footprint was massive within a niche commu-nity prior to the McDonald's collaboration, but a certain subset of followers could only truly participate at a distance, watching celeb-rity, company, or influencer videos on platforms like TikTok and Instagram. After the fast food toys emerged, so did a new stream of videos that "unboxed" or opened the toys live for viewers, a popu-lar form of content creation across social media. In the case of the "adult" Happy Meal, the toy itself almost didn't matter, and, indeed, it was difficult to find enthusiasm for the figurines across McDon-ald's social media groups at the time; the product moved based on novelty and access to a stratosphere of 21st-century fad-dom that initially was financially out-of-reach. At the time of the Teenie Beanie Babies promotion, the Cactus Plant Flea Market sensation would have been next to impossible. Pre-social media, fad items had to be within reach of at least the middle class in order to ensure the "quick spread" that defines them. TikTok, Instagram, Facebook, and Twitter brought with them a sort of fad virtual participation in which consumers could feel a part of a fad by scrolling through hundreds of influencer and celebrity videos surrounding the craze. While the fad products themselves remain desirable, they can take longer to get into consumers' homes, as their phones have already introduced a constant, fast stream of content that both scratches and exacerbates the itch for the items themselves. Whereas once upon a time it was difficult for the spread of a fad to move quicker than its items themselves, social media can run circles around that speed, making the physical items truly secondary to the online buzz surrounding them.

While the kids' meal toy genre is not a fad, I posit that they are directly linked to a modern trend that has been accelerated by online spaces. So-called "blind boxes" or "unboxing toys" are small collectibles that come inside a box that reveals nothing about the contents inside. The boxes may show consumers the range of possible toys, but the specific item within remains hidden—keeping buyers "blind" to the collectible—until opened. In many cases, even after the owner opens the box (or, in some cases, opaque plastic bag), the toy remains obscured by another layer of bagging or cardboard. Collectors chase specific rare toys, though, when pulls are truly randomized, outcomes are so luck-of-the-draw that even the most casual of consumers could stumble into a 1-in-24, 1-in-48, or even 1-in-100 item. These blind boxes are priced below the MSRP of many mainline toys, and can typically be found by the registers in comic book and collectible shops, making them ideal impulse buys. In fact, this is exactly how I have wound up with a small but mighty collection of these toys over the years. I am not what one might call a fan of them. The thought of spending ten dollars on a toy I cannot even see, and may already have, seems excessively frivolous, but

I also have not always resisted the siren's song of potentially getting the rare Captain Picard vinyl figurine (in his shore leave attire!) from Titans Vinyl Figures' *Star Trek: The Next Generation* "Make It So Collection." The odds of getting that toy were one in forty, making it the hardest of the wave to find, and, when I pulled it on a particularly early purchase, the rush of feeling like, somehow, there was a council of the Rare Toy Gods decreeing that I, the most nonchalant of blind box buyers, should have this scarce piece hooked me. I bought several more before getting fed up with the repeated doubles and then turning to eBay to buy the already-unboxed characters I really wanted. In this way, it is helpful that the blind box market contains myriad waves across many properties for whom there is constantly new product. Consumers who may feel they have depleted one particular line—either successfully pulling all the characters they desired, or losing interest after too many failed attempts at this—generally have several others they can choose from as a "fresh start." While some blind boxes are more popular than others, the many YouTube accounts devoted to the process of unboxing these items demonstrates fervent interest in the overall category. The channel Lorien's Toy Box has roughly 1,300 videos of just blind box openings and has drawn a following of approximately 112,000 subscribers. The channel Paul & Shannon's Toy Reviews features over 5,000 videos of the same, and has a base of 1.86 million subscribers. Rhia Official's account is a bit more varied, but is still founded on unboxing videos, and has a following of 9.9 million subscribers.* And all of this just scratches the surface of blind box social media influencing on one particular platform. Still, it suggests significant digital participation in this fad—which, itself, has perhaps been around long enough to graduate out of fad-dom and into something with greater cultural staying power.

I illustrate, in-depth, the footprint of the blind box trend so as to present this as a way the kids' meal toy play pattern has moved

---

*Derek Johnson notes, "Already by 2014, CNN reported that the number of unboxing videos on YouTube had increased 871 percent in four years, with users having produced 6.5 years of footage in the previous year alone" (Johnson 169).

beyond fast food chains and into this new realm of popular collectible consumption. Blind box collectors are essentially doing the same thing many kids' meal consumers do, except without the food. Both pay to receive a toy "blind," or unseen and unchosen by themselves, and derive pleasure from simply finding out which item they were given. In both cases, these toys are smaller and cheaper than typical action figures and dolls found on store shelves. Both toys come surrounded by material—lists, package art, supporting posters and displays—that announce all of the possible items that might be collected from this particular promotion. Finally, kids' meal toys and blind boxes both rapidly release their waves, moving quickly, compared to their pricier alternatives, so that collectors can speed off to their next hunt without losing interest in the format. Specific examples of kids' meal commercials that include unboxing elements similar to those of today's YouTube videos include the 1991 McDonald's *Back to the Future* Happy Meal ("X-Ray Mode" shows a hand going into the box to pull out a specific toy in the ad), the 1995 Halloween McDonaldland Tapes and Toys Happy Meal (in which kids remove a toy from their food container), and the 1994 McDonald's Epcot '94 Adventures Happy Meal (which mimics the modern unboxing video almost exactly). Given all of these similarities, and the fact that the blind box trend in the United States took off after a long-established tradition of similar toy consumption through kids' meals, it would not be unreasonable to read kids' meal toys as a launchpad for this fad.

The market also bears this connection out. YuMe Toys is a major producer of, among other items, blind boxes. They have created unboxing toys for the Batman, Harry Potter, and Stranger Things licenses. In 2020, I toured the YuMe booth at Toy Fair, and their Batman offerings specifically caught my eye. These blind boxes allowed consumers to receive one randomized Batmobile and Batman figurine from across the entire span of the superhero's massive omnibus. I noticed that the way in which the Batmobiles separated—horizontally dividing top from bottom—such that the little Batman could be secured inside had a simplicity and playfulness that reminded me of kids' meal toys, specifically the way McDonald's 1992 Super

Looney Tunes Happy Meal promoted figurines of Bugs Bunny and the gang that could snap into plastic superhero costumes that came apart vertically, back-and-front, into halves. It was then that the representative giving me the tour told me about YuMe's origins as an international manufacturer of kids' meal toys. This made it clear to me that the design strategies they employed as kids' meal toy producers directly led to their success as blind box collectible makers. Kids' meal toys often craft small-scale figurines that speak to bigger toy lines but stand out in that they have one or two novel play features (the snap-on costumes, the water-squirting Pokémon) thrown in. YuMe understood this from experience, and aligned their Batman line with gimmicks frequently seen in kids' meal toys in order to produce blind boxes that both latched onto a broader trend and presented consumers with a familiar, intuitive play pattern.

This means that kids' meal toys interact with fads in two primary ways: they translate fad items into a format that would traditionally fit with the convention of fast food promotions, and they more generally utilize styles, features, and strategies that have greatly informed the current blind box craze. Therefore, kids' meal toys, while perhaps better seen as a more permanent category of toy overall, sit on the border between fad and fixity. They offer cheap, easy, available access to fads that are sometimes financially, locationally, and/or materially out of reach. This becomes most evident when the kids' meal promotion has latched onto a fad that has spread both broadly and quickly across the most cutting-edge channels of its time (eBay in the 1990s, TikTok and other social media in 2023). While these fad kids' meal promotions sell quickly they emerge, the kids' meal toy does not disappear when the fad does, it simply moves on to a different property, which is not a fad on the level of its predecessor. Because kids' meals also contain the communal, survival experience of eating, their entire purpose does not rest upon a fad. They can steadily simmer on non-fad toys, cheaply made and received as a charming bonus, while still performing their role as affordable, quick meals exceptionally well (health concerns perhaps aside). Kids' meals are but one portion of a fast food chain's menu, similar to the way the toy aisle is just one part of a big box store. Just like people will always go to Target for, say, patio furniture, consumers will always go to a McDonald's for a Big Mac. If the Target happens to have the latest trend toy, or if the McDonald's offers a fad promotion, the increased interest will naturally help the company's bottom line, but, in both cases, corporate survival is not solely staked on the fad. In this way, kids' meal toys can respond to, and participate in, fads without attaching their staying power to them.

CHAPTER 8

Finding McDonaldland

Kids' Meal Toys as Take-Home Props
of (Appropriated) Immersive Fast Food Theater

> "When smells of vodka and despair permeate absolutely
> everything, also imagine, just for example, just going off
> the top of my head here, that you spent the last three
> months trapped in a house with the woman of your
> dreams and her husband; you've been sleeping all day and
> sleeping all night; the work around the farm is beginning
> to pile up, and you're starting to wonder if your entire life
> is based on a lie. Now open your eyes! Welcome home."
> —Three Day Hangover's *Drunkle Vanya*, an immersive,
> booze-fueled version of Chekhov's *Uncle Vanya*

> "NARRATOR: Sure, you've got places to go, people to see,
>   but—why not pop over to Burger King and find out
>   how to join the Kids Club?
> "IQ: Details are specified in the Kids Club newsletter.
> "NARRATOR: You can find out how to get a membership
>   card, stickers, autographed pictures....
> "JAWS: And have lots of fun, non-stop!
> "KID-VID: With, or without your pop!"
>   —1989 Burger King Kids Club commercial

Previously, I noted Jaap van Ginnekin's analysis of the branded
lapel pin to describe how an object from a specific event—the French
Open, in the case of these pins—becomes a fad when it commemo-
rates one's attendance and begins to act as shorthand between others who had been there, too. One is not generally inclined to consider
eating at a fast food chain an "event" in the way the French Open is,
yet kids' meal toys do inherently signify a presence in one of these

restaurants, or at least an awareness of them. Kids' meal toys are exclusive to fast food chains, and, unless one buys them on the secondary market, a consumer would need to engage with the store in some way, whether in-restaurant, via the drive-thru, or delivery. Thus, for many who own kids' meal toys, these objects do signify that their collectors had "been there," which leads me to consider what the "there" actually is. It is not the French Open, but a scripted "production" does take place. Corporate language guides what cashiers say. A pre-built assembly line produces the food. Displays and advertisements promote current items, including kids' meal toys. In some cases, mascots make in-store appearances, and restaurants alter their decorations, at times radically, to plunge guests into the world in which the chain's products are not a commodity to be sold, but a naturally-occurring element of immersion, which, at best, transports one's senses into fantasy, or, at worst, uses rudimentary narrative to separate the customer from their money, thus discreetly serving Capitalist profit-making.

In this way, fast food restaurants appropriate the tools of theater in order to create novel experiences for guests, excitement for services offered, and spontaneous up-sells that help the corporate bottom line, as this chapter demonstrates. The "play" put on by fast food chains is not an artistic endeavor, though artistry is involved, but it is the "event" one participates in when they pass through a restaurant's doors. If one reads these theatrical elements as contributing to a fast food "event," then the kids' meal toy becomes a token of the experience, meant to be carried away by collectors young, and, at times, old, into their respective communities, branded with where they had been, advertising the space shared with them, and, ideally, its openness to further new audiences. Because this event comes with multiple take-away items—the toys, the food, the drinks—it cannot be a play that is watched from a distance. Instead, it is a sort of corporate immersive theater whose products are the point, but still disguised, sometimes quite cleverly, by an environment constructed around them.

By accessing immersive theater scholarship, one can see both how kids' meal toys help create this environment, and add to the

This 1968 "Ronald McDonald Theatre" box held a large meal and could be converted into a cardboard puppet theatre, materially representing an early marriage of the stage and fast food.

corporatization of the craft in a way that betrays the spirit of the theatrical style. Immersive theater, in the purest sense of the term, defines productions where the audience experiences elements of the play's emotional core such that they feel plunged into the world that, otherwise, might live at a distance onstage. A common example is Punchdrunk's *Sleep No More*, in which Shakespeare's notorious Scottish play is told as an immersive noir in which the audience drifts through a hotel, interacting with actors, props, and each other along the way. This immerses the show's audience in the textures of the narrative's fantasy world in order to create fuller escapism and allow for more individualized experiences within a range permitted by the production. But immersive theater does not always have to involve the full takeover of a building, complete with destination rooms with takeaway items and solo exploration. Production company Three Day Hangover just needs a room and a few drinks for its immersive editions of classics. Their November 2015 production of *Tartuffe* had actors leading audience members to different parts of a room, interacting with different scenes, and their beverages of choice, along the way. It was clearly of a lower budget than *Sleep No More*, but was just as successful at immersing the audience in its world through participation, movement, and connection. Through these core components, immersive theater works on a large- or small-scale, so long as its audience becomes involved with the production's structured-yet-open fantasy world.

Theater scholars argue that the novelty of recent immersive plays have led to others attempting to capitalize on the term. In the abstract to "The Post-Immersive Manifesto," Jorge Lopez Ramos, et al., state, "Over the past decade, 'immersive' has arguably been one of the most overused terms to describe theatre productions that aim to involve audiences in unconventional ways. With the mainstream success of specific 'immersive' productions, this trend goes beyond the theatre and arts industry" (Lopez 1). As of 2023, the aforementioned *Sleep No More* continues to draw crowds, as it did when it opened in its current form in 2009. "The Post-Immersive Manifesto," being published in 2020, refers to the catalyzing effect this show had on others like it "over the past decade," so much so that the very word "immersive" became a sort of code for new, individualized theater that could easily be made profitable. It is this promise of money that propelled the term into spaces beyond the arts, as Lopez indicates. Recent activity in the fast food world confirms this. In May of 2023, Burger King announced its "Burger King X Spider-Verse Immersive Restaurants" that invited guests to "immerse themselves in the Spider-Verse" in anticipation of the film *Spider-Man: Across the Spider-Verse* (Average Socialite). To this end, select stores were redecorated, special paper crowns were printed to represent a fusion between the Burger King brand and Spider-Man's mask, a new Whopper was created, and the chain produced toys that were offered in kids' meals between May and June that duplicated action scenes from the movie in miniature. The immersive experience, here, is the restaurant. The exterior featured the chaotic blues and reds that defined the animation style of the film. "Graffiti" of Spider-Man symbols adorned the windows. The store entrance was remade into a sort of portal that led to a busy interior of the comic book hero bounding across walls. The exclusive Whopper was similar to the conventional one, but it was colored red, one of the main colors of Spider-Man's suit. While the company defined all of this as equivalent to an "immersive" experience, one imagines it would leave the theater scholar unfulfilled.

At their core, fast food chains' "immersive" experiences omit the emotional centers vital to immersive theater in order to front-load the products being sold. In 2019, McDonald's advertised their Summer Festival Tour, an event that typically offers McFlurry's to attendees, as an "immersive McNuggets experience," by which the company meant there would be "a McNuggets maze, AR McNuggets lenses, and a 360[-degree] spinning photo experience" ("McDonald's announces"). The point of this roll-out was to shift the Summer Festival Tour away from the McFlurry and toward the sale of McNuggets. There is hardly room for the kind of catharsis embraced by immersive theater in that, and there was not meant to be. McDonald's Senior Brand Manager Hannah Pain said, "Younger festival goers cherish experiences over material things, so immersive activation like the McNuggets Sharebox experience is sure to drive brand love for McDonald's" ("McDonald's announces"). To decode that: Pain is essentially suggesting that today's generations do not need physical take-aways from events as much as they want memorable, or Instagrammable, experiences, and the more "immersive" those experiences are—or, the more they surround all senses—the more unforgettable they will be. Admittedly, this perspective saddens the part of me that finds so much joy in the physical promotion item; however, this notion is not new.

In 1998, B. Joseph Pine II and James H. Gilmore wrote the influential article "Welcome to the Experience Economy" for the Harvard Business Review. Their thesis, which later became a larger book, argued that the younger generation of the time, Millennials, found greater value in experiences than products offered by brands. In this article, which later became a larger book, they stated, "Today we can identify and describe this fourth economic offering because consumers unquestionably desire experiences, and more businesses are responding by explicitly designing and promoting them" (Pine II). Hannah Pain, above, basically took this late-'90s idea and placed it onto the Generation Z and Generation Alpha crowds that McDonald's hoped to attract in their 2019 Summer Festival Tour. To her, the song remains the same as when Pine II and Gilmore originally sang it: the experience *is* the product. While Pine II and Gilmore could not have foreseen the seduction of social media virality (or the possibility thereof), they did highlight the fact that experiences, unlike physical promotional items, are individual; they are unique and internal to each person who immerses in them (the authors even use a "theatrical play" as an example of this). As Percival Hornak notes in his dissertation on immersive theater, Pine II and Gilmore demonstrate that the Experience Economy begins with commodity. In other words, a company starts with a product they want to sell. To distinguish their brand from others, companies will next stress the service they offer as a way to stand out from their competition. From this "Service Market" springs the "Experience Market with theatrical underpinnings" (Pine II). The Experience Market, which drives the Experience Economy, includes everything that surrounds the purchase of a product, from company interaction, to design of stores, to sights and smells absorbed while browsing, to, now, virtual engagement with social media and other online content.

The Experience Market opens the door, therefore, for additional costs to be charged to consumers for their participation. Most simply, this can be seen through the service plans commonly sold in big box stores in order to guarantee a product purchased. For example, Target seems intent on selling me a roughly $4.00 "service plan" whenever I buy a $20 action figure, though why a solid block of plastic should ever need service I cannot comprehend. More extravagantly, such cost takes the form of admission into brand events, a price that, once, primarily took the form of money, but, now more than ever, could be calculated in terms of digital assets instead. Social media influencers are routinely shipped "experiences" via elaborately designed boxes to be opened live in front of their followings.

Chapter 8. Finding McDonaldland

When McDonald's promoted their 2019 40th Anniversary Happy Meal, toys were sent to influencers like Instagram's @yeahfoodbeer, who made engaging content unwrapping each one. Beyond this, influencers and the general public are sometimes invited to ticketed events with the expectation that similar posts will be made. Finally, a modern Experience Market price can simply be paid through the transmission of data. In 2023, McDonald's offered free french fries for National French Fries Day (July 14), but only if one downloaded the company's app. Apps create a specific experience for consumers virtually on their devices, but only after a certain amount of personal data is input into them upon sign-up. After that, data can be collected on eating habits and other purchases as customers continue to interact, and, as Forbes noted in 2017, McDonald's did just that. This data becomes a commodity for the company that collects it, and the exchanged service or good, typically a far less valuable item like french fries, allows the consumer to feel as though they have, in some way, found a "hack" or workaround to paying the full cash price that those not as in-the-know regarding the app must fork over.

With such profit in the virtual realm, fast food giants have every reason to house their Experience Markets inside apps and digital programming. Kids' meal toys offer invitations to this sort of engagement by containing QR codes that, when scanned, bring consumers to an active virtual experience such as a game or online animated character. In 2020, for instance, McDonald's issued the Mickey & Minnie's Runaway Railway Happy Meal, in which QR codes accompanied small toys of the Disney characters enjoying various theme park rides. One was meant to scan the code within the McDonald's app in order to access digital play features and exclusive character content intended to further immerse users in the world of Disney. However, in this case, consumers found that the QR codes, when scanned outside the McDonald's app, led to pages with error messages, or, for some, search results for staple guns (Norris).* This prompted McDonald's to pause the distribution of these toys such that the QR code cards could

---

*An error one might love if reading fast food toys through the lens of Legacy Russell's Glitch Theory, perhaps!

be removed from circulation. This promotion highlights the way in which these Happy Meal toys were intended, chiefly, not to provide an open door into a virtual play space, but to encourage downloads of McDonald's data-collecting app so as to guarantee the immersive experience aided by online games offered its parent company a substantial digital commodity in return. Had this not been the governing desire, the QR codes would have worked via any app that could read them, as that would be the most direct route to the linked Disney games. While this one example shows an ultimately fumbled final act, plenty of other kids' meal toys, like McDonald's Squishmallows promotion, are accompanied by much more successful QR codes that transform the toy premium from the takeaway item to a conduit for further Experience Economy immersion for the consumer and valuable data collection for the corporation.

Though conversations around app-based data collection, Experience Economies, and immersion in virtual experiences shrink the role of the kids' meal toy such that it becomes primarily a way to support these broader online efforts, they are also very new. However, this does not mean fast food chains' investment in immersive experiences is limited to today. In fact, before this prioritization of "experiences over material things," physical takeaway items scaffolded and represented the immersive event of fast food restaurant dining in far more crucial ways. In studying McDonald's restaurant events of the 1970s, '80s, and '90s, one sees local franchises as reliant on corporate products to immerse consumers not just in a corporate construct, but their own communities. During these decades, McDonaldland was a key component of McDonald's immersion. "McDonaldland" describes the fictional place in which McDonald's corporate mascots like Birdie, Grimace, Hamburglar, Mayor McCheese, Officer Big Mac, the Gobb'lins (later the Fry Kids), and, of course, Ronald McDonald reside. VHS tape films, video games, conventions, numerous products available both in restaurants, catalogs, and department stores like Sears (via the "McKids" brand), comic strips, Happy Meal toys, and a global ad campaign transported McDonald's guests to McDonaldland, where menu items played a central role. Hamburglar stole hamburgers, Officer Big Mac bore the name of McDonald's signature sandwich, Chicken McNuggets came alive, Grimace hoarded shakes, Birdie (the Early Bird) plugged breakfast, and Ronald McDonald was the face of the Happy Meal. This entire world was built so that consumers could feel that eating at McDonald's represented their immersion in a bigger, theatrical fantasy world that elevated the significance of menu items beyond their practical functions. The result of this was an experience that embedded in the nostalgia of many of McDonaldland's youngest guests, moving the consumption of a hamburger from the forgettable to the remarkable, as it was tied to interactions with a world beyond the mundane, where yellow-clad clowns and purple monsters romped through sunny fields of talking food. At the turn of the millennium, McDonald's began phasing out the emphasis on McDonaldland, removing many characters from consistent appearances on TV and in promotional items. As of 2023, a few of those personalities placed on the backburner have begun to reemerge, most notably Grimace, whose "birthday" was celebrated by a special, berry-flavored shake. Perhaps there is no better proof of McDonaldland's induction into nostalgia than the fact that, as news radio station 1010Wins reported on July 27, 2023, the Grimace Birthday shake went viral on TikTok, and contributed to a 94 percent rise in sales for the chain compared to the same period in the previous year (*1010Wins...*). Because the world of McDonaldland was so immersive, and then virtually decimated in the early 2000s, the slow roll-out of its characters' reappearances evoke memories in many of when this unique, exclusive world consumed them. And it wasn't just that McDonaldland invited guests to buy McDonald's products; McDonaldland characters invested in consumers' lives, too.

Before apps made immersion virtual, McDonald's restaurants regularly held in-store visits from McDonaldland mascots that established a symbiotic relationship between guest and character. Through meet-and-greets and coupon giveaways, the McDonaldland live appearances got guests to further their relationship with the fast food chain. However, as seen through McDonald's trayliners of the 1970s, '80s, and '90s, these visits were also used to promote community events. One June 1992 trayliner expresses this relationship particularly well. This trayliner, which could be found on trays handed to guests for dine-in eating, is hyper-local. On the bottom right corner of one side, it advertises specific McDonald's locations in the Milwaukee, Wisconsin, area. Above this is a "McDonald's Calendar of Community Fun." It is a conventional calendar, except many of the dates are filled in with various local happenings. For example, the June 15 slot reminds guests of an American Legion meeting at 7:30 p.m. Other dates advertise events more relevant to younger consumers, like June 19th's "South Shore YMCA Teen Dance" notice. These all appear alongside McDonald's-specific action items like June 16th's request that kids call the "Ronald McDonald Hotlines.... For a message from Ronald McDonald" ("McDonald's Calendar of Community Fun"). Trayliners like this paint a specific picture of McDonald's role in its guests' lives: as a corporation, they want McDonald's and McDonaldland to exist not only in-store but also within consumers' day-to-day routines. By putting seemingly unrelated community events next to prompts to engage further with McDonaldland, McDonald's implicitly suggests that these are one in the same. This is useful for McDonald's because they presumably understand that we are typically never more immersed than when we are performing our day-to-day routines. If the theater of McDonaldland can make cameo appearances there, McDonald's immersion, and therefore the company's built-in purchasing suggestions, will be nearly constant. Where immersive theater productions like *Sleep No More* end at the exits of the buildings they are performed in, McDonald's tries to extend the immersion past any boundaries, allowing it to fluidly exist in the "real" worlds of consumers.

The reverse side of the June 1992 trayliner furthers this synthesis cleverly. It features a reworking of The Lovin' Spoonful's song, "Do You Believe in Magic?" The tune clearly remains the same, but it includes lines like, "You'll always have a friend wearing big red shoes" in place of the original's hints at how the infectious joy of music might lead to a successful date. Below the music, whose lyrics and notes are both written out, one sees a child and Ronald McDonald playing the song on an Golden Arches–shaped piano. Surrounding them are additional children and McDonaldland mascots Birdie, Grimace, the Fry Kids, McNuggets, and anthropomorphic hamburgers. This suggests that there is no boundary between the fantastical characters of McDonaldland and the real-world children that would likely see an illustration like this. Where one side of the trayliner presents a day-to-day look at how McDonald's supports (or invades) life, the other envisions one event where our everyday world bends such that McDonaldland exists within it.

But these promotions are, by necessity, transitory. The fast food served will be eaten, and guests will proceed with their days. Adults will go to work, and kids, especially prone to short attention spans, will go to school. Yesterday's lunch will become a detail faded from memory. Therefore, the physical Happy Meal toy takes on a special role. It, like van Ginnekin's lapel pins, represents the fact that its owner partook in not just the consumption of food, but the entire world that came with it, which was made immersive by in-store appearances by McDonaldland characters. As we know from the 1978–1979 *Chicago Tribune* Ronald McDonald comic strips, Ronald McDonald appearances were well-publicized and hyped. The July 22, 1979, strip ends with a panel of Ronald McDonald saying, "Ronald will be at the McDonald's at 724 Rollins Rd. in Roundlake Heights for the Grand Re-Opening, Saturday, July 28 at 1 and 5!" ("McDonaldland"). In fact, in-store appearance announcements for Ronald McDonald comprise the last panel 42 times, the far majority of strips published weekly for one year. This number even excludes the amount of final panels that did not announce in-store appearances, but did drive consumers to McDonald's by promoting other games and in-store events meant to craft a theatrical space beyond its food. By ending the comic strips in these ways, McDonald's created a synthesis of McDonaldland fantasy narrative, the first four panels, and concrete ways in which this world exists in that of the consumer, the final in-store announcement panel. Theoretically, one could read about Ronald's adventure with Uncle O'Grimacey on Sunday, and then ask him about it the following week at a given restaurant. While adults may not conventionally find this sort of interaction appealing, kids used to dissolving the border between fantasy and reality could immerse in exactly this manner. The in-store appearance announcements in the Ronald McDonald comic strips, though numerous, had a once-in-a-lifetime tone about them. The specificity of date, address, and time(s) made one feel that, if missed, Ronald McDonald might be absorbed back into McDonaldland forever, despite the fact that he would likely be appearing at another site the following week. McDonald's encouraged this type of blink-and-you'll-miss-it excitement through its calendars, which were also promoted in these '78-'79 comic strips, as well as given out on trayliners like the one discussed above. There, one had all the information needed to mark a store appearance, or remember an event, like the Ronald McDonald hotline notice from June 16, 1992. But all of these components—time, food, appearances—are temporary. They are meant to get consumers into the restaurants, but they cannot be the reminder that makes them come back. This is where the promotional item, like the Happy Meal toy, comes in. The Happy Meal toy acts as a souvenir and a reminder. It can signify not just lunch, but a trip to McDonaldland, in which perhaps one conversed with Ronald McDonald himself. Then, through that association, the toy is able to remind its owner of the immersion they experienced when the object was obtained, encouraging them to recreate the event, a task with which they will find McDonald's all too willing to assist via its repeated advertisements for more appearances, in-store games, prizes, and theatrics.

This interaction qualifies as what some call experiential theater. Experiential theater differs from conventional theater in that it asks its audience to experience their surroundings, as opposed to observing them. It is closer, and perhaps interchangeable with, immersive theater, but the term "experiential" side-steps the overuse of the term "immersive," which, as mentioned earlier, has become heavily broadened to the detriment of its specific meaning. Scholars have defined experiential theater inclusively, though, as not only a produced, intentional, theatrical endeavor but also a component of daily life. As William W. Lewis and Sean Bartley write in their *Experiential Theatres*,

> An experiential encounter might be something as seemingly simple as purchasing a warm morning beverage or playing with tactile artifacts that enhance the educational benefits of a science museum or something as complex as interfacing with the multiple ways a marketing campaign has designed connections between a narrative component of a film, a live theatrical event using augmented reality, and the packaging of a consumer toy based on a character from the film [Lewis 1].

Chapter 8. Finding McDonaldland

In other words, these *experiencers* go beyond the role of spectator in that they engage with an "encounter" up-close and with a number of their senses. "Purchasing a warm beverage" at, say, a McDonald's might include smelling and tasting the drink, as well as seeing the corporate logo on the cup, and perhaps noticing the unique advertising material for a current promotion, other customers playing a game, families partaking in an in-store character appearance, and other aspects unique to not just this chain, but the specific store location at which they have decided to stop. Furthermore, the "complex" experience may also occur within a McDonald's, as, for example, a child might interact with a McDonaldland Happy Meal toy, associating it with play, Ronald McDonald (who, again, may be just steps away from the experiencer), and the entire source text from which the object is derived. After the fact, the toy may translate nicely into an "artifact," or, more accurately, a memento of the experience. Here, too, it should be said that, while this chapter has largely centered around McDonaldland and the specific toys, services, and products generated to support McDonald's in-house fantasy realm, there is no reason the same significance could not be placed onto other kids' meal toys, so long as they are accompanied by some semblance of an experience that actualizes a textual narrative thought relegated to a screen or page.

But though this broad version of experiential theater can contain kids' meal toys and the experiences fast food chains build around them, the corporations who deploy such tactics do so to meet Capitalist ends, which, in many ways, omits some of the deeper qualities of experiential theater. Primarily, experiential theater aims to foster collaboration on a profound and intentional level, and the time and care put into this process would not necessarily serve a sector of business termed "*fast* food." As Lewis and Valerie Clayman Pye write in their *Experiential Theatres* chapter, "Frameworks for Making and Performing in Experiential Performance," "Nearly all the experiential theatre practitioners we have surveyed and interviewed argue for a greater emphasis on collaborative processes and interdisciplinary connections when developing their works" (Lewis and Bartley 25). This indicates that, while experiential theater can go beyond the traditional stage, it pushes for connection between creators and experiencers. Such connection, like that which occurs frequently in the experiential work of theatermaker and game designer Jessica Creane, is found at the bottom of a journey into social critique, planned chaos, personal interrogation, structured intermingling, and theatrical vulnerability on behalf of the maker. Lewis and Pye outline a three-step process for devising such work: "Think," "Make," "Check" (30). In the "Think" stage, creators conceive the broad strokes of their endeavor, with special attention paid to the "intended experience" of experiencers. The "Make" stage scaffolds the experience through the designers establishing the "rules" of the performance and attempting to account for "affordances," or ways in which individual experiencers might go outside those parameters. Finally, the "Check" phase tests aspects of the creation to discover whether or not their intended reception replicates in a live audience. Zooming out, one may see some similarity between these steps and the ways in which kids' meal toys and fast food chain experiences are brought to life. Toys and experiences are "thought," or conceived with play features and intended takeaways at the center of the work. They are then "made" through promotional material such as translites, store displays, and ads which tell future consumers how to experience the forthcoming products and/or events. And they are "checked" through test markets and small groups which tell corporate executives whether their intended experience comes through in practice. However, while this translation exists, experiential theatermakers may be given pause by the impersonal nature of it all. McDonald's does not, ultimately, want guests to "experience" their restaurants, make meaningful connections with others, or ask deep questions of their own existence; they want people to buy their offerings. That end goal is incompatible with much of the theory behind experiential theater. As such, one would much more accurately describe the fast food chain's relationship to experiential theater as appropriation, or a successful yet hollow application, than genuine investment.

This is because deeper connections form when participants linger in a story, exploring it on their own terms, which would slow down, catastrophically, the profit-making potential of fast food spaces. One sees this more meaningful bonding most vividly in video games, where maps are rendered with rigorous detail so that players can, as Jonathan Gray indicates, "dawdle in some spaces where a film charges" (Gray 191). In other words, video games allow users to learn more about a film's "world" through details they now have time to look at, handle, and appreciate. This lingering becomes educational, allowing players to sometimes learn answers to plot holes left unfilled by other media in the franchise. Gray and Henry Jenkins both use *The Matrix* as an example of a case where this sort of exploration happens, though they disagree slightly on its effect. For Gray, the video game *Enter the Matrix* is "a warning to transmedia and paratext developers" as playing it was too essential for one's understanding of the third franchise film, *Matrix Revolutions*. By holding so much knowledge of the franchise's world, it excluded from the full *Matrix* experience anyone who had not played the game. For Gray, it did not "allow audiences to explore a narrative," but rather "requir[ed] that they explore that world" (Gray 196). The distinction is important. Audiences who are allowed to explore a world are subject to lower stakes than those required to do so. If participation in all transmedia elements is mandatory to gaining a full understanding of the narrative, all who do not have the time or ability to absorb those many paratexts are boxed out of that level of appreciation. Jenkins, however, is a little kinder to *The Matrix*'s transmedial approach, saying, "Each step along the way has built upon what has come before, while offering new points of entry" (Jenkins 97). Even though Jenkins, too, sees this transmedia immersion as a stair step process, he finds that, if a paratext performs to the best of its medium, it can be a gateway into the narrative as well (98). So this raises the question of what a fast food promotion paratext can do at its best. While such promotions, such as kids' meals, can succeed financially for their parent corporations, this success necessitates a relatively shallow experience.

Jenkins and Gray both wrote about *The Matrix* before the release of its fourth film, *The Matrix Resurrections*. This is important, here, because *Resurrections* had a fast food promotion at Denny's restaurants. This campaign included no physical paratexts, instead being exclusively a feature of the chain's app. One could access the matrix by "jacking in" to the Denny's app which would, through "glitches," offer not must-know truths about the world of the films, but free and discounted menu items at the restaurants.* If one saw *Resurrections* without accessing the Denny's promotion, their experience would be unchanged. More importantly, though, if one ate at Denny's without engaging with the film promotion, they would not lose anything beyond perhaps a coupon. It is here where one sees why fast food "experiences" cannot be more profound. If one is, as Gray said, "required" to participate in a promotion in order to fully appreciate a chain's products, those outside the campaign would be less likely to buy those items, feeling excluded from a story so essential to their consumption. If, however, a chain engineered a promotion where one was "allowed" to explore a promotion or "immersive experience," but *not* doing so held no bearing on their enjoyment of the restaurant, there would be far less risk of losing money on those who did not immerse, while increasing the likelihood of gaining profit from those who did. To do this, such experiences must be relatively flimsy. One likely does know of the mascot Ronald McDonald, but, even if a consumer does not, buying a Big Mac will not depend on this knowledge. Similarly, though kids' meals attempt to incorporate products with wide appeal, one's lack of awareness of a particular promotion will not impact their enjoyment of the food, as they are not required to participate in a complex, immersive experience to get it.

Therefore, though a kids' meal toy can be a souvenir of an immersive/experiential "event" of sorts, that moment rarely gives the item its emotional weight. One of my students is a repeat experiencer of the immersive play *Sleep No More*. She has collected jars of screws, bolts, and other small items from the set of the show across all of her visits (this is permitted by the production). Showing me photos of

---

*Russell's idea, presented in Chapter 5, that the glitch provides opportunities to thrive outside a system is truly made literal here, as these (intentional) glitches sent customers bonus coupons— not deep, personal growth, but perhaps the best a Denny's could do.

the containers, she spoke of each with great reverence, evoking specific emotions felt during the various evenings she spent immersed in the world. Rarely when interviewing kids' meal toy collectors do I come across the same phenomenon. Their prized kids' meal toys do elicit strong feelings and deep connections, but usually not in relation to an in-store event experienced when receiving the object. Far more typical are memories linked to the toy's role in the owner's life after they had left the restaurant and began to incorporate the item into their imaginary play space. Though, as the long list of in-store Ronald McDonald appearances suggests, live events and immersive worlds were built by fast food corporations to an extent, they are not, in my experience, significantly tied to the souvenir objects experiencers take home with them. This may be linked to the ways in which corporate immersive experiences strip away the intentionality, connection, and emotional truth finding so central to the theater practitioners mentioned in this chapter, as preserving them is not essential to achieving the desired financial end fast food chains seek. Remarkably, however, kids' meal toy owners still find ways of storing these theatrical elements in their most prized items through cathartic play, fan communities, and emotionally resonant collecting. In this way, the true experiential theater is crafted not by the corporations who spend high dollar amounts to construct immersive stores, but by guests who, through little to no monetary expenditure of their own, imbue the physical takeaway objects from those events with their own emotional selves.

Conclusion

Completing the Collection

This book began as an exploration of kids' meal toy pasts. By reaching far, perhaps absurdly far, back into the realm of ancient food "giveaways," such as they were, I aim to describe cultures that have, in some ways, always been fascinated by objects that can prolong the by-definition temporary experience of eating. The coin in the *vasilopita*, the *fève*, the cookie's fortune, and other such food-encased surprises use unexpected whimsy, scaffolded by tradition, to create an impact that extends farther than digestion, and into territory that is at times political, at times divine, and typically rooted in fate.

Modern kids' meal toys lower the stakes. They do not tend to tie themselves to images of, say, the Baby Jesus, nor do they portend future events. Instead, they replace representations of gods and kings with corporations telling mass market narratives. King Cakes and fortune cookies still exist, of course, but, now, they orbit paper or plastic toys that rotate monthly and beckon, to varying degrees of success, interested parties of all ages but especially the young, into buildings equipped with, once, playgrounds and party rooms, and, now, easy-access ordering screens to facilitate the collision of bodies and food. In the process of doing so, these fast food corporations embed directly into consumers' nostalgia, thereby divorcing the restaurants from their practical functions in order to plant them in a brainspace that houses, for many, constructs of childhood, "simpler times," and the joys of surprise toys. For those who identify with this, how fast food restaurants are today will never compare to the ways they used to be. If the *vasilopita* took the religious route to the deeply personal, fast food restaurants and their toys used corporate marketing to arrive at the same place. Once there, it becomes diffi-cult to see the kids' meal toy as anything other than "mine." The toy speaks to an aspect or aspects of one's own history, identity, and/or fandom, and its role as a cultural, mass produced object fades into erasure. We are, figuratively, the centers of our own universes, and the toys rattling around in our pockets are there with us, not in a Chinese factory, or a board room meeting, or a sculptor's table, or on the 10 o'clock news. But this is where cultural studies like this can come in. They both validate the private experiences of kids' meal toys and elucidate the broader ways in which the objects fit into larger leg-acies, cultures, contexts, and histories. Scholarship serves this role in the best and biggest of circumstances, as, after all, even Earth itself was once thought to be the center of the universe until, as Stephen Hawking reminds us, scientific scholarship located us in relation to the Sun, and then that star in relation to all the others, all while tak-ing nothing away from individual experiences of our shared planet. If large-scale scholarship like this can articulate truths about our place among the galaxies, small-scale work like my investigation into kids' meal toys can teach us both how to name the emotional effects such portable objects have on our unique selves and see past that individ-ual catharsis so as to appreciate a global phenomenon whose impacts are felt on exactly that scale.

But: lower stakes. The entire known universe will not depend on a book about kids' meal toys. Rather, studies like this, which both make theoretical connections between its subject and established lit-erary scholarship and collect academic work around fast food pre-miums, bring out of the shadows a product for which mystery is its biggest selling point. Kids' meal toys appear with meals as a surprise, a bonus that many child consumers anticipate only in the most gen-eral sense until they unbox their specific, secretly preordained item. When fast food toy advertising reaches these kids, they are in a par-ticularly vulnerable state, perhaps not even able to comprehend the persuasive nature of commercials (Calvert). Once in the restaurant, the toys they will be given seize upon another aspect of child psy-chology: an interest in collectability. As studies by Anna R. McAlis-ter and T. Bettina Cornwell find, all kids' meal toys are not created equal. Those that are distinctly collectible—in other words, clearly part of a unified set—succeed more often than toys that seem unconnected to one another (McAlister). This is perhaps best exemplified by the 1999 McDonald's *Inspector Gadget* Happy Meal, or the *Mystic Knights of Tir Na Nog* Happy Meal of that same year, which included with each character one piece of a larger dragon figure that could only be completed if all premiums were bought. Since then, this became a common practice in mainline action figures from companies like Hasbro, who include "Build-a-Figure" parts with their Marvel superheroes for the same purpose. If this type of collectability was potent enough to drive kids back to fast food restaurants for premiums whose source material they may not have been devoted fans of, there is no reason not to capitalize on it when there is a $20–$30 action figure purchase at stake. But as McAlister and Cornwell note, this type of draw does not necessarily happen consciously. Preschool age children were given options in their studies that ranged between no toy, a non-collectible toy, and a collectible toy. Most kids leaned toward the collectible choice even in cases where this toy was paired with less appealing "healthy" food, though they admit children leaned into this far more when they already owned a piece from the set in question—a testament to what the authors call the "motivational power that collectible toy premiums hold for some young children" (McAlister 203). While this might imply some kids made this decision in order to complete a set, others may not even be fully able to articulate why they chose as they did. I think it may be because children are at least a little aware of what Brian Sutton-Smith articulates when he states, "Whatever toys may have originally signified to their makers (in plastic or wood), when children play with them this signification is often destined to be destroyed" (Jenkins 145). As discussed in Chapter 6, when kids play with a toy, paratext becomes text. They have the power to transform their playthings into a limitless range of roles. When that object is one with whose source property they are unfamiliar, as in a kids' meal toy from a promotion to which they have no attachment, this transformative power becomes necessary as the desire is not to fit the toy into its parent narrative, but the child's. It is this kid-made narrative that takes priority in such play, and, at an age where so little power rests with them, such prioritization and transformation is empowering, novel, and, yes, *fun*. Add to this the hype created by toy packaging that prevents seeing which prize one garnered until a satisfactory amount of digging has occurred, and there exists an entire system that, top to bottom, uses mystery to influence the choices that ultimately sell kids' meals. However, as one grows, it is common for these cheap objects to be lost unless they are bestowed with some sort of special meaning by their owner. With that, it is easy to lose interest in solving their mystery, too. As new toys emerge and nostalgia brings old ones back into the fold, though, it is important to recognize that this system of production still thrives. Because of this, new ways of "reading" our kids' meal toys become ever more urgent.

Relieving the kids' meal toy of (some of) its cultural mystery also defangs its role as societal scapegoat. As noted in this book's introduction, by the controversy over the McDonald's 1992 *Batman Returns* Happy Meal, these toys can become saddled with cultural anxieties over child safety and appropriateness. When this happens, media coverage shifts away from the issue(s) raised and toward the sensationalism of these fears infiltrating toys that are, in the case of kids' meals, consumers' only options when ordering such a menu item from a fast food restaurant. Conversely, as the McDonald's 1992 Food Fundamentals Happy Meal demonstrates, these toys can also contain a corporation's interest in pushing back against parental concerns surrounding, for those specific toys, "child obesity." There, the toys became frontline soldiers in a public relations fight to plant McDonald's firmly on the side of health and nutrition. In both cases, the focus on the toys avoids the larger, more impactful questions. Demanding recalls of *Batman Returns* toys creates a far simpler task than addressing meaningful gun reform and mental health access. This simplicity is seductive. It convinces some that achieving the former is a step in the direction of making the latter redundant. Similarly, the creation of the Food Fundamentals line, with its embrace of the American Dietetic Association and active, "healthy" food figurines, imagines that as a solution to problems linked to economic disparity, racism, food deserts, and healthcare affordability. It can only fall short, but the already-mysterious nature of the kids' meal toy makes it the perfect breeding ground for such fallacy. If these toys are objects that appear as if out of the ether, then what they contain is equally vexing. With this unknown comes the possibility that they may contain something insidious. However, an actual understanding of the toy industry along with an acceptance of the spectrum of ways these premiums actually function within society sheds light on even the darkest crevasses of Food Fundamentals' Ruby the Apple's hollow body. By understanding kids' meal toys, one understands them as both (para)textual and vessel-like, capable of telling stories and absorbing one's own at the same time.

While many of the stories from kids' meal toys' past are still urgent, modern kids' meal toys have altered the narrative. There are fewer of them, currently. Fast food restaurants like Taco Bell, Roy Rogers, Pizza Hut, Subway, and others no longer offer kids' meal toys, with Taco Bell's former CEO Greg Creed saying the premiums "had an insignificant impact on system sales" ("Taco Bell Discontinues"). McDonald's and Burger King now use a sizable number of cardboard and paper-based toys in an effort to address environmental concerns, with the former chain aiming to make the switch more completely by 2025 (Russ). The overall impact of this may not be knowable for years after the move is fully made, but it is striking in its focus on the practical materials in, not the content of, fast food premiums. Where once one might have imagined such an "environmentally-conscious" toy being a plastic globe with a smiling face on it, here, the interest is more in sustainable, recycled materials regardless of what the item depicts. The current strategy seems more meaningful, though not without its naysayers. Social media sites are flooded with consumers announcing their disdain with the shift, largely rooting their protest in nostalgia. Reddit, for example, has many such posts, just one of which, titled, "McDonald's toys are paper and cardboard. I hate that my kids are getting ripped off." has 738 upvotes and 329 comments, mostly in agreement, including one boldly asserting, "Reddit. Where nostalgia comes to die" (u/AButtFacedMiscreant). All the while, McDonald's tests the waters of said nostalgia through sudden bursts of McDonaldland characters reemerging in new forms through "adult" Happy Meals—a concept that is notably not new, but is novel in the sense that it now is an attempt to sell childhood memories back to grown-ups—and Halloween buckets reminiscent of those issued in the 1980s and '90s. Thus, the current kids' meal toy market is in a state of flux: some of it is disappearing, some of it is changing, and some of it is reemerging. This is all the more reason to take seriously its origin story, as where the kids' meal toy came from, and what it culturally means, can inform where it goes.

That destination is likely not a single point. With apps controlling more and more of a restaurant's consumer experience, and "drive thru" and delivery orders making in-store kitsch less relevant, chains will likely prioritize connectivity to digital features. Kids' meal toys are currently gateways to this via the QR codes that frequently accompany them, such as the Squishmallows McDonald's promotion scheduled to hit the United States market in December of 2023. These small plush toys will contain paper QR codes that will direct users to online content that supports play. While "directed play," or the ways in which a toy leads its owner to engage with it, once concerned only a toy's physical features, modern playthings incorporate guidance to app- or web-based supplementals that create opportunities for engagement that demote the material object to URL delivery device and prioritize the transferal of data from the consumer to the corporation providing the latter with a stockpile of profit-driving information that was far more difficult to obtain thirty years prior. But with the QR-ification of recent kids' meal toys comes a new adult appeal that is less concerned with such a link to the digital realm.

Nostalgia currently invests adult consumers in kids' meal toys unlike any time before. This is, in many ways, the first era in which the kids' meal toy has become an object many adults the world over remember from their childhoods. Though available prior, these toys erupted in the 1980s and maintained growth into the '90s. The children of those years have now grown up, and many of them are searching for the characters and objects that they excavated from the bottom of a greasy bag so as to eat a meal with the otherworldly. These memories drove adult collectors to McDonald's restaurants as

Conclusion

they rolled out their 2022 Cactus Plant Flea Market "adult" Happy Meal, they are currently accelerating the Grimace renaissance ushered in by said fast food chain's birthday celebration thrown for the purple former shake-stealer, and they combine with other adult collector fandoms to reunite grown-ups with the experience of chasing prized restaurant-based figurines like the DC Super Heroes "keshi"-style toys available from Wendy's as of this writing. Because of the influence of adult collectors, restaurant strategy will likely evolve over time to best include this new demographic of customer. After all, 2023's *Barbie* film is currently Warner Brothers' highest-grossing global release of all time. All McDonald's needs to do to get a piece of that deep-fried apple pie is figure out how to unlock the core memories of adults who discovered Barbara Millicent Roberts in their 1990s Happy Meals, and of course figure out the contracts that might materialize that nostalgia in the present. This is, fundamentally, a question of what happens when an object designed to be hyper-temporary and disposable sticks around for long periods of time. Of all the "in-betweens" kids' meal toys live in—domestic and foreign, collectible and playable, text and paratext, educational and dubious—this is perhaps the most consequential: temporary and "permanent."

This binary-breaking aspect of kids' meal toys may be the most compelling reason to include them in interdisciplinary literary studies. As literary theory starts to consider the current meanings of texts such as memes, social media posts, viral videos, and other content that rotates monthly, daily, or hourly but still persists in some areas of the zeitgeist for longer, kids' meal toys, which have been essentially physical memes since the early 1970s, can provide an earlier framework for understanding and analyzing the socio-cultural engines that drive these more modern phenomena. When Richard Dawkins coined the term "meme" in 1976, he described a cultural element that exists both by *mimesis,* or reproduction, and copying akin to the behavior of a *gene.* This came to embody, among other components that comprise socio-political experiences the world over, texts that are born into the realm of disposability but, through Eline Zenner and Dirk Geeraerts call "diffusion through competition

200

and selection," manage to survive perhaps even past their shelf lives. Zenner and Geeraerts go on to reference the example of "Killroy was here," the World War II-era captioned illustration that subsequently popped up in disparate civilian places during the war and after it, finding success through its malleability, recognizability, and nostalgic appeal (Zenner 168). "Killroy was here" was a meme that one could both alter and still use to trigger a certain familiarity, as readers can simultaneously get the reference and be curious about the reason for its existence within a novel context. Kids' meal toys provide a corporate version of the same experience. Despite the fact that they either resemble well-known in-house mascots or popular licensed characters, it is still entirely possible to detach kids' meal toys from their textual parents, injecting the text of play into these paratexts. As stated in Chapter 6, my *Pocahontas* Governor Ratcliffe toy was easily separated from its source narrative, as I was unfamiliar with the film that gave it origin. This plus the toy's cheapness, both financially and compositionally, allowed me to use it as fodder for the materialization of my imagination, an empowering, playful process I craved. Ratcliffe was the villain in my stories, though not quite the same villain he is in his original media, but he could have just as well been a hero, a turncoat, a lover, or a sidekick. Each of those outcomes, and many more, is possible, just as "Killroy was here" could come to represent almost anything. Memes like these may have an original meaning, but they do not contain inherent meaning, leaving them open to play, the action perhaps better studied via the kids' meal toy "meme" than the two-dimensional ones. Maybe, then, in some ways, all of language is a kids' meal toy, arriving as if by surprise into our lives from a distribution engine that dispersed it long ago, surviving only by our consistent engagement with it, thriving in play, connecting bodies through the smallest of scales, disappearing, and yet, somehow, not.

Once again I remind myself, however: lower stakes. A book like this is unusual. It will not sit with the scores of price guides and collectors' catalogs that wonderfully populate bookshelves and Kickstarter campaigns. It cannot provide an inventory of specific kids' meal toys the way some website databases can. It does not seek to

Conclusion

assign monetary value or boast about a large collection in the vein of certain social media groups. As such, some may find such a project off-putting. Kids' meal toys are where many—and I also include myself in this group—go to forget books such as this, which analyze, deconstruct, and deepen aspects of the world used to escape it. It can be easy to feel that such escapism, especially that which is encased in the colorful plastic shell of a surprise toy, should not be prodded too much. It is for fun, and fun alone. However, I contend that this *is* fun. Meaning-making is yet another form of play. That it is word-based and connected to theory and history does not lessen the joy of interaction. Much like Richard Feynman describes the scientist's view of a flower, which appreciates the atoms and the molecules and the chemistry and biology of the plant, as an experience of joy and wonder, so is the literary plunge into the realm of kids' meal toys. The more such objects are invited into academia, the more exciting its scholarship becomes. In my classes, I primarily work with college freshmen who are reluctant writers. They want to be proficient at the craft, but are unsure sometimes of exactly how. When I use kids' meal toys in my classroom as writing prompts, their attitude toward writing shifts massively for the better. The same student who will turn in a blank piece of paper out of anxiety over how to begin their writing will instantly produce pages telling me, in-line with my writing prompt, the story of their toy, as they have invented it, and proceed to read their creation aloud in class. This type of enthusiasm is hard to come by, and the ways in which our playthings can still infect us with it into adulthood should be preserved and utilized. The same can be said for academic writing around kids' meal toys. Where some literary theory may be unapproachably dense, kids' meal toys can provide concrete, familiar gateways that make the scholarship more alluring. In other words, it is not because kids' meal toys are such esoteric objects that a project like this is undertaken, but because they are not.

Ultimately, I am articulating the kids' meal toy, an object of little articulation in every sense. Stuart Hall's "Articulated Theory" teaches us that the word "articulate" can mean "to utter, to speak forth, to be articulate," but it can also mean "a connection that can make unity of two different elements" (Gray 203). In toys, the latter definition of "articulate" applies most often, where one talks about the joint of an action figure, say, which unified an arm with a torso. In Toy Studies, we preserve that meaning, but add to it the act of connecting the object itself to the many scholarly theories that can deepen its significance and explain its cultural role. It has always struck me that we, as human beings, mass produced smaller versions of ourselves not only for worship but also for play. We have, in the kids' meal toy, given them out to children with the food that sustains them amidst a backdrop of Capitalist profit-making, artistic creation, and socio-political regulation, and this process, one that unites so many elements of life, alarmingly produces little discussion in the scholarsphere. I hope this book catalyzes more in this area, and helps begin to understand what compels us to turn to our food for objects of personal significance.

After all, we are still searching for the coin in our *vasilopitas*, the fortune in our cookies, the toy with our meals. Whether the kids' meal toy endures or not, our desire to be gifted an otherworldly surprise while participating in the mundane surely will. This much is clear through the media we create. Luke Skywalker works on a (moisture) farm until he learns of his heroic fate and potential abilities. Katniss Everdeen lives in poverty, going through the motions of life in Panem until her sister is chosen as a tribute, a selection she cannot allow. Joseph Campbell's Hero's Journey is exactly this: the ordinary turned adventurous through a "call to action." Kids' meal toys do not whisk anyone off on a Jedi adventure, but they also do a little bit. Through a surprise bonus item, an average lunch can be transformed into every bit of a Campbellian escapade. In 1995, when my Happy Meal treated me, a die-hard Power Rangers fan, to a kid-sized bracelet that resembled the communicators used in the then-new feature film, for which McDonald's was running a promotion, I ceased to be a child eating a hamburger. I was Jason, calling Zordon, summoning my Zords, and protecting the planet against the evil Ivan Ooze. My surroundings were a restaurant, but the stage in my mind was far more fantastical. No money was exchanged for this item—and my tiny mind could not process fully how it was paid for through

Conclusion

the price of the meal—so that left only one remaining logical option: it was bequeathed unto me the same way the communicators were given to the chosen Power Rangers by a mystical floating space head. While perhaps that reasoning does not follow as one ages, at the time, it was as real as the french fries in my greasy fingers. This experience afforded me the *feeling* of main character energy in my own fantasy narrative, if not the actual arc. But this collapse of the ordinary as induced by the sudden appearance of a bonus toy boon does not limit itself to childhood. Even now, finding a toy, kids' meal or otherwise, after months of searching and anticipation feels more like a divine discovery and less like a financial transaction. There is magic in these moments—magic that started with a kids' meal toy.

Supplement—Kids' Meal Toys
in the Classroom
A Lesson Plan

In addition to theoretical exploration, I have found practical, pedagogical use for kids' meal toys in the classroom. Whether attempting to hook reluctant writers into the craft, or honing the skills of seasoned playwrights, kids' meal toys incorporated into writing exercises have helped my students grow their creative processes and produce work of depth. In this brief supplement, I will provide a lesson outline, with reflections, that demonstrates one way that I have effectively used kids' meal toys to teach creative writing. My classes typically run between two and three hours, so the plan, as described, is built for that time frame. However, it could be broken up so as to fit a shorter period.

Kids' meal toys are ideal for classroom use because they can be cheaply acquired, and even offered to students as prizes upon completion of their writing. Substantial lots of kids' meal toys frequently appear on eBay within the 10–20 dollar range, and, as you will see from the parameters of my writing exercise, sourcing is aided by the fact that purchased premiums need not be from a specific promotion. In fact, the more varied and generic the toys are, the better. In-package toys work better than loose examples as a student-writer is able to reflect upon the process of freeing their plaything from its container, possibly providing more fodder for their writing. Additionally, given the Covid-19 pandemic, the sanitary nature of a fresh toy can reassure recipients that they are not handling a used and potentially germ-laced object. In this way, the fact that they may, should supply allow, keep their toy not only gives them "rewards" for writing but also reinforces the notion that these toys will not be re-used, again aligning with 2023 health initiatives. It would, therefore, be ideal for new-in-bag toys to be bought; however, loose and sanitized toys will also be sufficient.

Once I collected enough toys so that each of my students may have one, I plan for class. The objective of this writing exercise will be one of synthesis: I want my students to synthesize the "story" of a toy with their personal experiences, thereby creating a hybrid piece of writing. Typically, I'll start class with a discussion about favorite toys. I'll ask, "Which toys do you remember playing with as a child?" "What made that toy special?" "Where did that toy come from?" These questions get students flexing their storytelling muscles before really putting them to use. It also forms connections between students as two people who have never spoken to each other prior suddenly bond over playing with the same toy. This discussion can take between 10 and 20 minutes.

After that, I tell the students that we will first read a story by someone who likely had similar important experiences with her toys. To model this, I have used Sandra Cisneros' "Barbie-Q." Essentially a piece of flash fiction, the story combines a narrator's experience with poverty, and its impact on her access to toys, with the character of a Barbie doll who has been mutilated by a fire. Ultimately, the narrator accepts the doll despite its flaws, a lesson that can be extrapolated beyond the bounds of the plaything's melted plastic shell. While the full-size Barbie doll in the story is not a kids' meal toy, Barbie did appear in several McDonald's Happy Meal promotions, and, sometimes, those particular pieces are even among the options when students select their toys in the next part of the lesson. So, though Cisneros' work does not directly involve a kids' meal toy, it is connected enough to still be relevant to a lesson that uses them. Students read and annotate "Barbie-Q" in class, after which we discuss the story. While students list their observations about theme, character, tone, setting, and plot, I take notes on the board. Once the discussion is over, we take a moment to reflect on what is compiled. This portion of the lesson takes approximately 45 minutes to one hour.

A Lesson Plan

After this, I tell my students that we will now try our hands at this type of writing. In order to do so, though, we will need toys. It is then that I walk around my classroom, box of toys in hand, and have each student pick one at random. They invariably want to see their options, but, in true kids' meal toy fashion, it is kept a surprise. Occasionally, students will trade after seeing their toys, an action ignited automatically in both classrooms and restaurants.

Often enough, students will voice confusion over the toy they have received. Students that are recent immigrants, especially, may express concern that they are, understandably, not familiar with a character rooted in American pop culture. "That's okay," I say, "You will not have to write the story of that character as it is in the movie or TV show it came from. Instead, everyone will make up their own story based on whatever strikes them about their toy. If you know the source text of your toy, and want to reference it, you can, but, if you don't—even better. You'll get to create it from scratch!" This usually puts students at ease. It is then that I instruct students to open their toys and "tell me the story of that toy." As stated previously, there is a lot of room for creativity in this process. Virtually anything a student crafts inspired by their object will qualify. I give students between 10 to 15 minutes for this, emphasizing that this may not be enough time to fully flesh out their stories, but that is not the point. The point is to see what you might create in that amount of time, however rough.

After time is called, I have students switch gears. In the next 10–15 minutes, they are to "write the most important story from their lives." After saying this, I assure them that the story they choose does not have to be the absolute most important story that they have lived, as it may be too overwhelming to rank them this way, but just any story from their lives that has been meaningful. They write, and, as they do, I will typically observe them playing with their toys. One student, who I will refer to as Matt, got very into the play feature on his He-Man figurine from Sonic's April 2022 *He-Man and the Masters of the Universe* promotion. This worked to Matt's advantage, though, as the sword-slashing button became something of a fidget toy as he powered through intense emotions that went into his brief memoir. This evokes another quality of kids' meal toys: the ways in which they are stress relievers. With typically a single action feature, kids' meal toys ask consumers to play with them one particular way again and again. This repetition can have a calming effect, as it did for the student at the center of this reflection.

Once this time period is up, I give one final prompt: "Put the character you made in your first story in the personal plot you wrote for your second story. Is your character a hero who saves you? Are they an antagonist you fight? Are they totally aloof and unaware of your plight?" This is where the synthesis happens. Here, students do essentially what Cisneros did when she put a Barbie doll in the middle of her catharsis around poverty and beauty norms. Students will often ask if they might use their character in a way I did not cover in my opening questions, and of course they can. Any way in which their creativity pulls them is appropriate, here. This final prompt is given 10–15 minutes, just like the others.

If there is time, I will ask students if they would like to volunteer to share their third prompt responses. Often times, there are takers. Some abstain due to the personal nature of their work, which is, naturally, entirely acceptable. In these share-outs, I have heard such unique and well-developed stories that extend far past students' previous page counts. It is as if these stories poured out of them. When they interact with an object, their imaginations latch on to the limitless potential of the toy, and they find they cannot stop writing. It is in these sessions that I have heard students like the one I will refer to as Rachel, who described a warrior-type toy she received. She stated, in her story, that her toy had a masculine body, but, within it, was contained a woman. This woman was not terribly concerned with gender, but was frustrated by the fact that the man whose likeness surrounded her kept getting all the credit for winning fights that she actually won. Rachel's story became the tale of the inside versus the outside, but not in a way I've ever read before. Instead, for her, it was less about identity and more about getting proper credit.

At the end of the lesson, we take a moment to appreciate the sheer volume that students have written. While writing is usually more about depth than breadth, it is meaningful for a beginner student to discover that page counts that once seemed daunting flew by when they were writing from a place of passion and inspiration. By being the objects that sparked that creativity, kids' meal toys demonstrate that they have a power far deeper than their disposability might suggest. They are vessels for emotion, catharsis, bonding, and, as such, story. Kids' meal toys—safety-tested, affordable, and pre-bagged—surely have myriad uses within classrooms, with this lesson being just one option. Because of this, I hope teachers of many fields and levels find ways of incorporating kids' meal toys into their lessons.

References

Ayres, Ian, and Antonia Rose Ayres-Brown. "Unhappy Meals: Sex Discrimination in Toy Choice at McDonald's." *William & Mary Journal of Women and the Law,* Vol. 21, Issue 2, 2015, pp. 237–273.

Barnes, Brooks. "Movie Ticket Sales Sagging? Time to Bring Out the Toys." *The New York Times,* May 22, 2017. https://www.nytimes.com/2017/05/22/business/media/at-warner-bros-former-disney-exec-leads-new-charge-on-merchandise.html.

Baudrillard, Jean. "The System of Collecting." *The Cultures of Collecting.* Edited by John Elsner and Roger Cardinal. Harvard University Press, 1994, pp. 7–24.

Bealer, Tracy. "The Same Aisle: The Intersection of Resistance and Discipline in Brony Fandom, or, Friendship Is Mythological." *Articulating the Action Figure.* Edited by Jonathan Alexandratos. McFarland, 2017, pp. 58–70.

"Beef and Burgers FAQs." *McDonald's,* 2017. https://www.mcdonalds.com/us/en-us/faq/burgers.html.

Benjamin, Walter. "The Work of Art in the Age of Mechanical Reproduction." *Illuminations.* Edited by Hannah Arendt, translated by Harry Zohn. Schocken Books, 1969, pp. 1–26.

Berfield, Susan. "How McDonald's Made Enemies of Black Franchisees." *Bloomberg,* Dec. 17, 2021. https://www.bloomberg.com/news/features/2021-12-17/black-mcdonalds-franchise-owners-face-off-with-fast-food-restaurant-over-racism.

Berger, Joseph. "Goodbye, Tickle Me Elmo; Hello, Beanie Babies." *The New York Times,* Mar. 14, 1997. https://www.nytimes.com/1997/03/14/nyregion/goodbye-tickle-me-elmo-hello-beanie-babies.html.

Betancourt, Michael. *Glitch Art in Theory and Practice: Critical Failures and Post-Digital Aesthetics.* Routledge, 2017.

Bissonette, Zac. *The Great Beanie Baby Bubble.* New York: Portfolio, 2015.

Bloomberg. "Hair Pulling in the Doll House." *Bloomberg,* May 1, 2001. https://www.bloomberg.com/news/articles/2005-05-01/hair-pulling-in-the-dollhouse.

Brody, Alan, et al. *Peculiar Capitalism: Fast-Food Franchising and Entrepreneurship in Postwar America.* George Mason University, PhD dissertation, 2020.

Broeske, Pat H., and Anne Thompson. "Hawking 'Batman.'" *Entertainment Weekly,* July 10, 1992. https://ew.com/article/1992/07/10/hawking-batman/.

Bruce, Scott. *Cereal Boxes & Prizes: 1960s.* Flakeworld Publishing, 1998.

Burger Chef Book Cover. Burger Chef, c. 1965. Promotional item.

Burger Chef Promotional Rings. Burger Chef, c. 1970. Promotional item.

Burger King Kids Club Adventures. Vol. 1, Issue 1, Mar. 1990.

Burger King Kids Club Commercial. VHS tape, 1990.

"Burger King Recalling Pokémon Toys' Containers." *Associated Press,* Dec. 28, 1999. https://www.deseret.com/1999/12/28/19482732/burger-king-recalling-pokemon-toys-containers.

"Burger King X Spider-Verse Immersive Restaurant, NYC." *Average Socialite,* May 15, 2023. https://www.averagesocialite.com/nyc-events/2023/5/15/burger-king-x-spider-verse-immersive-restaurant-nyc.

References

Calvert, Sandra L. "Children as Consumers: Advertising and Marketing." *National Institute of Health,* 2008. https://pubmed.ncbi.nlm.nih.gov/21338011/.

Carey, Bill. *Fortunes, Fiddles and Fried Chicken: A Business History of Nashville.* Hillsboro Press, 2000.

Chapman, Tom. "A Not So Happy Meal; How McDonald's Destroyed 'Batman Returns' and Cost Tim Burton His Job." *Geeks,* 2018. https://vocal.media/geeks/a-not-so-happy-meal-how-mcdonald-s-destroyed-batman-returns-and-cost-tim-burton-his-job.

Chatelain, Marcia. *Franchise: The Golden Arches in Black America.* New York: Liverlight, 2020.

Chief Marketer Staff. "McDonald's Under Fire for Report Card Ad." *Chief Marketer.* Dec. 7, 2007. https://chiefmarketer.com/mcdonalds-under-fire-for-report-card-ad/.

China Labor Watch. "The Other Side of Fairy Tales." *China Labor Watch,* Nov. 20, 2015. Chinalaborwatch.org.

"Continue to Offer High Quality Happy Meal Toys & Initiate Toy Recycling Program." *Change.org* petition, Jan. 20, 2022. https://www.change.org/p/mcdonald-s-recycle-happy-meal-toys-and-continue-to-offer-high-quality-toys.

Crosby, Shawn. Interview. Conducted by Jonathan Alexandratos. Oct. /Nov. 2021.

Darren. "Who Is the Largest Toy Distributor in the World?" *Plastic Toy Factory.* https://www.plastictoyfactory.com/who-is-the-largest-toy-distributor-in-the-world/.

Flager, Madison. "Happy Meals Will Start Having Disney Toys in Them Again." *Delish,* Feb. 28, 2018. https://www.delish.com/food-news/news/a58483/disney-toys-are-coming-back-to-happy-meals/.

Freud, Sigmund. *Beyond the Pleasure Principle.* Translated by CJ M. Hubback. London: The International Psycho-Analytical Press, 1922.

Garrett, Frances, et al. "Narratives of Hospitality and Feeding in Tibetan Ritual." *Journal of the American Academy of Religion,* Vol. 81, No. 2, June 2013, pp. 491–515.

Gray, Jonathan. *Show Sold Separately: Promos, Spoilers, and Other Media Paratexts.* New York University Press, 2010.

Gray, Jonathan W. *Civil Rights in the White Literary Imagination: Innocence by Association.* University Press of Mississippi, 2014.

"A Guide to Plastic in the Ocean." *National Ocean Service.* https://oceanservice.noaa.gov/hazards/marinedebris/plastics-in-the-ocean.html.

Haracz, Mike [@chefmikeharacz]. "What Is in McDonald's Beef???" Sept. 16, 2023. tiktok.com/t/ZT8rqfr9U/.

Harrison, Richard. "The Fantastic Paper Man: Heroic Proportion, the Ideal Body and Me." *Secret Identity Reader: Essays on Sex, Death, and the Superhero.* Edited by Lee Easton and Richard Harrison. Wolsak & Wynn, 2010, pp. 113–134.

Harrison, Rebecca. "Star Cistems Will Slip Through Your Fingers: Glitches, Malfunctions and Errors as Modes of Queer Resistance in Star Wars." Realizing Resistance Episode II: Uncharted Galaxies, DCSC. May 7, 2021. Online.

Hautzinger, Daniel. "How Tom Burrell Convinced Corporations That 'Black People Are Not Dark Skinned White People.'" *WTTW/PBS,* June 28, 2018. https://interactive.wttw.com/playlist/2018/06/28/tom-burrell.

Henderson, Jamala. Foreword. *Geek Elders Speak: In Our Own Voices.* Edited by Maggie Nowakowska and Jenni Hennig. Forest Path Books, 2021, pp. 6–9.

Hobin, Erin P. "The Happy Meal Effect: The Impact of Toy Premiums on Healthy Eating Among Children in Ontario, Canada." *Canadian Journal of Public Health,* Vol. 103, Issue 4, July 2012, pp. 244–248.

Howe, Sean. *Marvel Comics: The Untold Story.* New York: Harper Perennial, 2013.

International Franchise Association. "The History of Modern Franchising." *IFA.* https://www.franchise.org/blog/the-history-of-modern-franchising#:~:text=This%20method%20of%20down%2Dstream,traditional%2C%20product%20or%20trademark%20franchising.&text=In%20the%20United%20States%2C%20many,franchisor%2C%20dating%20franchising%20to%201851.

References

Jekanowski, Mark D., et al. "Convenience, Accessibility, and the Demand for Fast Food." *Western Journal of Agricultural Economics*, Vol. 26, Issue 1, 2001, pp. 58–74.

Jenkins, Henry. *Comics and Stuff*. New York University Press, 2020.

Jenkins, Henry. *Convergence Culture: Where Old and New Media Collide*. New York University Press, 2006.

Johnson, Derek. *Transgenerational Media Industries: Adults, Children, and the Reproduction of Culture*. University of Michigan Press, 2019.

Jones, Robert, Jr. "Humanity Not Included: DC's Cyborg and the Mechanization of the Black Body." *The Middle Spaces*, Mar. 31, 2015. https://themiddlespaces.com/2015/03/31/humanity-not-included/.

Kellaway, Mitch. "Birth of a 'Brony': A Queer Man Watches *My Little Pony*." *Huffington Post*, Feb. 2, 2016. https://www.huffpost.com/entry/birth-of-a-brony_b_4647905.

Kidd, Anastasia. Interview. Conducted by Jonathan Alexandratos. Aug. 23, 2023.

Kinder, Marsha. *Playing with Power in Movies, Television, and Video Games: From Muppet Babies to Teenage Mutant Ninja Turtles*. University of California Press, 1991.

"King Cake History." *Randazzo King Cake*, 2022. https://randazzokingcake.com/history.

Klayman, Ben. "McDonald's Stand by 'Cursing' Happy Meal Minions." *The Sydney Morning Herald*, July 11, 2015. https://www.smh.com.au/entertainment/movies/mcdonalds-stand-by-cursing-happy-meal-minions-20150711-gia2gr.html.

Lee, Jennifer 8. "Solving a Riddle Wrapped in a Mystery Inside a Cookie." *The New York Times*, Jan. 16, 2008. https://www.nytimes.com/2008/01/16/dining/16fort.html?_r=1&pagewanted=all.

Levin, Diana E., and Nancy Carlsson-Paige. "Marketing Violence: The Special Toll on Young Children of Color." *The Journal of Negro Education*, Vol. 72, No. 4, 2003, pp. 427–437.

Lewis, William W., and Sean Bartley. *Experiential Theatres*. Routledge, 2022.

Lobel, Orly. *You Don't Own Me: The Court Battles That Exposed Barbie's Dark Side*. Norton, 2018.

Lopez Ramos, Jorge, et al. "The Post-Immersive Manifesto." *International Journal of Performance Arts and Digital Media*, Vol. 16, Issue 2, 2020, pp. 196–212.

Mao, LuMing. *Reading Chinese Fortune Cookie*. University Press of Colorado, Utah State University Press, 2006.

Marx, Gary, and Douglas McAdam. *Collective Behavior and Social Movements: Process and Structure*. Prentice Hall, 1994.

McAlister, Anna R., and T. Bettina Cornwell. "Collectible Toys as Marketing Tools: Understanding Preschool Children's Responses to Food Paired with Premiums." *Journal of Public Policy and Marketing*, Vol. 31, Issue 2, Sept. 1, 2012, pp. 195–205.

"McDonaldland." Comic strip. *Chicago Tribune*, Dec. 30, 1979.

"McDonaldland." Comic strip. *Chicago Tribune*, Jul. 22, 1979.

"McDonald's Announces Festival Tour with Immersive McNuggets Experience." *Marketing Communication News*, June 6, 2019. https://marcommnews.com/mcdonalds-announces-festival-tour-with-immersive-mcnuggets-experience/.

"McDonald's Calendar of Community Fun." *McDonald's*, June 1992. Trayliner.

"McDonald's Worker Stole Beanie Babies, Police Say." *Orlando Sentinel*, June 7, 1998. https://www.orlandosentinel.com/1998/06/07/mcdonalds-worker-stole-beanie-babies-police-say/.

"McNugget Happy Meal." *My Fitness Pal*. https://www.myfitnesspal.com/food/calories/happy-meal-4-chicken-mcnuggets-small-fries-diet-coke-apple-slices-60992243.

Menagerie. Vol. 1, Issue 17, 1981.

Meyersohn, Rolf, and Elihu Katz. "Notes on a Natural History of Fads." *American Journal of Sociology*, Vol. 62, Issue 6, May 1957, pp. 594–601.

Mills, Amanda. "The Disparities Between Zines and Commercialism." *Kennesaw State University College of the Arts*, Jan. 27, 2016. https://www.artsatl.org/opinion-disparities-zines-commercialism/.

References

"Misleading Vintage Ads About the Dietary Benefits of Sugar, 1950s–1960s." *Rare Historical Photos,* May 24, 2022. https://rarehistoricalphotos.com/sugar-vintage-ads/.

My Favorite Shapes. Created by Julio Torres. HBO, Aug. 2019.

"Nintendo Putting 25M Into Pokemon Promotion." *New York Daily News,* Aug. 26, 1998. https://www.nydailynews.com/1998/08/26/nintendo-putting-25m-into-pokemon-promotion/.

Norris, Sean. "McDonald's Pauses Disney Promotion Over Issues with QR Codes Included in Happy Meal Toys." *Print and Promotion Marketing,* Nov. 24, 2020. https://www.printandpromomarketing.com/article/mcdonalds-pauses-disney-promotion-over-qr-codes-printed-on-cards-included-with-happy-meal-toys/.

1010Wins News Broadcast. Produced by Ben Mevorach. WINS, July 27, 2023.

Pantano, Joshua. "Why Are Kids Obsessed with Horror?" *The Ithacan,* Nov. 3, 2022. https://theithacan.org/45477/life-culture/popped-culture/column-why-are-kids-obsessed-with-horror/.

Park, Alex. "The Wartime Roots of the Global Fast Food Boom." *The Conversationalist,* 2022. https://conversationalist.org/2022/09/01/the-wartime-roots-of-fast-food/.

Parrott, Fiona. "Death, Memory, and Collecting: Creating the Conditions for Ancestralization in South London Households." *Unpacking the Collection.* Edited by Sarah Byrne, et al. Springer, 2011, pp. 289–305.

Pearce, Susan M. *Museums, Objects, and Collections.* Smithsonian Books, 1993.

Pfeiffer, Annie. *To the Collector Belong the Spoils: Modernism and the Art of Appropriation.* Cornell University Press, 2023.

Piepmeier, Alison. "Why Zines Matter: Materiality and the Creation of Embodied Community." *American Periodicals,* Vol. 18, No. 2, 2008, pp. 213–238.

Pine, Joseph, II, and James H. Gilmore. "Welcome to the Experience Economy." *Harvard Business Review,* July–Aug. 1998. https://hbr.org/1998/07/welcome-to-the-experience-economy.

Price, Cortney. "The Real Toy Story: The San Francisco Board of Supervisors Healthy Food Incentives Ordinance." *Journal of Food Law & Policy,* Vol. 8, Issue 2, pp. 347–362.

Robertson, David C., and Bill Breen. *Brick by Brick: How LEGO Rewrote the Rules of Innovation and Conquered the Global Toy Industry.* Crown Business, 2013.

Rogers, Kate. "McDonald's Settles Discrimination Lawsuit with Herb Washington." *CNBC,* Dec. 16, 2021. https://www.cnbc.com/2021/12/16/mcdonalds-settles-discrimination-lawsuit-with-herb-washington.html.

Russ, Hilary. "McDonald's Happy Meal Toys to Go Green Globally by 2025." *Reuters,* Sept. 21, 2021. https://www.reuters.com/business/sustainable-business/mcdonalds-happy-meal-toys-go-green-by-2025-2021-09-21/.

Russell, Legacy. *Glitch Feminism: A Manifesto.* Verso, 2020.

Saint Basil Academy. "The Vasilopita (Saint Basil's Bread)." https://stbasil.goarch.org/about/vasilopita.

San Francisco Government Health Data. "Health Disparities Dashboard." 2017. https://sf.gov/data/health-disparities-dashboard.

San Francisco Health Improvement Partnership. "Overweight or Obesity." *SFHIP,* 2018. https://sfhip.org/chna/community-health-data/overweight-or-obesity/.

Sanders, Scott R. *Burger Chef.* Arcadia, 2009.

Schiffman, Lawrence H. *Sectarian Law in the Dead Sea Scrolls: Courts, Testimony, and the Penal Code.* Chapter 8, "The Communal Meal." Brown Judaic Studies, 2020.

Scott, Willard. *The Joy of Living.* Ballantine, 1983.

Seiter, Ellen. *Sold Separately: Parents and Children in Consumer Culture.* Rutgers University Press, 1995.

Shobe, Dané. "Your Favorite Toys Were Created by David Vonner." *Sun Hero Magazine,* Vol. 1, Issue 1, June 2023, pp. 24–30.

Shuman, Amy. "The Rhetoric of Portions." *Western Folklore,* Vol. 40, No. 1, Jan. 1981, pp. 72–80.

References

Smith, Vanessa. *Toy Stories: Analyzing the Child in Nineteenth Century Literature.* Fordham University Press, 2023.

Sulem, Matt. "When Were These 24 Iconic Fast Food Restaurants Founded?" *Yardbarker,* Sept. 21, 2023. https://www.yardbarker.com/lifestyle/articles/when_were_these_24_iconic_fast_food_restaurants_founded_092023/s1__37779777.

Taback, Simms. *Joseph Had a Little Overcoat.* Viking Books for Young Readers, 1999.

"Taco Bell Discontinues All Kids' Meals." *Taco Bell,* July 13, 2013. https://www.tacobell.com/news/taco-bell-becomes-first-quick-service-restaurant-to-discontinue-kids-meals-and-toys-nationally.

Temple, Norman J. "The Origins of the Obesity Epidemic in the USA—Lessons for Today." *National Institute of Health,* Oct. 12, 2022. https://www.ncbi.nlm.nih.gov/pmc/articles/PMC9611578/.

Thomas, Susan E. "Value and Validity of Zines as an Art Form." *Art Documentation: Journal of the Art Libraries Society of North America,* Vol. 28, No. 2, Fall 2009, pp. 27–36, 38.

"Topics of the Times; Unhappy Meal." *The New York Times,* July 13, 1992. https://www.nytimes.com/1992/07/13/opinion/topics-of-the-times-unhappy-meal.html.

"The Tradition of Mardi Gras King Cakes." *King Cake,* 2022. https://www.kingcake.com/history.

"20 Things You Didn't Know About Star Trek: The Motion Picture (1979)." *WhatCulture.* https://whatculture.com/film/20-things-you-didnt-know-about-star-trek-the-motion-picture-1979?page=18.

"2008 MCDONALD'S STAR WARS THE CLONE WARS SET OF 18 HAPPY MEAL FULL COLLECTION TOYS VIDEO REVIEW." *YouTube,* Apr. 16, 2013. Uploaded by FastFoodToyReviews. https://www.youtube.com/watch?v=tctlUJfNOzs.

u/AButtFacedMiscreant. "McDonald's toys are paper and cardboard now. I hate it." *Reddit,* 2021. https://www.reddit.com/r/RandomThoughts/comments/sgb9fy/mcdonalds_toys_are_paper_and_cardboard_now_i_hate/.

"Un homenaje a la creadora de de la Cajita Feliz—Yoly de Cofiño." *YouTube,* 2021. McDonald's Guatamala. https://www.youtube.com/watch?v=CVifIcmYQlw.

United States Court of Appeals, Ninth Circuit. *Sid & Marty Krofft Tele. v. McDonald's Corp.* Google Scholar, 1977.

United States District Court for the Northeastern District of Ohio, Eastern Division. *Herbert L. Washington v. McDonald's Corp.* Pfeiffer Wolf, 2021.

United States Government, Centers for Disease Control and Prevention. "Fast Food Statistics." *CDC.*

United States Government, Centers for Disease Control and Prevention. "Genes and Obesity." *CDC.* https://www.cdc.gov/genomics/resources/diseases/obesity/obesedit.htm.

United States Government, Centers for Disease Control and Prevention. "Overweight and Obesity Statistics." *CDC.*

Van Ginnekin, Jaap. "Fads and Crazes." *Fashions and Hypes,* Vol. 16, Issue 2, 2003, pp. 132–137.

Varner, Steve. "Interview Request." Received by Jonathan Alexandratos, June 8, 2021.

Watterson, Bill. *The Days Are Just Packed: A Calvin and Hobbes Collection.* Andrews McMeel, 1993.

"What Is a Zine?" *University of Texas Libraries,* Sept. 8, 2023. https://guides.lib.utexas.edu/c.php?g=576544&p=3977232.

White Scripts and Black Supermen: Black Masculinities in Comic Books. Directed by Jonathan Gayles, performances by Dwayne McDuffie, John Jennings, et al. California Newsreel, 2010.

"Who Put the Baby in King Cake?" *Brain Stuff.* Podcast.

"Who Really Invented the Happy Meal?" *InspireIP.* https://inspireip.com/who-really-invented-the-mcdonalds-happy-meal/#:~:text=Both%20Bob%20Bernstein%20and%20Dick, Happy%20Meal%20box%20in%201987.

References

Williams, Meredith. McDonald's Newsletter. Feb. 1989.

Windsor, J. "Identity Parades." *The Cultures of Collecting.* Edited by John Elsner and Roger Cardinal. Harvard University Press, 1994, pp. 49–67.

Winnicott, D.W. *Playing and Reality.* Routledge, 2005.

Zakarin, Jordan. "Tim Burton on 'Batman,' 'Edward Scissorhands,' and the Teen Fans of 'The Nightmare Before Christmas.'" *Yahoo,* Dec. 22, 2014. https://www.yahoo.com/entertainment/tim-burton-on-batman-edward-scissorhands-and-105875262422.html?guccounter=1&guce_referrer=aHR0cHM6Ly93d3cuZ29vZ2xlLmNvbS88&guce_referrer_sig=AQAAAE9R-8Ag7yljPG6fhebr7XP08q9ku2V17dqi_a_Rit5b3jByP7zMd85yNIWQaa533BF6bpFtVxknThDsPWOUphQT_r7eD-aRyEIZpOs7KM3vlfytqGdYuG8hiNwOK7c9h4rfOZG4zHt0ItzEdwvIQhxYZ1Vmsl3q_w4HWXgA3jAm.

Zenner, Eline, and Dirk Geeraerts. "One Does Not Simply Process Memes: Image Macros as Multimodal Constructions." *Cultures and Traditions of Wordplay and Wordplay Research,* Edited by Esme Winter-Froemel and Verena Thaler. De Gruyter, 2016, pp. 167–194.

Index

217

Index